AN AMERICA FIRST
APPROACH TO U.S.
NATIONAL SECURITY

AN AMERICA FIRST APPROACH TO U.S. NATIONAL SECURITY

Fred Fleitz, Editor
Lt. Gen. (Ret.) Keith Kellogg
Congressman Michael Waltz
Secretary Rick Perry
Secretary Robert Wilkie
U.S. Trade Rep. Robert Lighthizer
Acting Secretary Chad Wolf
Morgan Ortagus
Ellie Cohanim
Steve Yates
Michael Rigas
Sam Faddis
Doug Hoelscher
Sam Buchan
Robert Law
Adam Savit

ISBN-979-8-9905031-0-6

*An America First Approach
to U.S. National Security*
is published in the United States by the
America First Press,
a division of the America First Policy Institute

May 9, 2024

THE AMERICA FIRST POLICY INSTITUTE
1455 Pennsylvania Ave. NW
Suite 1200
Washington, DC 20004
Phone: 202-637-3690 | Email: info@americanfirstpolicy.com
For more information, please go to AmericaFirstPolicy.com

Contents

Foreward..1

Introduction...5
   By Fred Fleitz

1. Defining the America First Approach to U.S. National
   Security...13
   By Lt. Gen. (Ret.) Keith Kellogg

2. America First and the Use of U.S. Military Force.....................29
   By Congressman Michael Waltz

3. There Can Be No America First Without the Shield of the
   Armed Forces..41
   By Robert Wilkie

4. America First and Homeland Security...63
   By Chad Wolf and Robert Law

5. America First, Russia, and Ukraine...75
   By Lt. General (Ret.) Keith Kellogg and Fred Fleitz

6. Communist China: A Singular Threat and a
   Comprehensive Challenge for America First Security
   Policy...97
   By Stephen Yates and Adam Savit

7. America First, Israel, and the Middle East..............................121
   By Ellie Cohanim

8. America First, NATO, and US Alliances: Why America
   First is Not Isolationism..141
   By Morgan Ortagus

9. Bad Trade Policy Endangers American National Security 159
   By Robert Lighthizer

10. Energy Security is National Security: America First and
    the Importance of an American Energy Powerhouse..........167
    By Rick Perry and Sam Buchan

11. The America First Approach to U.S. National Security
    Requires Fixing America's Intelligence Community 187
    By Sam Faddis

12. The Right Team, Prepared to Meet Global Challenges
    and an Emboldened Administrative State................................203
    By Doug Hoelscher and Michael Rigas

About the Authors...223

Endnotes 227

Index..247

Foreward

I n the closing days of the Trump Administration — or more properly, what will probably be the first Trump Administration — a handful of veterans of his White House knew what the celebratory Left of early 2021 did not. We knew that the Trump era was not a mere passing moment in American history, and its issues and principles weren't going away. The man who incepted it drew upon deep and enduring themes in American life and inheritance, and there was no erasing them — despite the Left's best efforts to that end. Whatever was to happen, to any one of us, the movement that put President Trump in office was now a permanent feature of American life and civics. So what next for it? None of us could walk away: we didn't have the right. Fortunately, neither did we have the desire. There would be a next chapter, and there was work to do now.

Out of that understanding was born the America First Policy Institute (AFPI). In the years since its creation, we have done our best to keep the charge handed to us: to keep the America First agenda alive, to develop it, to expand it, and to ready it for its inevitable return to governance. Being the fullest expression of the American people and their values, that agenda is never a theoretical exercise. We do not possess the expectation of power so much as we are conscious of the responsibility of it. When that moment comes in any one of our tomorrows, the agenda and its execution will be ready — because AFPI did its work today.

Front and center in that work is the responsibility for conceiving and shaping a new era of thought in American national security. That is the point and purpose of the book you hold in your hands now. The imperative could not be more stark, for we live in a moment that historians may well describe in generations to come as prewar. The past generation of American strategic leadership has, with some exceptions, mostly failed in its core duty: to defend and preserve a secure and prosperous America. From the absolute summit of American global power and security at the close of the Cold War, in which American sea power guaranteed global navigation, American airpower reigned unchallenged, American land power was incontestable, American diplomatic power dictated outcomes, American alliances secured prosperity and security for Americans, and American economic power assured the American way of life, we have endured a precipitous descent.

The combination of hubris and ideology that took root in elite circles in the flush years of the 1990s reoriented American power and American strategy toward disastrous ends. Our armed forces, instead of being kept strong for their own sake, were transformed into laboratories of progressive experimentation. Our economic strength, instead of fueling American prosperity and community, was outsourced to antagonists and enemies in the name of market efficiency. Our alliances, instead of securing America and Americans, became ends in themselves, unexamined and too often unenforced. Our leadership, instead of understanding its responsibility to secure and steward the American people, dissociated itself from that heritage and embraced a basket of propositions and values unmoored from the American inheritance, finding more in common with the elites of other nations than the people of their own.

Over three decades onward, the results speak for themselves. War and rumors of war sweep the globe, and the United States — the indispensable nation for freedom across two and half centuries — is seen as weak, uncertain, and rudderless. The examples are myriad. Freedom of the seas is over, as the United States Navy finds itself unable to stop mere Yemeni tribesmen from closing the Red Sea to traffic. American industrial supremacy is over, especially in the naval arena, as a single Chinese shipyard can produce more tonnage than the entire United States. Our merchant-marine fleet is shrunk to near nonexistence. Hostile powers overfly American airspace with impunity. Our technological superiority is blunted by a defense-industrial complex that takes decades to produce major weapons systems that may or may not prevail against rapidly iterated foreign systems. Major great-power war in Europe for the first time since the Second World War tests our alliances, and American policymakers find themselves unable to arrive at a strategy or even a desired end. Asymmetric warfare confronts and confounds America from the Middle East to Africa, to — most critically — the Western Hemisphere itself, where Mexican cartels and the

Mexican state together engaged in armed aggression against American communities in America.

Watching it all, the People's Republic of China prepares for war — and its moment to displace the United States of America as the world's premier power.

We must understand two major things about this state of affairs, so desperate and so perilous for America. The first is that this weakness is a choice — and it is a choice made by specific men and women, mostly but not wholly in Washington, D.C. — who lead America's national security apparatus but do not have American interests at heart. They are a persistent and, they think, permanent group who control the levers of American strength and engagement forever, regardless of partisan control or change in administration.

We must prove them wrong.

The second thing we must understand is that we can make a different choice. The sources of American strength still exist: our inheritance of liberty, our geography, our industry, and surpassingly, our people. Where they are diminished, they can be restored. We are not finished as a nation nor as a global power after a mere two and a half centuries. A country that was made on an April morning when simple militiamen decided to take on the regulars of a global empire will not be undone by Yemeni tribes, nor by Mexican violence, nor by Russian infantry, nor by the Communist Party of China. The only true existential danger to America is American leadership unworthy of the Americans. We can change that leadership — and we can chart a path back to the greatness that is our right.

This book shows the way.

For America First, always.

Brooke Leslie Rollins
President and CEO
America First Policy Institute

America First Press

Introduction

By Fred Fleitz

America First is the bold and successful approach to government by the Trump Administration that put the interests of the American people ahead of the so-called establishment. It empowered Americans, served as a voice for the people, and helped revive the American dream. America First made our country a better place by bolstering our economy, establishing energy independence, and securing the U.S. homeland. Despite the efforts of the current administration to reverse the accomplishments of this successful approach to government, it is clear today that the America First approach to governing has transformed American thinking about government. It is here to stay.

This book discusses a crucial component of the America First approach to governing—America First policies to protect our nation's security.

This approach was driven by the failures of recent U.S. administrations to implement national security policies to defend and protect American security and prosperity. It is an approach that rejects conventional thinking and the positions of the foreign policy elite and U.S. government foreign affairs careerists. This approach significantly improved American and global security through decisive presidential leadership and policies that focused on the interests of our nation and its people. It helped bring about a time of peace for our country and, for the first time in 20 years, the U.S. did not enter a new war abroad.

President Joe Biden made a deliberate decision to reverse President Trump's successful America First approach to U.S. national security and revert to the failed policies of the past. Coupled with Biden's incompetent leadership, the results for U.S. and global security have been catastrophic. The world today is without question far more unstable and dangerous than it was when President Trump left office.

For our nation's survival and safety, it is urgent that we return to the successful America First national security policies of the Trump Administration.

To accomplish this, this book has two purposes. First, to fully explain the America First approach to national security and how it can better protect our nation and promote global security. Drawing on a set of leading national security experts that includes a U.S. congressman who serves on the House Armed Services, Foreign Affairs, and Intelligence Committees, five former cabinet members, and three former U.S. intelligence officers, this book provides detailed analyses of how the America First approach succeeded in addressing a wide range of national security threats and issues in the last administration and the consequences of the Biden Administration's reversal of these policies.

Second, this book's experts provide bold America First solutions for a future U.S. administration to implement so it can address the serious national security threats facing our nation today.

In Chapter 1, General Keith Kellogg, Co-Chair of the America First Policy Institute's Center for American Security, sets the stage for this book with a detailed discussion defining the America First approach to U.S. national security based on his service as a highly decorated U.S. Army officer and his experience implementing the Trump Administration's successful foreign policy in his positions as National Security Advisor for the Trump Administration and as National Security Council Chief of Staff. General Kellogg's analysis also reflects his work at AFPI to defend and develop America First national security policies. General Kellogg, who often was in the Oval Office while President Trump made crucial national security decisions, explains the origins and development of the America First approach to national security, how such policies were successfully employed by the Trump Administration, and how a new administration can restore this approach as soon as possible.

Following General Kellogg's chapter are two chapters with extraordinary analysis by two military experts—U.S. Representative Michael Waltz (R-Fla.) and former Secretary of Veterans Affairs Robert Wilkie—on what is arguably the most important element of America First concerning national security: its implications for the U.S. military and national defense. Drawing on their vast military and government experience, the authors explain the urgent need for the U.S. military to be focused on its core mission of warfighting and deterrence in order to defend the vital national interests of the United States and that there can be no America First without the shield of the U.S. Armed Forces. Waltz and Wilkie also express their alarm at the damage being done to our military by the Biden Administration by subjecting military personnel to social engineering and the radical "diversity, equity, and inclusion" (DEI) ideology and call for these policies to be immediately ended and reversed by a new administration.

In Chapter 4, former Acting Secretary of Homeland Security and AFPI Executive Director Chad Wolf and Director of the AFPI Center for Homeland Security and Immigration Robert Law describe why putting the security of the American people first means making the defense of the U.S. homeland an absolute priority. The authors discuss at length why the unsecured southern border during the Biden Administration is a serious national security threat. They explain how this administration's reversal of the Trump Administration's successful border security policies is responsible for an unprecedented surge in illegal aliens and a sharp increase in drug trafficking, human trafficking, and terrorist suspects across our southern border. Wolf and Law also discuss protecting U.S. infrastructure and threats from cyberwar and domestic terrorism. Their solutions stem from the important work Wolf and Law are doing for AFPI to analyze threats to the U.S. homeland and provide policy answers to protect it.

Following the homeland security chapter, General Kellogg and I discuss in Chapter 5 one of the most challenging national security problems facing the United States today: the Russia-Ukraine War. We explain the Biden Administration's serious policy failures before the war that made this war inevitable and its policies after it began that have prolonged it and caused this conflict to become a stalemate. We also present America First solutions that could have prevented this war and provide a framework on how to end it. I believe this is an important chapter that could help guide a future president to end the killing in this war and put Ukraine on track to becoming a prosperous and secure nation.

As serious as the war in Ukraine is, it is not the top national security threat to our country. That threat is China, which is discussed in Chapter 6. The lead author, Steve Yates, is Chair of AFPI's China Policy Initiative. Steve also was a Deputy Assistant to Vice President Dick Cheney for National Security Affairs and a National Security Agency analyst. Co-authoring this chapter is Adam Savit, Director of AFPI's China Policy Initiative. According to Yates and Savit, the Chinese Communist Party (CCP) represents the most comprehensive threat to U.S. national security since the fall of the Soviet Union. The essential difference between the two is that the CCP is far stronger economically and culturally and is embedded into nearly every aspect of American life. Their analysis looks at how the threat from China has grown over the last three years and presents tough America First national security policies to counter this threat and lower tensions with Beijing.

The stark deterioration in stability and America's crucial relationship with Israel are addressed in the next chapter. The author is Ellie Cohanim, former U.S. Deputy Special Envoy to Monitor and Combat Anti-Semitism for the Trump State Department and Senior Fellow with Independent Women's Forum. Cohanim discusses the extraordinary success of the Trump Administration's America First Middle East policies, which included defying the foreign policy establishment with original approaches to promote regional security and standing firmly with Israel. The results were the Abraham Accords peace agreement and a much more secure and stable Middle East.

As Cohanim explains, the sharp increase in violence and instability in this region since President Trump left office is a direct result of diminished U.S. leadership and deterrence because the Biden Administration reversed Trump's initiatives and returned to the failed policies of the Obama Administration, especially appeasing Iran. Cohanim notes that weak U.S. leadership in the Middle East during the Biden Administration has created opportunities for American adversaries such as China, Iran, and Russia to expand their influence at America's expense. Cohanim believes it is urgent that a new president in January 2025 bring security and stability to the Middle East with decisive America First national security policies that reestablishes America's regional leadership and strong relationship with Israel and counter Iran's malign influence with a "Maximum Pressure/Maximum Support" strategy.

In Chapter 8, former spokeswoman for the Trump State Department and founder of Polaris National Security Morgan Ortagus addresses the crucial question of U.S. alliances and NATO. Ortagus explains how the America First approach to national security requires that the United States work closely in alliances but also that alliance members pay their fair share of the costs of mutual defense. Using her experience working for President Trump, she also debunks false allegations that the America First movement is isolationist. To maintain its global leadership, Ortagus believes strong relationships and transactional alliances are a critical element of the America First approach to U.S. national because they contribute to a future of strength and continued prosperity and are our greatest comparative advantage over our adversaries.

President Trump's foreign policy also prioritized a comprehensive reset of our global trade relations. In Chapter 9, Robert Lighthizer, who served as the U.S. Trade Representative under President Trump, explains that going forward, America First foreign policy must revolve around two key principles: mutual defense and balanced trade. Lighthizer highlights how long-standing American trade policies have endangered our national security both by transferring American wealth and technology to our adversaries and by eroding our defense industrial base. A successful American First foreign policy, he details, must act to reverse both of these trends.

Closely related to economic security is energy security. This is discussed in Chapter 10 by former Trump Administration Secretary of Energy Rick Perry and Samuel Buchan, who served as a senior advisor to Perry and Energy Secretary Dan Brouillette. Buchan is currently a Senior Fellow with AFPI's Center for Energy and the Environment. Perry and Buchan argue energy security is national security and that it is crucial for U.S. security and prosperity that America be an energy powerhouse. Although the authors call the United States an energy superpower, they say it is unclear whether this status can be sustained in a policy environment increasingly defined by a myopic fixation on climate change as an existential national security threat. Perry and Buchan are critical of the Biden Administration for ending President

Trump's America First energy policies which made our nation energy independent. They call on U.S. leaders to recognize that U.S. energy security is equivalent to national security, and the most impactful means of beginning this process is to empower industry to innovate, access, produce, transport, and export the vast energy potential of this great nation.

Sam Faddis, who served for many years as a CIA operations officer and manager, makes the case in Chapter 11 that the corruption and politicization of America's intelligence agencies are undermining national security and hurting our political system. He argues that because an America First approach to government means responsible and ethical management to put the American people and their interests first, our intelligence agencies must be managed responsibly. Faddis says U.S. intelligence is at a tipping point and warns that major intelligence failures, meddling in domestic politics, politicization of intelligence, and social engineering within intelligence agencies have alienated the American public and our elected officials. He puts forward several crucial recommendations to restore responsible management to intelligence agencies and keep them out of U.S. politics.

The final chapter discusses why a future president must name strong and capable national security officials who believe in the America First approach to address the national security threats and issues discussed in this book. This chapter was co-authored by AFPI's Doug Hoelscher and Mike Rigas. Hoelscher is Chair of AFPI's America First Transition Project and previously served as Director of White House Intergovernmental Affairs in the Trump Administration. Rigas is Vice Chair of AFPI's America First Transition Project and was Acting Director of the Office of Personnel Management and Acting Deputy Director for Management at the Office of Management and Budget in the Trump Administration. Drawing on their extensive work for the America First Transition Project to prepare policies, management directives, and personnel actions so a new America First administration can hit the ground running in January 2025, they discuss the urgency to find the right leaders who can successfully operate in the challenging national security space to implement an America First agenda. They note that a new America First president likely will face opposition from entrenched national security careerists determined to resist change in U.S. policies on China, the Middle East, energy security, intelligence, and other issues. Hoelscher and Rigas argue that to carry out America First national security policies, a new president must appoint and nominate tough, resilient foreign policy officials. These officials must be ready to confront bureaucrats who are willing to go to any lengths, even breaking the law and their oaths, to thwart the president.

It is my hope that you will find the analysis by this book's expert authors informative and that it will help you understand how the America First approach to U.S. national security can solve the growing number of serious national security threats facing our nation today. It also is my fervent hope that this book will not just serve as a guidebook for a new U.S. administration in 2025 but will help lay a foundation for American foreign policy for many years to come.

I am very grateful to AFPI President Brooke Rollins and AFPI's Executive Director Chad Wolf for their support of this important project. I would like to thank the 15 experts who drafted chapters for their extraordinary reasoned and careful analysis and important recommendations. Special thanks go to my colleagues with the AFPI Center for American Security General Keith Kellogg and Gloria McDonald for the many hours they put into this project. I also want to thank many other patriots who helped review and prepare this book, including Ben Boychuk, David Bernhardt, James Carafano, Gordon Chang, John Mills, Sam Faddis, Michael Faulkender, John Gentry, James Gilmore, Callista Gingrich, Christopher Hull, Kay Bailey Hutchinson, John Hurley, Pete Hoekstra, Steve King, Ron Johnson, Christopher Landau, Natalie Leaman, Morgan Murphy, Jonathan Pidluzny, James Sherk, Adam Schindler, Ken Timmerman, Josh Treviño, Kristen Ziccarelli, and Adrian Zuckerman.

America First Press

1.

Defining the America First Approach to U.S. National Security

By Lt. Gen. (Ret.) Keith Kellogg

When Donald J. Trump announced his candidacy for President on June 16, 2015, he issued a promise to put America first and "Make America Great Again." This call to put America first came from a political outsider who, like many Americans, recognized the void created by the U.S. foreign policy establishment and national security apparatus in which the interests of the American people were often left neglected as our government built its priorities around securing international hegemony and carrying the weight of all other nations – often at the expense of our nation and people. Today, we are at a historic crossroads. There are but two options. A current Biden Administration national security policy that is filled with equivocation or a policy of America First.

Before President Trump, the U.S. foreign policy establishment and national security apparatus had adopted a status quo approach to how America should engage in the world. This status quo meant America's continual entanglement in endless engagements abroad as a primacy rather than focusing first on our citizens. The distinction and the clarity of America First were missing. America's domestic security was left vulnerable through open border policies, a faltering economy, a lack of energy independence, a weakened defense establishment, and a lack of clarity when it came to our vital national interests.

In the last generation, American strategic leadership, with few exceptions, has largely failed in its primary duty of safeguarding a secure and prosperous America. Since the height of American global

13

dominance at the end of the Cold War, when American sea, air, land, diplomatic, and economic powers were unparalleled, we have witnessed a significant decline. This decline, caused by a lack of strategic foresight compounded by ineffective leadership, has led us into a perilous situation not seen since 1939.

During the prosperous years of the 1990s, a combination of arrogance and ideology influenced decision-making within elite circles of governance, American power and strategy were redirected toward uncertain objectives. Instead of maintaining a robust military, it became a platform for progressive experiments focusing on diversity, equity, and inclusion. Economic prosperity was sacrificed in pursuit of market efficiencies by outsourcing to competitors and adversaries. Alliances, originally meant to ensure American security and prosperity, became unquestioned priorities in themselves. Leadership, rather than embracing its responsibility to protect and guide the American people, distanced itself from this tradition and adopted a set of values detached from American heritage, often aligning more with international elites than with the American people.

The consequences of these decisions are evident three decades later. Conflict and instability plague the globe, and the United States, once seen as the beacon of freedom for over two centuries, is now viewed as indecisive and adrift. Numerous examples highlight this decline: the erosion of freedom of navigation at sea, the loss of American maritime industrial supremacy to China, the depletion of our merchant-marine fleet, and the impunity of hostile powers in American airspace. Technological superiority is undermined by a sluggish defense-industrial complex, while major powers engage in conflict, testing the resilience of American alliances without clear strategies or objectives.

Furthermore, U.S. engagement with our allies had become imbalanced, with prominent disparities between America and contributions by its allies in alliance structures, such as NATO and trade agreements. Despite this being the case for years, the foreign policy establishment – Democrats and Republicans – tolerated the unequal burden sharing between the U.S. and its allies, and those who spoke out against it were denounced as isolationists.

14

As a result, a "uni-party" consensus had been formed on U.S. foreign policy. Prior to the announcement of Trump's candidacy in June of 2015, the American people were continually given a choice between "neocon" Republicans who advocated for hawkish responses to conflicts, endless U.S. military deployments abroad, and "democracy building," and Democrats guided by liberal idealism and globalist-oriented foreign policy objectives. Despite these being presented as two distinct choices, these approaches toward U.S. engagement abroad were more unified than they were distinct from each other.

Under the Bush Administration, America was led into a twenty-year military campaign in the Middle East. A war that had become endless and only ended with the true debacle of our retreat under pressure from Afghanistan.

And while America spent two decades in Afghanistan to fight a "global war on terror," conducting nation-state building exercises, we neglected the emergence of China as a global power.

America's endless war campaigns in the Middle East, therefore, was a critical turning point in our nation's history. It should have been a wake-up call that our national security apparatus was not working for the interests of the American people, and in many ways, it was actually working against them.

This solidified the reality that the United States had adopted a status quo regarding its engagement in the world. Regardless of whether it had a Democratic or Republican Administration, the United States pursued interventionist and globalist approaches to world affairs that increasingly resulted in more, not less, regional instability.

When the Obama Administration engaged in regime change in Libya in March 2011, supporting the overthrow of Muammar Gaddafi, it generated a domino effect of instability in the region. Libyan insurgents quickly filled the power void created by the U.S., ISIS gained a stronghold in the region, and it started a migrant crisis of Libyan migrants surging to Europe.

While justified under different names and undertaken by presidents from both political parties – humanitarian interventionism, democracy promotion, preemptive military engagement, these interventionist approaches of regime change, backing proxy forces, and endless military campaigns became the standard of the U.S. foreign policy establishment.

The question for many Americans was whether this status quo approach made the world safer and was it in the best interest of the American people.

America's diplomatic embrace of an interventionist approach to national security – instead of utilizing nation-state diplomacy and statecraft tools to avoid the outbreak of new wars and to mediate preexisting conflicts – increasingly led America down a path of strategic overreach as these efforts consumed our nation's resources while neglecting the homeland.

In his book "The Rise and Fall of Great Empires," Paul Kennedy warned of this "strategic overreach," by which he warned that when nations invest more of their vital resources in building empires abroad than they do in prioritizing their own nation, it inevitably leads to their decline.

The interventionist status quo of our foreign policy establishment was leading America down this path of decline and "strategic overreach" that Professor Kennedy warned about.

The U.S. foreign policy establishment and national security apparatus of the past were representative of a broken system that was not working for the vital national interests of the average U.S. citizen. It also had increasingly pivoted away from our constitutional framework and embraced externally -oriented foreign policy objectives. As a result, the U.S. had lost sight of core principles of effective national security policies: the prudent use of military force, the sanctity of nation-state sovereignty, the importance of nation-state level diplomacy, and most importantly, the need to prioritize the security and prosperity of our nation first.

President Trump understood the folly and the high price in blood and treasure of the uni-party's policies. This led to a revolutionary new approach: the America First approach to U.S. national security.

The America First policy framework of the Trump Administration was a necessary recalibration of our national security apparatus and foreign policy establishment. The Trump Administration established a clear list of goals to put our nation back on a pathway to security and prosperity and put the interests of Americans first.

The Trump Administration's America First national security policy priorities were:

- Preserve our national sovereignty, both physically through secure borders and legislatively through policies that protect U.S. sovereignty from encroaching international institutions.

- Rebuild American strength and prosperity through a strong economy, safe communities, secure supply chains, and energy independence.

- A strong U.S. military refocused on warfighting and deterrence and ensure the prudent use of military force.

- Lead through a peace-through-strength approach by prioritizing nation-state-level engagement and using bold diplomacy.

- Work closely in alliances and with U.S. allies by ensuring that our allies carry their weight in defending their regions.

- Keep our nation out of endless wars.

- Address the growing threat posed by Communist China, which had been neglected for decades as a threat.

This America First approach is not isolationist nor a retreat from America serving as the leader of the free world. It is an approach, however, that rejects the pervasive view of our broader foreign policy establishment that the United States' focus should be on developing a hegemonic empire abroad and being a world policeman while failing to take care of our nation and citizens first.

Rather than retreating from our engagement in the world, the America First approach seeks to redefine U.S. engagement to ensure that all international arrangements where the United States is involved have concrete benefits for the American people. President Trump's transactional approach to diplomacy sought to remedy the unequal burden sharing of the past and was a call for our allies to pay their fair share so the cost of regional security did not disproportionally fall on the American taxpayer.

At its core, the America First policy framework was neither Republican nor Democrat but instead reflected principles of populism and was based on the constitutional premise of "We the People." This means the U.S. government is accountable to the American people directly, and its primary function is to preserve and defend the American people's constitutional rights, security, and interests first.

This America First doctrine for U.S. national security is a choice to preserve national sovereignty and maintain a Constitutional Republic and a necessary safeguard from the rise of globalism, which has increasingly framed America's and the international community's approach to foreign affairs.

SECURING A STRONG AMERICA FIRST

The call to put the interests and security of our own nation and citizens first is not unique to America alone. Every nation-state leader has the duty to prioritize the affairs of its nation. The United States, however, has largely adopted a different position toward this matter. Ever since the U.S. became the default leader of the free world after World War II, America has adopted the responsibility of maintaining the international order, providing for the security of our allies, and deterring adversaries globally. As a direct result, the United States disproportionately contributes to international organizations. When other nations are faced with crises, it is the United States that takes the primary role, economically and militarily, in coming to their aid. We have seen this play out most recently in the wars in Ukraine and Israel, where U.S. aid far exceeds the combined aid of other nations.

America's embrace of being the leader of the free world has meant our nation's resources are often invested in the affairs of the world while the interests of our nation is ignored, if not neglected. As an example, while European NATO states like France and Germany decline to fund their defense programs at agreed levels, they spend freely on expansive social welfare programs.

America First means promoting peace through strength to protect American security with effective national security policies led by an engaged U.S. president who exercises decisive leadership. We had that with President Trump. Unfortunately, President Biden's weak leadership and national security policy incoherence, which includes designating climate change as the primary threat to U.S. national security, falls far short of effective and decisive national security leadership. This has undermined America's standing as a great power. This also has resulted in a world that is much more unstable and dangerous than when President Trump left office in January 2021.

The Trump Administration most notably pivoted to prioritizing the security of our own nation's borders, specifically by securing our southern border and stopping the flow of illegal migrants into our nation by use of all diplomatic, economic, and military means available.

The Trump Administration rebuilt our military, strengthened our national economy, secured our supply chains, and achieved energy independence. Due to this dramatic improvement in our domestic security, the U.S. was better positioned to engage outwardly from a position of strength.

Under the Biden Administration, we have seen the consequences of what happens when a president fails to prioritize our nation and its people. Pursuant to its green energy agenda, America has lost its ability to provide for our own energy needs. As a result, the U.S. has been forced to turn to other nations to fulfill our energy needs. As a result, President Biden's mismanagement of the domestic economy and energy production has directly contributed to historic levels of inflation.

The America First approach to U.S. national security is, therefore, not a retreat from engagement in the world, nor is it ending America's position as leader of the free world. Instead, America First is the policy framework that ensures America remains a strong nation first, so it can engage outwardly from a position of strength and ensure that America is fulfilling its primary duty – protecting the interests of the American people.

AMERICA FIRST IS NOT AMERICA ALONE – HOW THE U.S. WORKS WITH OTHER NATIONS FOR THE BENEFIT OF AMERICANS

In its 2017 National Security Strategy (NSS), the Trump Administration established the criteria for America's engagement with other nations and international institutions. The NSS set a new standard that every U.S. multilateral arrangement must "achieve better outcomes" for the American people.[1]

In international arrangements and alliances, the first question raised by President Trump was how they would secure and advance American interests and would reap tangible, concrete benefits for the American people.

The criteria that all international arrangements must result in benefits for the United States were crafted in response to one of the glaring and systemic flaws in America's engagement abroad: the unequal burden sharing between the United States and our allies.

The NATO alliance is representative of this issue. NATO was originally built as a collective defense pact, in which under the Washington Treaty, all NATO members under Article 3 agreed that "...separately and jointly, by means of continuous and effective self-help and mutual aid, will maintain and develop their individual and collective capacity to resist armed attack". In the 2014 Wales Declaration, agreed to by all member states, each nation committed to spend 2% of their GDP on Defense. Fully two-thirds of NATO's members still do not meet this agreed-upon goal after ten years.

Due to Russia's war against Ukraine, we have witnessed a shift in NATO member defense spending as many members recognized the need to reach their 2% GDP spending requirement. However, the problem of unequal burden sharing from our NATO allies remains. Even today, U.S. aid to Ukraine is equivalent to all other NATO members combined.[2]

The America First national security policy framework seeks to address this unequal burden sharing from our allies to ensure that Europe's defense and deterrence against an emergent Russia do not fall disproportionally on the American taxpayer. President Trump sought effective security partners, not states dependent on the United States.

As a businessman, Trump instinctively recognized that economics is at the core of successful policies and that alliances can only succeed when all sides are equal partners with equal participation. It was on this basis that President Trump sought transactional relations with other nations. When President Trump met with foreign leaders, for example, the first question he would ask them was what the trade imbalance was between our two nations.

President Trump also recognized that transactional relationships with nations that may be authoritarian or have poor human rights records are often necessary to promote the interests of the United States. Under this approach, the Trump Administration successfully pursued transactional working relationships with Russia, China, and North Korea that advanced U.S. interests without endorsing their governments.

The America First approach to national security pursued by the Trump Administration also ensured that U.S. sovereignty was preserved amid our involvement in international organizations that have increasingly adopted globalist objectives.

As described in the Trump Administration's National Security Strategy, the America First approach toward multilateral institutions is that the U.S. should leverage these institutions when they offer opportunities to advance American interests. However, it also clearly asserted that "it should be clear that the United States will not cede sovereignty to those that claim authority over American citizens and are in conflict with our constitutional framework."[3]

This meant the United States should always make its own national security policies and not give the United Nations or any foreign entity a veto over them. Central to an America First approach to national security is the preservation and sanctity of nation-state sovereignty. America cannot be ruled by edicts given by centralized powers and unelected bureaucrats who hold different ideologies than those of America's founders. This conviction that putting America First fundamentally means protecting America from encroaching external structures and organizations that seek to subvert or replace U.S. sovereignty was articulated by President Trump in his 2019 address to the United Nations General Assembly when he stated: "The future does not belong to globalists. The future belongs to patriots. The future belongs to sovereign and independent nations who protect their citizens, respect their neighbors, and honor the differences that make each country special and unique."[4]

That is the very conviction of America First: that the United States will work with our allies to advance American interests. The U.S. will leverage international organizations when they offer clear ways to secure U.S. interests, but America will never be subordinate or beholden to any international institution in which the "consent of the governed" is replaced with the rule by unelected elites or when these institutions pursue objectives contrary to American interests and constitutional rights. President Trump demonstrated this when he withdrew the U.S. from the Paris Climate Accords and the UN Educational, Scientific and Cultural Organization (UNESCO) because he believed they were in direct violation of U.S. interests and constitutional rights.

DELIVERING "PEACE THROUGH STRENGTH" WITH BOLD DIPLOMACY

One of the defining characteristics of the America First approach to national security, and ultimately what separates it from the mistaken efforts of the U.S. foreign policy establishment, is the prioritization of bold diplomacy to advance our national interests.

As discussed previously, the U.S. foreign policy establishment has largely established a status quo approach to U.S. diplomacy in which nation-state level diplomacy often was not seriously pursued before resorting to military force. There also was a complacent mindset regarding the role of diplomacy to mediate longstanding conflicts, such as those in the Middle East.

The Trump Administration deployed a different approach: it prioritized nation-state level engagement and ignored the conventional wisdom of the foreign policy establishment.

The best examples of this concerned Israel and North Korea.

President Trump strongly embraced Israel as one of America's closest and most important allies. Unlike prior Republican and Democratic administrations, American diplomacy with Israel and Middle Eastern states during the Trump Administration was not constrained by failed and outdated positions of the foreign policy establishment and prior U.S. presidents.

Nothing could be clearer than his approach to our American Embassy to Israel. Previously located in Tel Aviv, the *Jerusalem Act of 1995* declared it as U.S. policy that the American Embassy be moved to Jerusalem. For years, multiple presidents declined to move the embassy in contravention of the law through continual waivers. Multiple U.S. presidents had promised, as candidates, to move America's embassy in Israel to Jerusalem. Despite U.S. Department of State concerns, President Trump actually moved the embassy in 2018. In 2019, President Trump followed with recognition that the Golan Heights, which Israel took control of in 1967, is part of Israel.

In January 2020, the Trump Administration unveiled its bold "deal of the century" Middle East peace agreement, which would have provided $50 billion in investment to the Palestinians, including $28 billion to Gaza. After the Palestinians rejected this offer, the Trump Administration in September 2020 announced one of the most ambitious diplomatic initiatives in history: the Abraham Accords peace plan which normalized relations between Israel and four Arab states. This agreement went forward because the Trump Administration negotiators convinced these Arab states of the economic and security benefits of normalizing relations with Israel and that the Palestinians should no longer have a veto over Middle East peace efforts.

This agreement was one of President Trump's greatest foreign policy successes and has proved to have staying power despite lukewarm follow-on support from the Biden Administration. In addition, although Saudi Arabia has not yet joined the Abraham Accords, this agreement helped significantly improve relations between Israel and Saudi Arabia and opened the door to an Israeli-Saudi normalization agreement, possibly in the near future. That very normalization could be key to resolving the conflict between the Jewish state and Palestinian aspirations.

On North Korea, President Trump combined a comprehensive all-of-government policy, American strength, tough sanctions, and aggressive diplomacy to convince North Korean leader Kim Jong Un to suspend his nuclear and missile tests and agree to personal diplomacy with him.

This resulted in three historic meetings between the two leaders and a significant reduction in tensions with North Korea. The culmination was the dramatic personal crossing of the Armistice Line between South and North Korea by President Trump, an action no previous American President had accomplished or even attempted.

Regrettably, the Biden Administration rejected President Trump's approach to North Korea and abandoned serious diplomacy with the North. This led to a huge surge in North Korean missile tests starting in 2022 and reports that the North is preparing to conduct a seventh underground nuclear test. Although Biden officials finally expressed interest in senior-level meetings with North Korea last summer, North Korean officials ignored these offers, and it seems unlikely the Biden Administration can repair the damage their neglectful policies have done to U.S.-North Korean relations anytime soon.

THE ROLE OF THE U.S. MILITARY IN THE AMERICA FIRST APPROACH TO NATIONAL SECURITY: PROTECT AMERICANS, DETER OUR ADVERSARIES, & KEEP OUR NATION OUT OF ENDLESS WARS

The U.S. military has a clear mission: deter our nation's adversaries and, when necessary, fight and win our nation's wars. This two-fold objective of warfighting and deterrence is vital to protecting our vital national interests and keeping Americans safe.

America's ability to maintain credible deterrence is made possible by our having the world's most powerful military force on earth and a Commander-in-Chief who has the competence, resolve, and will to use this force when necessary. This credible deterrence is crucial to thwarting our nation's adversaries and keeping our nation out of unnecessary wars. Equally important to our military's mission is having a military force capable of achieving decisive victories over the adversary when all other levels of statecraft and deterrence have failed. This strategically focused mission objective of warfighting and deterrence is what our military was designed to carry out.

However, recent events have steadily and progressively pulled our military away from carrying out its core mission and intended purposes.

Most notably, the war in Afghanistan led to a dramatic shift in our military. After the 9/11 attacks, the Bush Administration led the U.S.

military into what would become a twenty-year military campaign in Afghanistan. What started as a mission directive to defeat the Taliban and al-Qaeda developed into using the U.S. military in global democracy promotion efforts and nation-state building exercises. These were essentially attempts to transform other nations into the likeness of the United States. As a result of deploying the military for operations outside of its intended purposes, it was set on a path of defeat. After twenty years spent in Afghanistan at the expense of $2 trillion, the United States ultimately left in defeat when President Biden ordered a failed withdrawal in 2021. Despite having the conditions-based Doha Agreement in place, the poorly planned withdrawal ended in a debacle with the loss of 13 American servicemen and women.

While we spent twenty years with our nation's primary effort dedicated to the Middle East, we took our eyes off the leading threat to America's national security: Communist China, which continued to execute a strategy of militarized global expansionism.

Today, our military has become further removed from its primary purpose of warfighting and deterrence as it has become consumed by social engineering and social justice politics. The far-left Diversity, Equity, and Inclusion (DEI) ideology is now engrained across the U.S. military. It generates a focus on race and gender theory over effective warfighting. The most obvious result is the lack of recruiting success of the Army, Navy, and Air Force. The young men and women of America are "voting" with their feet by not going into our Nation's military recruiting centers.

The Biden Administration has also targeted U.S. servicemembers in ways unprecedented in our nation's history, such as directing internal investigations to hunt down "extremists" in the military and discharging over 8,000 U.S. servicemembers congruent to the administration's ill-advised vaccine mandate.

Our military is now facing a historic recruitment crisis we have yet to see in our nation's history, with the military experiencing the lowest number of recruits since the creation of the all-volunteer forces in 1971. We cannot ignore nor negate the role that the Biden Administration's politicization of the U.S. military and the influx of DEI ideology.

It is clear we have lost sight of the intended role and use of our military, particularly from our foreign policy establishment, which has neglected the principle that warfare should be used only as a last resort – when all other avenues have been exhausted.

The America First approach to national security recognizes the critical mission the U.S. military plays to protect the security of our nation and its vital interests by upholding its intended mission objective of warfighting and deterrence.

During the Trump Administration, we saw a pivot to return our military to its core mission. The Trump Administration issued an Executive Order in September 2020 banning the teaching of Critical Race Theory in the military to keep our forces focused on warfighting.[5] The message to commanders: warfighting is your number one mission.

A major goal of the Trump Administration's national security policy was keeping America out of endless wars. For President Trump, this issue was at the core of putting America First as he recognized the toll that endless wars had on our servicemembers and our nation's resources. Endless war campaigns in the Middle East, for example, magnified a Veterans crisis in our nation, and a policy priority was therefore set on taking care of our veterans and keeping our servicemembers out of new wars.

President Trump understood that U.S. engagement in endless wars was an economic burden that was unsustainable for the United States to continue. The U.S. defense budget has continued to rise but increased largely to sustain our endless war campaigns abroad rather than rebuild and modernize our military.

In his 2020 State of the Union address, President Trump delivered a quote that captured his mentality toward deploying military force: "You will never escape American justice. If you attack our citizens, you forfeit your life."[6] While President Trump's priority was on keeping America out of unnecessary wars, President Trump was willing to use military force when American lives and American interests were at stake. The elimination of Islamic Revolutionary Guard Corps leader General Qasem Soleimani demonstrated the level of escalation of U.S. military force President Trump was willing to take when American lives were at stake. The strategy behind this operation was clear – super escalate to a point where Iran would be forced to retreat and recognize the U.S. was willing to deploy its military force at a level that Iran had yet to witness.

A further principle of the use of military force that was used in the Trump Administration that kept our nation safe from adversaries without bringing America into protracted conflicts was deploying military force decisively and with a pre-determined end-state. We saw this mission carried out successfully through the defeat of ISIS's force structure in Iraq and Syria in 2010. The U.S. military went in with the clear goal of eliminating ISIS's force structure in the region, and we did not depart our military's mission from that objective to pursue vague policies of the past, such as conducting nation-state building exercises.

In alignment with the America First policy priority of prudent use of military force and keeping our nation out of endless wars, the Trump Administration recognized the importance of rebuilding our military and maintaining the most powerful military force on earth. At the same time, Trump recognized that efforts to rebuild the military and maintain the world's most powerful military force could not simultaneously contradict the goal of keeping America out of unnecessary, endless wars. Throughout his administration, President Trump cautioned against those who sought to generate new wars as the first response to nation-state conflicts, including cautioning our nation's defense industrial base and contractors. As President Eisenhower first cautioned against the "unwarranted influence" our vast and powerful military arsenal could yield on foreign policy decisions, President Trump demonstrated how the U.S. can rebuild our nation's military while also keeping us out of unnecessary wars.

AMERICA FIRST AS THE PATHWAY FORWARD

Today, the United States is facing a series of challenges at home and threats abroad.

The Biden Administration's open-border policies have created a perilous national security crisis with the illegal entry of over 6.4 million unvetted individuals into the United States. China and the cartels continue to exploit our porous border by pouring deadly fentanyl into our communities, which now is the leading cause of death for young Americans. Moreover, inflation and the rescinding of America's energy independence continue to deteriorate America's domestic strength and prosperity.

Abroad, the United States is faced with a series of regional conflicts that continue to escalate and unravel into broader implications, including Russia's ongoing war against Ukraine, China's encroachments on Taiwan, Israel's war of survival against Hamas, Iranian-backed proxy groups creating regional conflicts, and Iran's potential nuclear proliferation. Moreover, China, Iran, Russia, and North Korea are developing an axis of power poised against the United States that challenges America's ability to preserve and defend our vital national interests.

America is, therefore, at a pivotal moment, and we as a nation have to choose which pathway to take. The choice for America is clear. For the first time in over a century, we have two clearly defined options: the failed foreign policy of a Biden Administration or a Trump policy of America First. America First, an approach with a record of success, offers us a proven pathway forward today.

2.

America First and the Use of U.S. Military Force

By Congressman Michael Waltz

U nder an America First Administration, the United States must focus its military power on deterring the peer threat of China. The lessons of the past 30 years, combined with changes in the way wars are fought, suggest new principles for the use of force: a realism about its ability to change foreign cultures, the need to use the maximum possible resources against the most vital collection of goals, and a need to use the full spectrum of United States political, economic, and military power to buttress the core military challenge of balancing a conventional peer adversary.

CONTEXT

The wars in Iraq and Afghanistan were seminal moments for our country. After the collapse of the Soviet Union, the United States stood at the pinnacle of its national power. Its economy far outpaced that of the rump Russian state, struggling to learn from its former adversary, and China, still in the halfway house of Deng Xiaoping's reforms and the aftermath of Tiananmen Square. American diplomatic and political power was no less supreme. Thorny diplomatic conflicts were muted, like in Northern Ireland. Communist-supported terrorist movements around the world which had deviled the US and its allies quickly adapted to peace, like the Palestine Liberation Organization (PLO), or were subjugated by US allies, like Colombia and the Fuerzas Armadas Revolucionarias de Colombia (FARC) narco-terrorists.

And most impressively, the U.S. military had just inflicted a crushing conventional defeat on Saddam Hussein in the Gulf War, reflecting the revolution in military affairs that represented a fusion of US technological and military power. The victory over Iraq in 1991, though dangerous for our servicemen, was so unexpectedly lopsided and dominant that it augured a new era of American military dominance.

That display of military power was used, effectively, in conjunction with a clear set of guidelines that came to be called the Weinberger doctrine, after President Ronald Reagan's Secretary of Defense Caspar Weinberger. Implemented by the Reagan Administration in the wake of the Vietnam War, the Weinberger Doctrine said, in short, that the U.S. military should only commit military power if its vital national interests were threatened; that power should only be used overwhelmingly, with the intention to win; with clear political and military objectives; and only as a last resort. In Iraq, the first time, the result was an overwhelming success, and the triumvirate of military, political, and economic power presaged the new American age.

It is clear now that this moment was wasted. In an era of unsurpassed national power, the mission of the United States began to go astray. Egged on by civilian ideologues, the Clinton Administration began to commit U.S. military power to humanitarian interventions divorced from our national security interests. The Powell-Weinberger doctrine of short, massive applications of force for clear goals was scrapped. After the terrorist attacks of September 11, 2001, American forces were given a new task: combat terrorism with freedom. They were to combat terrorism by spreading democracy in the heart of the Arab world, one of the most repressive places on earth, and in the remoteness of Afghanistan, perhaps the least developed country in the world.

These wars, even their supporters would agree, did not turn out the way we had hoped. The second Iraq invasion went quickly, as did the first, but was followed by a bloody and meandering counterinsurgency. Saddam was replaced by an Iraqi political coalition that was Shia-dominated first and democratic-dominated second. Today, despite over 5,000 U.S. servicemembers killed, Iraq has fallen almost totally under the control of Iran and its militias. In Afghanistan, of course, the Taliban is again in charge. Two decades of costly counterinsurgency warfare may have protected the U.S. homeland from additional 9/11-style attacks, but certainly has not produced the long-term results that we hoped for.

NEW PRINCIPLES

Perhaps no question is more telling in military affairs and the modern political environment than: "What did you learn from the wars in Iraq and Afghanistan?" For some people, the answer is nothing: the story is one of a righteous war, a somewhat stumbling occupation followed by a heroic surge to save the day. But for the Obama-Biden Administration pulling the troops out too early, in 2011, which permitted ISIS to establish a violent caliphate and Iranian influence to regrow, the war would have been a success.

There is some truth to that. There were paradigm-shifting innovations made in US military doctrine – the way we fight counterinsurgencies – how to fight them at all and the way we conduct direct action operations. The rapidity of the intelligence exploitation and raid cycle that exemplified American counterterrorism operations in Iraq, Afghanistan, and around the world did more than any single tactic or weapon to dismantle al-Qaeda and win the war on terror.

But that narrative of the last 20 years of war is not the whole story. There were critical failures: in mission scope, as well as execution, in military as well as political leadership, that helped squander the unipolar moment across a thousand wadis and the Arghandab river valley. Now our rivals are far closer to military parity with us, particularly today, with an aggressive China actively seeking to replace the United States as the primus inter pares, our use of force must be very different from that of the past thirty years.

I served multiple tours in Afghanistan as a U.S. Army Special Forces officer, a Green Beret. I came away from the wars with the conviction that America's military power must not be expended recklessly, in pursuit of the fever dreams of academics and think tanks in the Washington, DC national security establishment. What we learned, among other things, was that American power was finite, even in the post-Cold War environment, and that changing the political culture of foreign countries was far more expensive than we thought, not least in the lives of our soldiers. Rather than trying to make over foreign countries into what we wanted them to be, which yielded little value for the amount of money invested, we need to adopt new principles for the use of military force. These include a new focus on political results, a re-establishment of deterrence, a capacity to wage full-spectrum warfare, integration of allied capabilities, and a focus on people as the bedrock of national power.

The Prussian military theorist Carl von Clausewitz famously stressed the importance of remembering that warfare is intended to support political ends. Success in the 21st century will require integrating military power into our efforts nationally to achieve political results, not just military victory. Military victories abounded in Iraq and Afghanistan but left us with little left at the end. Force must be committed for clear goals, in the American national security interest, with a realistic appreciation of the costs of war and the limits of American military power. These principles partially reflect a return to our Reagan-era doctrines, but informed by our most recent experiences. They also are emblematic of the need to husband and employ military force in the most efficient possible way to contest the power, globally of the Chinese Communist Party.

The full-spectrum threat of China takes its most acute form in the shape of a conventional military danger to US-allied and partner nations of the Pacific Rim where 50% of global GDP is generated. High-intensity war with a peer competitor would burn through such large amounts of resources and strain the United States military to its maximum capacities that every measure must be taken to prioritize these costs over ancillary requirements. Our military must be focused on protecting our homeland, securing supply chains vital to our economy, defending against asymmetric threats such as cyber and space that result in catastrophic damage to our way of life, and deterring near-peer competitors that are developing capabilities to defeat us.

This focused application of military power means making the utmost use of our allies. Allied countries can dramatically reduce the strategic burden on the United States if they are allowed to contribute in their own way. Particularly in Asia and the Middle East, nations will project power in different ways from that of the United States. Under the Trump Administration NATO nations were pushed to contribute more to their defense budgets, the Quadrilateral Security Dialogue (an informal defense and economic arrangement comprised of the United States, Japan, Australia, and India known as "the Quad") was strengthened, and

Middle East nations pulled into alignment with Israel through the Abraham Accords. Coalitions like the Abraham Accords countries will help contribute to global security by balancing regional adversaries like Iran but also require broader left and right limits to pursue these goals in their own way and with maximum latitude.

Longtime allies like Japan recognized the growing threat from China and made the difficult political decision to nearly double its defense budget. Contrast this approach with NATO countries where only a third of them are living up to their 2% defense commitments despite a land war on their doorstep. We can be friends and allies but also have tough conversations about burden sharing for collective defense. The US literally can no longer afford to go it alone with the interest on our national debt eclipsing the defense budget

There is also a critical need for the foreign policy of the United States, particularly its use of military force to reflect the will of the people. More than that, however, it should lend disproportionate weight to the opinions of those who actually fight its wars. The manufacturing towns of the Midwest that send their sons to the infantry should have just as much say as the policy shops of the Beltway. The use of military force cannot be an elite subject – it is one that everyone must have a say in, especially its soldiers. This requires a commander-in-chief who explicitly and regularly explains to the American people the national security interests at stake that require their blood and treasure. It also means significant Congressional engagement in matters of war and peace through mechanisms like the voting on Authorizations of the Use of Military Force with limits and sunsets. Congress must protect its constitutional prerogatives through oversight and avoid funding wars "off the books" with funding mechanisms like Overseas Contingency Operations (OCO) funds that existed for the wars in Afghanistan and Iraq outside the budgetary process.

If the populace isn't engaged, the foreign policy of the United States will have little staying power, and the leaders who attempt to implement such a policy will soon find themselves removed from power. It is telling that in the 2016 Republican primary election for president, only two candidates were willing to urge more realism about the use of American power, and only one – Donald Trump – was willing to call the Iraq war a mistake. These two candidates were not coincidentally the most successful in the primary, and Trump, of course, was successful in the general election.

NEW TYPE OF WAR

These methods are shaped and lent additional urgency by the changing character of modern war. The victory over Iraq in the first Gulf War aside, the United States has not fought a conventional war against a near-peer adversary since Korea. The strategies and techniques employed in its counterinsurgency wars are radically different than against an adversary that can contest its supply lines, air and space domains, and the nuclear sphere as can China. Given this need to wage war as efficiently as possible, the US must focus on fighting in ways that maximize its strengths.

The nature of warfare has also changed. The conflict in Ukraine has been a key revealer of the nature of modern high-intensity warfare. In many ways, it has demonstrated a military shift like World War I: a rapid advance in military technology that seems to favor the defensive in war. It has made it far more expensive to mass conventional forces and conduct combined arms attacks.

The widespread use of unmanned aerial vehicles and the damage such weapons can inflict on military formations suggests that conventional operations, for the immediate term, may be of limited value. The United States began to use drones widely for intelligence, surveillance, and reconnaissance in Afghanistan and Iraq. The use of these systems was novel in that they were popularized across the force and that they were tactically controlled. Individual battalions, platoons, and even squads had access to their own UAVs and UAV-fed streams of battlefield intelligence. The U.S. also began to widely use larger armed drones, MQ-9 reapers, and others, to conduct counterterrorism strikes and close air support for units on the ground.

During the war in Ukraine, however, both Ukraine and Russia began to mix these two types of drones. They used large numbers of small, cheap, armed, disposable drones to cut apart formations and even small groups when they could find them, leading to a focus on fortification and concealment. This changing dynamic is part of the reason why Ukraine's counteroffensive has been less effective than many had hoped. The value of electronic warfare (EW) has also grown. Effective EW offers the potential to disable unmanned aerial vehicles before they can strike, jam sensors before they can communicate their data, confuse enemy GPS, and target command and control nodes based on their electronic emissions. The struggle to disrupt and protect all types of transmissions has become just as important as the struggle to disrupt and protect satellites in space.

The United States and the Western world encountered the same situation during World War I, when industrialized warfare with popular armies vastly increased the lethality of combat and temporarily made conventional tactics obsolete. This was eventually overcome by technology, with developments like the tank, but also by the innovative use of small, lightly armed, motivated infantry units to achieve tactical breakthroughs that then could be exploited strategically.

We are at something of the same impasse now. If our military is to achieve better results than it has over the past twenty years, it must adjust both its mission and its model of fighting. The political must be the utmost goal for U.S. forces: how to effect a political outcome, rather than a military one. Our adversaries have been experts at achieving political outcomes with a minimum of military force, while we have been experts since Vietnam at using a maximum of military force to achieve unclear political outcomes.

POLITICAL AND MILITARY

Somewhat ironically, these same principles about the use of force and the relationship of the political to the military are the same lessons that Russia believed it had learned during the democratic color revolutions of 2003-2005. After the widespread public riots against election rigging and corruption brought down Russian-allied governments in Georgia, Ukraine, and Kyrgyzstan, Putin and his senior leadership came to believe that the United States was waging political warfare against its allies.

The rapid regime changes in the Middle East that resulted from the Arab Spring demonstrations reinforced that view, contributing to a full-spectrum Russian doctrine of information, political, economic, and military conflict against the West. This was not precisely true – in fact, Russia's own support of corrupt autocrats in its near abroad fomented more than enough opposition and bad governance to cause a revolt. However, it was accurate in the assessment of the costs and benefits of different types of national power.

In a terrible irony for Moscow, Russia's experience in Ukraine has born out precisely its own hypotheses of modern war: that the political was more valuable than the military, that full-spectrum operations were more valuable than a conventional onslaught, and that the unconventional was far more cost-effective, for the results achieved than the conventional. Far better that Russia expended tens of thousands of its troops, trying to learn how modern wars were fought than the United States.

The United States under an America First administration, and particularly the Defense Department, must think of national power across all these spectrums. It must focus intently not just on where to use American power but how, and which type of power to use. We must shape the battlespace to reduce the need for military force, and to contest political influence with great power rivals like China and regional rivals like Iran. Weakness is contagious: weakness invites aggression by our rivals, and that aggression raises significantly the cost of defending our vital national interests.

Power springs from population, as well. Iran has spread a wide swath of influence over much of the Middle East not by formally annexing it but by successfully leveraging political doubt about responsibility and escalation among the states that might counter-balance it. Russia has attempted to rebuild its sphere of influence over the past two decades in former Soviet territories by utilizing the legitimacy claims of ethnically Russian populations abroad to throw the question of national sovereignty into doubt. In certain cases, both Russia and China have attempted to move native ethnic populations into territory controlled by rebels or opposing nation-states, like Donbas. In Tibet and Xinjiang, Beijing has aggressively sought to replace native populations with ethnically Han Chinese inhabitants. The United States, with its unsecure southern border, must never allow itself to risk a great power adversary weaponizing migration to damage it politically and economically.

Knowing that asymmetric and political warfare is a favored and effective tool of its enemies the United States must secure its border for its own national security.

CLEANING UP THE MESS

The core of the national policy decisions about the use of military force remains a conventional, high-intensity war. Properly employed, overwhelming conventional military force can ensure stability by providing a credible deterrent such that the actual use of military force is not needed. Unfortunately, under President Biden, conventional deterrence has been totally eroded. The calamitous retreat from Afghanistan was a signal to our adversaries of American weakness, and they responded. In Europe, Putin launched a full-scale invasion of Ukraine, continuing the operations that first began in an unconventional way in 2014. The brazenness of this attack was unprecedented in the post-Cold War world. Russia's invasion of Ukraine in February 2022 was a global demonstration of the depth to which the Biden Administration's fecklessness has severely degraded American leadership and deterrence.

Russia's intent to devour Ukraine was not new. Vladimir Putin has invaded one of his neighbors under every U.S. administration since he came to power in 1999, except for one. Under President Trump, the Ukraine security situation was stabilized. Through an effective combination of lethal aid to Ukraine and sanctions on Russian oligarchs with effective diplomacy, backed up by a credible threat of military force, the political situation in Ukraine was calmed. By the last year of his administration, cross-border security incidents had dropped to a tenth of what they had been, and multilateral talks on peace under the Normandy format had restarted. What was new, under Biden, was that U.S. deterrence had completely collapsed. Our rivals no longer feared what the U.S. president might or might not do. Worse, Biden combined that weakness with a maximization of the political importance of Ukraine. Having spent every waking moment for the previous six years talking about the threat of Russia and the value of Ukraine, Biden then paused military aid and demonstrated U.S. ineptness in the Afghanistan withdrawal. Further, Biden slow-rolled Ukrainian military requests out of fear of provoking Putin, lifted sanctions on the Nord Stream II gas pipeline, rewarded Putin with a summit after the hacking of U.S. critical infrastructure in the colonial pipeline, and made critical mistakes by saying minor incursions may not generate a significant response. It was little surprise that Putin believed his 2022 invasion would be met with the same feckless response under Biden as his 2014 invasion was met with under Obama. Over $100 billion in US aid later and the war stalemated, we can congratulate ourselves that at least Russia didn't capture Kyiv. But it would have been far better for us, and Ukraine, if the war had not happened at all.

The collapse of America's military deterrent is particularly acute in the Middle East. The unchecked growth of Iranian power over the past two decades has created a significant threat to American interests in the Middle East. It has been U.S. policy for at least seventy-five years – and British policy, before then – to prevent the domination of the Persian Gulf by a hostile power. That is precisely the situation the region finds itself in today. The invasion of Iraq eliminated a critical counterweight to Iran. President Obama's precipitous removal of forces from Iraq in 2011 emboldened Iraqi sectarianism and Nuri al-Maliki's relationship with Iran. It also created a vacuum for the rise of ISIS. American muddling during the Syrian civil war allowed the rapid expansion of Iranian power. And perhaps most importantly, Obama's disastrous Iran nuclear deal flooded the Iranian government with money for its proxies while failing to significantly affect Iran's ability to dominate the Gulf.

Worse, by ensuring Iran an economic lifeline based on meeting weak nuclear proliferation goals – standards that were lower than the four UN Security Council resolutions Iran was already violating – the Obama Administration eliminated America's ability to sanction Iran effectively. It could no longer attach strategic conditions to economic relief, since that relief was guaranteed anyway, and made it functionally impossible to sanction entities that were clearly involved in proxy war and terrorism but had had their sanctions lifted by their association under the nuclear deal. Perversely, the American inability to use effective economic sanctions made it more likely that the U.S. would have to use military force to deter Iran or watch Iranian proxies destabilize the region.

This is particularly critical because our "by, with, and through" model has not been met with overwhelming success in balancing Iran. The model for how we develop a partner military has clearly failed. In the Middle East, the Lebanese and Iraqi armed forces are institutions that we believed would provide an effective counterweight to Iranian-backed militias. We have poured millions of dollars into developing those partner militaries and they are fundamentally incapable of competing with Iran and its proxies for influence. It has exacerbated the security crisis that the region faces under Biden.

The October 7 Hamas attacks against Israel are a product of this broken framework. The strength and deterrence of the Trump Administration helped blunt Iranian aggression and begin to roll back Iranian proxy warfare. Nowhere was this more evident than in the targeted killing of Iran's proxy field general, Qasem Soleimani. For every pundit who calls for the necessity of reigning in presidents with bureaucratic power, it is enough to say that President Trump's decision to hit the Qods Force leader was made against every single piece of bureaucratic and institutional advice. It was a bold decision that shocked the Iranian system to its core, short-circuited a cycle of escalating violence, and brought Iran's creeping regional aggression to a halt. In fact, the accumulated mistakes of the permanent bureaucracy with both Iran and other regional issues like moving the U.S. Embassy to Israel to Jerusalem suggests that U.S. policy towards Yemen should be reviewed: that in 2017 a coalition-led campaign to regain control over Yemen might have been a better outcome than allowing an Iranian proxy to gain control over yet another strategic chokepoint.

More broadly, the unprecedented economic sanctions that President Trump levied on Iran and the quick, bold deterrent strikes created the space to allow the Abraham Accords to be achieved. That is, they permitted the diplomatic outcome that Tehran abjured most and which would most imperil long-term Iranian domination of the Persian Gulf and the Middle East. Under Biden, this pressure has been reversed and Iranian influence has exploded across the region. The Abraham Accords have stalled. Iran's proxy Houthi militants have blocked the Red Sea to commercial traffic, and an Iranian proxy government has consolidated power in Baghdad. Thanks to the policies of the Biden Administration,

Israel stands isolated, under pressure, and isolation breeds aggression in the Middle East.

THE DAY AFTER

Stabilizing the Middle East and Europe will not be an easy task for the administration that succeeds the Biden presidency. The legacy of failure is so pronounced, and the expression of weakness is so absolute, that only a disciplined and sustained whole-of-government effort can reverse it. It will be even harder since those two missions need to be achieved while the U.S. military husbands its resources and rebuilds its deterrence for the primary threat, the People's Republic of China. China will present a continuing risk of a high-intensity threat that the U.S. military must be prepared and focused to combat. Integrating new principles for the use of military force, drawing realistic lessons from the successes and failures of the last three decades, and making the utmost use of allies and full-spectrum tools to limit the strain on our military is vital. It is a threat that the United States must be prepared to face and to defeat.

In an America First administration, it will.

3.

There Can Be No America First Without the Shield of the Armed Forces

By Robert Wilkie

At what point shall we expect the approach of danger? By what means shall we fortify against it? Shall we expect some transatlantic military giant, to step the Ocean, and crush us at a blow? Never! All the armies of Europe, Asia and Africa combined, with all the treasure of the earth (our own excepted) in their military chest; with a Bonaparte for a commander, could not by force, take a drink from the Ohio, or make a track on the Blue Ridge, in a trial of a thousand years.

At what point then is the approach of danger to be expected? I answer, if it ever reach us, it must spring up amongst us. It cannot come from abroad. If destruction be our lot, we must ourselves be its author and finisher. As a nation of freemen, we must live through all time, or die by suicide.

Abraham Lincoln's address to the Young Men's Lyceum of Springfield Illinois, January 27, 1838

When Donald Trump took office, America's armed forces were reeling from progressive indoctrination of our troops and budgets that sacrificed training and readiness for the ephemeral goals of fighting climate change, racism, and the baleful effects of fossil fuels. The threats to the future of our free republic—Communist China and militant Islam—were downplayed, if not ignored outright, by the Obama-Biden Defense Department.

The Obama-Biden years were also marked by the ahistoric appeasement of traditional adversaries—Iran, Russia, and China. The administration dispatched billions of dollars to Iran's ruling mullahs, promised Russian President Vladimir Putin we would go easy on him after the 2012 election, and signaled weakness to China by reducing our naval footprint in the Pacific. More ominously, the Obama-Biden Administration squandered American power by daring malevolent actors not to cross military "red lines" lest American reprisals be swift and devastating. The red lines were crossed repeatedly with no response from the White House. America was painted as the paper tiger that the communists and theocratic fanatics always claimed we were. In the meantime, wars expanded, and more Americans were put in harm's way.

Under the Obama and Biden Administrations, America's military has been overextended, undervalued, and insufficiently resourced. Obama's "third term" is worse because his successor, Joe Biden, is presiding over the most precipitous decline in American power and prestige in our history. It took Biden fewer than seven months to accomplish in Afghanistan what Jimmy Carter couldn't do in four years: make America an object of derision.[7]

Biden's failure to protect American troops needlessly placed in exposed desert outposts—supposedly to fight an ISIS enemy that Donald Trump vanquished—has created a crisis of confidence in our military and its reason for existence not seen since the dark days of street rage during the Vietnam War. American parents in regions of the country that have been hotbeds of military service see Biden's humiliation in Afghanistan and the needless deaths of Americans in the Middle East and ask the age-old question asked by a decorated Marine warrior: "Was it worth it?"[8]

Biden has placed this nation in needless danger by failing to fight back. That danger springs from within as thousands of young Americans refuse to consider the colors. Young civilians who might thrive in a military environment are also disenfranchised when educators and influencers discourage them from learning about military service and preparing for the honor of wearing America's uniform. Entire sections of the nation, particularly students at our "elite" universities, have checked out of military service. And radical politics are eating away at the vitality of those who already serve. Not once has the president or his vice-president gone to the country and said we want our best and brightest to serve our nation in the military. There is no higher calling.

Ominously, the Biden Administration is sapping our will to fight. Our ancestors were taught that we were Lincoln's "last best hope for man." They lived to advance the cause of Ronald Reagan's "shining city on the hill." America was the citadel of freedom worthy of sacrifice. Today, our citizens are taught that ours is a sordid legacy built on racism and oppression, and the only way to escape our past is to discard the patriotism of our forebearers. We are living the nightmare the young Lincoln predicted.

The Biden Administration has endangered our security by not sufficiently funding our military or making necessary long-term investments. It has undermined morale by lowering fitness standards and squandered tax dollars promoting social engineering in the military, including the radical diversity, equity, and inclusion ideology. The Biden Administration's incompetent management of the military has caused the most severe military crisis since Richard Nixon and General Creighton Abrams gave America the all-volunteer force in 1973.

PREPARING FOR A PEER-ON-PEER WARS ACROSS MULTIPLE DOMAINS

After a quarter century of training for and fighting insurgents and terrorists, the United States faces a four-headed adversary. One is already a threatening peer: China. Another, a near-peer that has been severely weakened by its bloody conflict in Ukraine, is Russia. The other two have the potential to cause severe damage in theaters vital for U.S. and allied security: Iran and North Korea.

Since the collapse of the Soviet Union, the Pentagon benefited from rapid and overwhelming conventional victories against small nations (Panama) and medium-sized countries with little military sophistication and incompetent leadership (Iraq and Afghanistan). The rapidity of the victory led Pentagon planners into the false security of preparing for two medium-sized regional conflicts that would repeat the on-the-ground military successes of previous decades.

The Trump Administration discarded the old military hobby horse that the next war will look like the last war.[9] Trump insisted that the Pentagon prepare for a peer-on-peer conflict, not a replay of Desert Storm and certainly not one that longingly looked for conflict determined by one decisive battle. Nevertheless, the two regional conflict models continue to dominate our current strategic and budgetary assumptions.[10] If anything, the war in Ukraine should open our eyes to the potential for a protracted conventional war in which the industrial capacities of the belligerents will be the deciding factor. Despite warnings from the Trump Administration, the Biden Administration still plans for quick conflicts that look like Iraq, and it continues the chimerical pursuit of wonder weapons to awe the enemy. The emphasis on capability over capacity will not work with China and may not work if Russia takes the proper tactical lessons from its initial debacle in Ukraine.

The corollary to the two regional contingency mindset is that the American defense industry scaled to the post-Soviet small-war construct. This consolidation of the defense industry after the Cold War stifled innovation. It was challenging to surge the production of much-needed conventional munitions, from artillery shells to precision-guided munitions. The gap was laid bare by the strain the system experienced by providing Ukraine with conventional munitions while husbanding weapons for the current conflict in the Middle East. Low budgets and inchoate strategic guidance make it difficult for industry to know when and where to accelerate weapons production.

During World War II and again during the Reagan Administration, the Defense Production Board was able to marshal American industry to meet national defense needs. The Pentagon administered strategic and budgetary guidance to direct the nation's industrial capacity. Without a healthy industrial base, the military enterprise will collapse. This is not 1941, where one trigger mobilized the latent power of America's industrial might. The mammoth plants of the mid-20th century no longer exist, nor can corporations the size of Ford and Boeing turn on a dime and switch from commercial to wartime production. We have an economy built on efficiency, not mass mobilization.

The Biden Administration and its cheerleaders in the media have heralded the arrival of the largest Pentagon budget in history for 2024.[11] The White House produced a budget matched only by Bill Clinton in 1999 as the smallest defense budget as a percentage of GDP since the end of the Korean War in 1953. In 2023, as the Pentagon's buying power was decimated by 6 percent inflation—meaning the budget was lower than the prior year's all-time low—the Biden Administration's priorities were reflected in double-digit increases for the Environmental Protection Agency, the Department of Energy, and the U.S. Department of Health and Human Services.[12] In short, the Biden White House placed climate change and welfare spending ahead of national defense. Biden sapped real dollar buying power with his government-manufactured inflation.

The China threat must be the driver of U.S. military readiness and recruitment, yet both have reached record lows. China in March 2024 announced a 7.2% defense budget increase, and Biden's response was to propose an under-strength navy, the oldest air force since the service was created, and an army that is at two-thirds of its required strength.[13]

The status of the United States Navy versus the Peoples Liberation Army Navy is illustrative, and the numbers become more stark given that the United States has global responsibilities. At the same time, China has focused on denying American access to the Asian littoral— particularly relevant in the case of Taiwan.

Beijing has been building a fleet for the type of force-on-force engagement the U.S. Navy has not seen since the battles off of Okinawa in 1945. After the fall of the Soviet Union, the U.S. Navy began a long transition to become, in many respects, merely a supporting element for the Marine Corps. The carrier strike groups have been stripped of their long-range anti-ship and anti-submarine strike craft that would be needed in a fleet action. Without them, $11 billion carriers would be vulnerable to a close-in Chinese anti-ship missile.[14]

We still have the qualitative edge in submarines, but China is the top shipbuilding nation in the world, according to the Department of Defense. The United States currently has just 10 shipyards. We must be able to flood the Western Pacific with submarines and, if need be, turn the power of guided missile submarines on the Chinese mainland. Without more boats in the water, the quantity will eventually overwhelm quality.[15] Beijing's fleet is being built by a robust Chinese military-civil shipbuilding industry, *"more than 200 times* more capable of producing surface warships and submarines" than the American shipbuilding industry, according to the Office of Naval Intelligence. (Emphasis added.)[16]

The U.S. Army is aging rapidly, suffered an 8 percent cut in modernization funding, and is at 62% strength under Biden.[17] The Air Force has 897 fighters—the lowest since the demobilization after World War II. It falls woefully short of the 1,200 necessary for a great power confrontation. And its bomber capacity is 64% of what is required.[18] The Marine Corps has the highest readiness and operational capability, comparatively speaking. However, the Corps' overall excellence is tempered by its small size and limited mission.[19]

Our defense budget must increase to post-World War II averages at a minimum, and our active and reserve components must expand. This also means returning to Trump-era energy independence to make oil and gas invulnerable to interdiction.

AMERICANS HAVE QUESTIONED THEIR MILITARY MANY TIMES IN THE PAST...

We have seen crises of confidence in our military before. On July 5, 1950, two companies of the 21st Infantry Regiment were rushed from garrison duty in occupied Japan to the hills of South Korea to slow down the invading army of the Communist North. They were wiped out. The 400 men of Task Force Smith became a metaphor for what happens when leadership is distracted, troops are out of shape, and either do not know how to use their weapons or their weapons do not work. General

Matthew Ridgway said at the time that the U.S. Army's mental and physical readiness before the Korean War was "shameful."[20]

It is also illustrative that as Task Force Smith collapsed—and the entire American-South Korean front along with it—it was African Americans who had been consigned to driving trucks and orderly and clerk duty who took up available weapons and, through sheer guts, halted the Communist tide long enough for the allies to regroup around the Pusan Perimeter. More than Harry Truman's order to integrate the military, those few men shattered every prejudice of the era and set the standard for the colorblind armed forces we extol today.

The aftermath of Vietnam also witnessed a catastrophic collapse in military morale coupled with the bottoming out of budgets during the Carter Administration. In the late 1970s, there was no money for training, and fuel and munitions ran out. At Fort Bragg, Americans witnessed the spectacle of Airborne and Special Forces units siphoning off gas from each other to survive. My father did not have the fuel to get his airborne battalion's artillery pieces from their marshaling areas to Pope Air Force Base—three miles away. But more devastating was the insertion of radical politics and criminality in the barracks—political activists and drug and biker gangs proliferated. Officers had to arm themselves to enter the barracks, even among elite troops. The post-Vietnam decline reached a sad and deadly conclusion in 1980 in the Iranian desert with the failed attempt to rescue American hostages in Tehran.

The dark days of the Carter Administration have returned with a vengeance, but this time, made more pernicious by the deliberate introduction of radical politics into the ranks, a concept anathema to the American military experience. The Biden Administration, through word and deed, has not only treated the armed forces as just another place to work but has made it a woke laboratory. The profession of arms is becoming a uniformed Great Society jobs program.

Forty-one million of those free Americans Lincoln heralded have put on the uniform since the first shots of the Revolution were fired on Lexington Green on that April morning in 1775. Since 1973, they have all been volunteers. More than 1 million have laid their lives on the altar of freedom. The American soldier has done more for world peace and the betterment of man than any fighter, government, or multinational organization in history. General Colin Powell put it this way:

> *We have sent men and women from the armed forces of the United States to other parts of the world throughout the past century to put down oppression. We defeated fascism. We defeated communism. We saved Europe in World War I and World War II. We were willing to do it, glad to do it. We went to Korea. We went to Vietnam. All in the interest of preserving the rights of people.*
>
> *And when all those conflicts were over, what did we do? Did we stay and conquer? Did we say, "Okay, we defeated Germany. Now Germany belongs to us? We defeated Japan, so Japan belongs to us"? No. What did we do? We built them up. We gave them democratic systems which they have embraced totally to their soul. And did we ask for any land? No, the only land we ever asked for was enough land to bury our dead. And that is the kind of nation we are.*[21]

Today, we are at a tipping point. We risk wasting the sacrifices of millions of our fellow citizens who fought believing that America was the last best hope of man.

Ronald Reagan knew what was at stake if we squandered that hope. He told a poignant story about an elderly Cuban man who rafted for 90 miles across the shark-infested Florida Straits to escape Castro's Island prison. When a young Coast Guard officer pulled him from the water, he said, "Boy, were you lucky." The old man said, "Me lucky? At least I had someplace to escape!"[22]

The Left has embraced identity politics and succeeded in exerting influence on college campuses, public schools, mainstream media, and, frighteningly, the leadership of our armed forces. A nation that is a beacon of liberty that countless fight and die to get to is now fixated on race and reducing all Americans to the category to which they have been assigned. In the civilian world, Jews are the latest victims of this intersectional madness, as segments within our country warp the facts and reality to fit their narrative.[23]

THE CRISIS OF CONFIDENCE IN THE U.S. MILITARY TODAY IS MORE DIRE THAN IN THE PAST

Despite the seriousness of the above and other examples of declines in popular confidence in the U.S. military, none of them come close to the challenges our military is facing today. Our military's uniformed whole is now divided along racial, sexual, and ethnic lines, emphasizing heightened individualism and obliterating unit cohesion and the military's foundational ethic as a colorblind meritocracy. Making this worse, the Biden Administration has emphasized these and other social engineering policies over maintaining and building the strongest possible U.S. military to protect our nation from a world of growing foreign threats that are collectively more menacing than the sclerotic Soviet Union ever was.

Last year, 160 retired admirals and generals sent a letter to Speaker of the House Kevin McCarthy warning that politically driven divisions in the military were a threat to national security. They argued that the "One Team, One Fight" battle motto describes a meritocracy-based military characterized by:

- a common mission and purpose;
- unqualified loyalty to the team and not to an individual's identity group;
- total trust and confidence in each other for their very lives, from the foxhole to the highest level;
- teamwork and camaraderie resulting in unit cohesion essential for warfighting readiness.[24]

The order of the day for the armed forces is diversity, equity, and inclusion. The prioritization of DEI and its underlying dogma, critical race theory (a concept rooted in cultural Marxism), over traditional military maxims such as "Follow Me," "Mass the Fire," "Strike Hard," "Noli Me Tangere," or "One Team, One Fight" is clear. Recruitment has reached a 50-year low.[25] The one service that has not seen a decline in its recruiting base is the United States Marine Corps. This service proudly heralds its ancient traditions, the grueling path one must take to wear the Globe and Anchor, and the fact that every Marine is a

49

warrior standing on the shoulders of those who have fought before. Unlike the other services, Americans have never seen Marines recruit using commercials that promote a social justice mission.

The American people's trust in a nonpartisan officer corps fell from 70% before the debacle in Afghanistan to 48% in 2022.[26] In an Army where 79% of those who serve come from military families[27], the current service secretary does not want second and third-generation recruits for fear of creating a warrior caste and warring against diversity.[28] Indeed, the Army secretary's six priorities for the service never mention fighting and winning battles against the nation's enemies, yet climate change is priority number three.[29] The Navy is now accepting recruits without a high school diploma or GED.

The Americans who have proudly sent their children to the colors are questioning why go down that road if the military is just another progressive petri dish. In the meantime, we confront a host of adversaries more threatening than the sclerotic Soviet Union ever was.

DEI is the antithesis of the American military ideal. The armed services are the greatest leveler in American society. If you perform, you are accepted. It does not matter where you come from or what color you are. I saw it as a youngster at Fort Bragg in the 1970s. My father's driver was an African American sergeant. His commanding officer, the major general leading the highly decorated and revered 82nd Airborne Division, was also black. If anything, the military was and is the manifest fulfillment of Martin Luther King Jr.'s dream. The military is the most "diverse and inclusive" segment of American society, and its only rival is professional sports in terms of awarding advancement based on merit. Sports are games, though; warfighting entails destruction and the possibility of death.

In 2021, Chief of Naval Operations Michael Gilday defended placing critical race theory tomes on his reading list for all ranks,[30] while Pentagon leaders defended instruction at West Point on topics such as "white rage" and "white fragility."[31] A progressive narrative of America's supposed fundamental flaws is infiltrating the U.S. military, threatening to undermine the meritocratic, apolitical nature of the institution, and jeopardizing our national security from the inside out. As the *Wall Street Journal* editorial board asked, "[W]hy is Kendi's 'How to Be an

Antiracist,' a book promoting sectarian racism, on a reading list with foundational naval classics?"[32] This is not, as the former CNO implies, about "open-mindedness." Anyone who has ever served knows that a suggestion from a superior officer is a command. Those "suggestions" from the Joint Chiefs of Staff form the core ethos of their services.

In 1791, Edmund Burke noted that the Jacobins were tearing down the foundations of French civilization in the name of *fraternité* and *egalité*. The Assembly ordained French youth to read from an approved list. "Nothing ought to be more weighed than the nature of books recommended by public authority. So recommended, they soon form the character of the age," Burke wrote.[33] Chances are the former CNO has not read "A Letter to a Member of the National Assembly."

Suppose you tell our young people repeatedly that their country's history is shameful and that its global legacy is repugnant. Is it any wonder they no longer flock to recruiters? As Senator Tom Cotton, a veteran of Iraq and Afghanistan, observed: "Every minute of training spent on charlatans like Ibram X. Kendi at best is wasted time better devoted to tactical and operation excellence, but at worst and more likely is a corrosive blow to the intangibles qualities needed to fight and win a war."[34] Moreover, such indoctrination pits soldier against soldier as one is identified as an oppressor and the other as the oppressed.

The imposition of progressive policies began in the Obama Administration when it declared climate change a more dire national security threat than Chinese Communism or militant Islam. Their progressive narrative of America's supposed fundamental flaws threatens to undermine the meritocratic, apolitical nature of the armed services from the inside out. DEI produces a system that expresses itself in proliferating legions of DEI bureaucrats at all levels of the uniformed services, breaking apart the common military identity and trust required to accomplish the mission.

Mike Pompeo, the former secretary of state and a captain of the corps of cadets at West Point, put it this way:

> *How can we ask young men and women who have decided to risk their lives for America, even die for America, to affirm that our country is inherently racist? How can we*

ask them to view their brothers and sisters in arms through the narrow prisms of race or gender? The clear and obvious answer is that we cannot—not without putting their lives at risk on the battlefield. A woke military is a weak military. Unfortunately, woke and weak are exactly what our military is becoming under Biden's leadership.[35]

It is not enough to criticize the intellectual and political underpinnings of DEI and CRT. One must see it in action to understand how it warms against our ability to deter the planet's bad actors and protect the homeland.

Traditional equal employment opportunity standards and educational practices have been supplanted by programs that promote discrimination by replacing equality with the latest college fad – "equity," which in practice means unequal treatment based on group identity.

On August 9, 2022, the Secretary of the Air Force issued a force-wide memorandum detailing the type of officers he would accept into the service in specific racial, sexual, and ethnic percentages. While claiming he supported merit-based applications, he said the Air Force needs only 43% of males with European ancestry as officers.[36] Meanwhile, Secretary Frank Kendall has presided over an Air Force that has traveled from "marginal to very weak" under his leadership based on the Heritage Foundation's 2022 Index of Military Strength.[37]

Ironically, even as the Air Force suffers a pilot shortage, partly because of its bureaucratic roadblocks, Kendall announced a specific plan to reduce the percentage of white pilots (currently 86%) by dropping prior flight training as a "plus" factor for selection. Prior completion of flight training is highly correlated to success in Air Force flight school.[38]

At the Air Force Academy, a "diversity and inclusion" slide presentation advised cadets to "use gender-neutral language and avoid terms such as mom and dad."

The Biden Administration started with a bang. Promotion boards and officer accession programs were ordered to implement DEI metrics in their decisions. This puts the military at war with prevailing Supreme

Court jurisprudence on this very matter. [39] The Biden Defense Department even admitted it uses racial preferences in amicus briefs it filed before the Supreme Court in the Harvard and North Carolina admissions cases. [40] Ivy League-style thought police have been unleashed on the Pentagon.

No sooner was President Biden sworn in than Secretary of Defense Lloyd Austin ordered an "extremism" stand down. The Pentagon began tirelessly searching for the purveyors of MAGA consciousness within the ranks.[41] For the first time in American history, a commander-in-chief used United States Marines not just as flanking sentinels but as political props as he excoriated half of the nation's citizenry as being a threat to the Republic. Air Force leaders at Minot, North Dakota, issued an all-airmen alert in November 2023, telling the force that attendance at a pro-Trump rally "could jeopardize their continued military service in the U.S. military" and to be cautious, especially because some rally-goers "could be confrontational to military members."[42] Does that type of action reject what separates the American military tradition from all others, including that of our closest ally, Great Britain? American soldiers were never asked about their political views. There was no political or religious litmus test under the Constitution until the Biden Administration took charge.

The Biden Administration's politics sowed distrust, fostering paranoia that one impolitic utterance might be reported as an extremist act. How can a military function cohesively if the leadership is telling troops to read books that label well over half the force as oppressors? In Beijing, Tehran, and Moscow, America's enemies began chortling. The search for nonexistent extremism was a distraction from the real-world military problems for which the Biden Administration had no answers.

In its investigation of more than 2 million active, reserve, and guard forces, the Pentagon found 100 "extremists."[43] The original Pentagon assessment was contradicted by a report that the secretary commissioned from the Institute for Defense Analysis. So embarrassing was the report to the administration's narrative that it was quietly released on Christmas Eve 2023. Researchers found that the "prevalence of extremists and gang-related activity that are reflected in court martial opinions is limited to fewer than 20 cases since 2012—excluding gang activity, that number falls to one a year."[44]

What the military experienced was a political inquisition. The report, signed by former Clinton Administration Pentagon officials, stated that "the risk to the military from widespread polarization and division in the ranks may be greater than the radicalization of a few members."[45] The Biden Administration does not understand that the nature of service creates an atmosphere that weeds out those disruptive to the mission. The culture of the team and, yes, survival keeps the ranks—ranks of all creeds and colors—focused on the mission.

The current climate is at war with the American military experience. With a few notable exceptions—George McClellan, George Custer, and Douglas MacArthur—the military has a long tradition of quiet service. Soldiers do not play politics. George Marshall and Dwight Eisenhower never voted.

Unless the trajectory changes, we will be stuck with an officer corps that looks to a woke political agenda rather than the precepts of fairness and merit that have seen this nation triumph against the most formidable foes.

War makes intractable demands on the mind as well as the body. When Franklin Roosevelt pulled George Marshall up the chain of command to become Army chief of staff on the eve of World War II, the inscrutable general promised the president he would vigorously overhaul the General Officer Corps and the officer promotion system. He was true to his word. Speaking to officer candidates in September 1941, Marshall laid out his precepts for leadership, noting:

> *When you are commanding, leading [soldiers] under conditions where physical exhaustion and privations must be ignored, where the lives of [soldiers] may be sacrificed, then the efficiency of your leadership will depend only to a minor degree on your tactical ability. It will primarily be determined by your character, your reputation, not much for courage—which will be accepted as a matter of course—but by the previous reputation you have established for fairness, for that high-minded patriotic*

purpose, that quality of unswerving determination to carry through any military task assigned to you.[46]

Marshall understood that brain and tactical ability alone were not enough to create the conditions for victory. "The 'starting line' for combat leadership is that one must accept, ignore, and discard the physical hardship accompanying it. Exhaustion is the innate price of participation. Thus, leaders should maintain a physical fitness level to fulfill their command duties despite fatigue."[47] Marshall cashiered senior officers and even some old friends because they were not physically fit. His ruthless culling of the leadership opened space for a new generation of soldiers—the generation that would win the war—including Dwight D. Eisenhower, Omar Bradley, George Patton, Matthew Ridgway, and James Gavin.

We are a long way from the Marshall model. DEI has been imposed upon physical readiness standards. Let us be clear: The call to go "Back to the Bayonet" is not a mandate to discriminate. It is a mandate to survive on the battlefield.

Because of the nature of its mission, the military discriminates. It is exclusive. You cannot show up and be a SEAL or an F-22 pilot any more than the average American is entitled to play in the NFL. The services discriminate because its members must meet physical requirements that most cannot meet to be ready to deploy and fight. Anyone who has seen the raw combat footage of young Americans struggling up the wet sand of Omaha Beach carrying a hundred pounds of gear while being strafed by German machine guns and pounded by mortars knows that this is not an ordinary profession. And, to knock down one popular DEI military shibboleth, future conflict will *not* be solely about pushing buttons. Americans will still need to hold ground, fly planes, and man the ships.

Of course, one size does not fit all. The fitness standards required of the Second Marine Division, the 1st Fighter Wing, or the 101st Airborne will be and should be different and more challenging than those required of yeomen, cyber warriors, or finance corps soldiers.

In the past, combat leaders had the leeway to add additional physical requirements that fit the fighting profile of the unit. For instance, the fitness standards of the 82nd Airborne were higher than for regular Army infantry formations because the troops of the All-American Division were required to jump out of airplanes with everything they needed to fight on their backs. The Army developed and eventually deployed a physical fitness test based on combat specialty in the last decade. The test consisted of six events, all chosen as a proxy for the types of strength soldiers need on the modern battlefield. The scientific standards were gender-neutral to assess who could serve in which Army positions objectively.[48]

This was the standard when Joe Biden took office in 2021. For instance, the Pentagon determined that the physical fitness test for field artillery would be most demanding because gunners routinely carry the most weight in the combat arms when moving shells. The artillery designation was based on comprehensive studies begun in 2013:

> *Scientists observed 28 field artillerymen from the 214th Fires Brigade June 4, as they performed an ammunition transfer, lifted the wheel arm assembly on an M777 155mm howitzer, recovered the spade trail arm and blade on the same howitzer, and set up a Gun Laying Positioning System.*

> *The same Soldiers also rotated through stations where they performed common warrior tasks: hand grenade throw, dragging a casualty and filling and moving sandbags to create a fighting position.*

> *The next day, another 28 FA (Field Artillery) Soldiers from the 75th FiB (Fires Brigade) performed the same tasks.*

> *The ammo transfer was a three-soldier task that required them to load 90 155mm rounds onto racks in an M992 Carrier Ammunition Tracked, or CAT.*

> *"Even though they can rotate positions, it's still pretty difficult because each round weighs 94 pounds," Dorman said.*

> *During the casualty drag, Soldiers shouted encouragement and suggestions as Specialist Andrew Gibson, C Battery,*

2nd Battalion, 5th FA, struggled to move a "victim," who weighed about 285 pounds with personal protective equipment.

"It was pretty tough—the mass of it," said Gibson, who had to drag the Soldier 15 meters as quickly as possible.[49]

The fitness standard the Army sought to implement had "no categories for male and female."[50] A science-based system ensured soldiers holding these physically demanding positions could survive under fire and continue contributing to the fight.[51]

Combat readiness and survivability are no longer fitness metrics. The Biden Administration has reduced physical fitness standards to the lowest possible common denominator, and commanders are prohibited from imposing higher unit requirements.

Ironically the Biden Administration's lowering of fitness standards devalues the progress American women have made in the armed forces by setting the bar so low. The sacrifice of young American women on the battlefields of Iraq and Afghanistan and by their counterparts fighting with the Israeli Defense Forces in Gaza were key to victories in combat. Indeed, retired Israeli General Amos Yadlin argues that Israel's own high training standards and the performance of Israeli women against Hamas have opened the door for Israel "to increase its fighting force by giving female soldiers an expanded role in combat operations."[52] Give young Americans a challenge and they will perform.

The Biden Defense Department desires "equitable" physical fitness standards. The Secretary of the Army so watered down combat fitness requirements that a pass for soldiers is now a 22-minute, two-mile run for men and a 23-minute two-mile run for women. The minimum push-up total each is now 10.[53] When Senator Cotton pressed about why the standards had disappeared, the Army secretary said, "We wanted to make sure that we didn't unfairly have standards for a particular subgroup that people, you know, couldn't perform. We didn't want to disadvantage any subgroups."[54] This is not about disadvantaging subgroups. It is about prevailing in combat. Civilian standards of fairness do not apply to warfare. Fair fights will get Americans killed.

There is no better riposte to the "equity" in readiness argument than the first woman to graduate Ranger School and the first woman to command an infantry unit: Captain Kristen Griest.

In an essay for the Modern War Institute at West Point, Griest argued that reverting to the lowest level of essential fitness will hurt the perception of women in the service, particularly those who desire to enter previously closed fields. She noted:

> *Reverting to gender-based scoring and reducing the minimum standard for combat arms will also hurt the women in those branches. Under a gender-based system, women in combat arms have to fight every day to dispel the notion that their presence inherently weakens these previously all-male units. Lower female standards also reinforce the belief that women cannot perform the same job as men, therefore making it difficult for women to earn the trust and confidence of their teammates. The original ACFT (Army Combat Fitness Test) promised some respite from these perceptions, but a reversion to gender-based scoring threatens to validate them. The answer is not to implement gender-based scoring or reduce the minimum standards for combat arms. Doing so would have both immediate and insidious impacts on combat effectiveness, as well as on women's credibility and potential... Failing to do so [implement high standards] will further marginalize women in these units rather than protect them and will hurt the Army rather than prepare it.[55]*

DEI and its military progeny are a danger to national security and warfighters. Faculty lounge social engineering experiments have no place in the armed forces. We know how to train, equip, and fight the battle. If we are to triumph against a new axis of evil, the military needs a radical overhaul. It will not happen overnight. We must restore our military to a place of honor and respect and recruit and retain the individuals who will meet the rigorous standards of excellence required for membership in the world's most formidable fighting force. America First means putting America's armed forces first.

POLICY RECOMMENDATIONS

Prepare for Peer-on-Peer Conflicts in Multiple Domains and on Multiple Fronts

- Dispose of the old regional contingency mindset and prepare for at least one, possibly two, peer fights on sea, air, and in space.

Restore Post-World War II Military Spending Levels

- Congress should incrementally return defense spending to the post-1945 average—6% of GDP—by the end of the next administration. Give the Defense Production Board the authority it had under Roosevelt, Truman, and Reagan to direct and scale industry for sustained production of weapons and munitions and the creation of redundant capacity to deploy and repair those weapons in the theater of operations.

Restore Standards of Lethality and Excellence

- Entrance criteria to military service and specific occupational career fields should be based on the needs of the positions. Exceptions should not be made for individuals already requiring medical treatment (e.g., suffering from gender dysphoria) for entry.
- Physical fitness requirements should be based on the occupational field without consideration of gender, race, ethnicity, or orientation. Commanders must be permitted to hold troops to the physical standards required by that combat category. One size does *not* fit all.

Eliminate Politicization, Reestablish Trust and Accountability, and Restore Faith to the Force

- Strengthen protections for chaplains to carry out their ministry according to the tenets of their faith.
- Codify language to instruct senior military officers (3 and 4 stars) to ensure they understand their primary loyalty is to the Constitution and to ensure the readiness of the armed forces.

- Eliminate Marxist indoctrination and divisive critical race theory programs. Abolish newly-established diversity, equity, and inclusion offices and staff and eliminate DEI courses and minors from the military academies.

Rebuild Recruiting and Retention

2023 was the worst recruiting year since 1973, and it will be worse in 2024. To reverse this trend, Congress and the next administration should:

- Improve military recruiter access to secondary schools and require completion of the ASVAB—the military entrance exam—by all students in schools that receive federal funding.[56]
- Restore high school and GED requirements for all recruits.
- Increase the number of Junior ROTC programs in secondary schools.
- Tie federal funding to schools to their willingness to allow JROTC, ROTC, and recruiters on campus.

Uplift the Military Family

Military service requires many sacrifices for families. To alleviate some of those burdens, Congress and the next administration should:

- Improve base housing and consider the military family holistically when considering change of station moves.
- Improve spouse employment opportunities and protections.
- Pick up on Trump-era recommendations that 19th-century-based rotation policies do not fit in the 21st century. To promote readiness and give the military family more stability, tours at major installations must be extended. It should be easier for troops to rotate from combat units to the school house to higher headquarters within the same installation to permit the family to put down roots.
- Audit all curricula and health policies in Defense Department schools for military families. Remove all inappropriate materials and reverse inappropriate policies.

- Improve Morale Welfare and Recreation facilities across the military for both soldiers and families.

The armed forces are the canary in the coal mine. If the military becomes another pawn in the woke revolution, we will fulfill Lincoln's dark prophecy: "If destruction be our lot, we must ourselves be its author and finisher."

4.

America First and Homeland Security

By Chad Wolf and Robert Law

The devastating terrorist attacks against our nation on September 11, 2001 forever altered the American way of life. On that horrible day, more than 2,600 Americans and hundreds of others from more than 50 countries died as two planes crashed into the World Trade Center towers in New York City, another plane struck the Pentagon, and a third plane went down in a field outside of Shanksville, Pennsylvania after passengers overtook the terrorists.

On November 27, 2002, Congress launched the 9/11 Commission to investigate and report on the events that led up to the terrorist attacks. The 9/11 Commission identified strategic failures among policymakers and intelligence officials. The 9/11 Commission Report states in part: "The 9/11 attacks were a shock, but they should not have come as a surprise...."[57] This included a failure of the legal immigration system under the Department of Justice's Immigration and Naturalization Service as the 19 al-Qaeda terrorists either had legal visas or had remained in the U.S. after overstaying visas while planning their attacks on U.S. soil.

The 9/11 terrorist attacks became a catalyst for fundamentally transforming the Intelligence Community, America's approach to counterterrorism, and immigration. Through the Homeland Security Act of 2002, Congress overhauled and restructured several U.S. national security agencies. This included establishing the Department of Homeland Security (DHS).[58] Congress established DHS with a core mission of safeguarding the American people, our homeland, and our values.[59] Within this restructuring of the federal government, nearly all of the immigration responsibilities held by the Immigration and

63

Naturalization Service were transferred to DHS as well as its three main components for handling them: U.S. Customs and Border Protection (CBP) for border security, U.S. Immigration and Customs Enforcement (ICE) for interior enforcement, and U.S. Citizenship and Immigration Services (USCIS) for legal immigration. The Department of Justice retained jurisdiction over the immigration courts, and the attorney general remained the final arbiter of legal interpretations of disputed immigration law.

AN UNSECURE SOUTHERN BORDER IS A NATIONAL SECURITY THREAT

The decision by Congress to assign DHS jurisdiction over immigration is a clear indicator that border security is homeland security. Prior to the Biden Administration, the administrations of Presidents George W. Bush, Barack Obama, and Donald Trump took steps of varying degrees of success to secure the southern border. By every metric, the Trump Administration was the most successful in utilizing the tools approved by Congress to secure the border and enforce U.S. immigration law. Specifically, the Trump Administration was the only administration to utilize the authority of Section 235(b)(2)(C) of the Immigration and Nationality Act (INA) to require illegal aliens to wait in Mexico until an immigration judge ruled on their asylum claim. The Trump Administration was also the only one to comply fully with the congressional enforcement tool known as expedited removal to streamline the deportation process of illegal aliens.

Unsurprisingly, the multifaceted enforcement policies of the Trump Administration led to record-low numbers of illegal aliens being apprehended at the southern border.

As a result of Border Patrol agents focusing their efforts on the border, Mexican drug cartels, human traffickers, and terrorists were disincentivized from trying to exploit the southern border as a mechanism to gain access to American communities. Throughout Trump's four-year term, only 14 aliens on the FBI's terrorist screening database were apprehended along the southern border.[60] Recognizing that bad actors may have infiltrated our country under previous administrations, Trump empowered ICE to fully execute its law enforcement responsibilities.[61] As a result, the Trump Administration removed over 1 million illegal aliens and increased deportations year-over-year until the COVID-19 pandemic disrupted the world in 2020. The trend of increasing deportations during the first three years of Trump's tenure is notable, particularly because sanctuary cities and states obstructed these efforts by shielding illegal aliens from removal and refusing to cooperate with ICE in clear violation of federal immigration law. Within this record level of removals, a significant number of national security and public safety threats were removed as well.

By contrast, the Biden Administration's ineffective border policies have made the U.S. the most vulnerable to a terrorist attack since 9/11. When Biden dismantled all of the effective policies of the Trump Administration, the cartels, human traffickers, and economic migrants quickly realized that no deterrent policies or repercussions stood in the way of crossing our southern border unlawfully.[62] Each year of the Biden Administration has been the worst ever recorded for unlawful border crossings, including a staggering single-month record of 301,982 illegal alien "encounters" in December 2023.[63] Although the southern border "encounters" in January 2024 declined to 176,205 illegal aliens, that is the highest January on record. Similarly, border encounters increased in February 2024 to 189,992 illegal aliens—the highest February on record.[64] Reportedly, at least 70 percent of U.S. Border Patrol agents are spending their time processing illegal aliens and releasing them into American communities instead of patrolling the border.

The implications for national security cannot be overstated. A total of 356 illegal aliens on the FBI's terrorist screening database, which includes known and suspected terrorists, were encountered along the southern border during the Biden Administration as of February 2024.[65] It is important to underscore that these are the aliens who did not realize the U.S. had their biometric or biographic information and had calculated that crossing the southern border was the easiest way to enter the country. The American people should be concerned about the nearly 2 million known "gotaways" who completely evaded the Border Patrol and have disappeared inside our country.[66] This set of illegal aliens presents profound national security threats when one considers the extraordinary steps they took to avoid detection when it has never been easier simply to surrender to the Border Patrol and be released into American communities.

AMERICA FIRST SOLUTIONS TO SECURING OUR BORDERS

The America First approach to U.S. national security recognizes that without a secure border, the United States is not a sovereign nation. While our immigration laws could always be modernized and improved, including overhauling the legal immigration system to better serve the national interest, there are sufficient existing authorities that the Biden Administration is refusing to use that the next America First administration should immediately implement to secure the border, end human trafficking, and defeat the drug cartels.[67]

To control the U.S. border and prevent exploitation by bad actors, we must reduce the flow of illegal aliens trying to enter the United States. The most effective way to do this is by resuming the Trump Administration's Migrant Protection Protocols (MPP), commonly called the "Remain in Mexico" policy. MPP succeeded by requiring illegal aliens to wait in Mexico throughout their immigration court proceedings instead of being released into American communities. The overwhelming majority of illegal aliens who claim asylum at the border make fraudulent claims in the hope of being allowed into the U.S. to either work or reunite with family members that came before them. By curbing the nationwide catch-and-release schemes of other administrations, opportunistic economic migrants will stop trying to exploit the asylum system. As the numbers decrease, more Border Patrol agents can patrol the lines and apprehend the dangerous actors who attempt to evade detection while crossing the border unlawfully.

DHS must also promptly resume construction of the border wall system to serve as a physical deterrent to unlawful crossings. With broad bipartisan support, Congress in 2006 passed the Secure Fence Act, which requires constructing physical infrastructure along the southern border. The Trump Administration constructed approximately 450 miles of a highly sophisticated border wall system, including fiber optics and access roads for Border Patrol agents, in high-priority locations despite facing challenges from Congress to provide the necessary funding. The Trump Administration had plans and materials to continue building the border wall system, but those contracts were terminated early in the Biden Administration. Physical barriers work, and the Biden Administration's refusal to adhere to the congressional mandate to construct the border wall has contributed to the ongoing humanitarian and security crisis.

While securing the border is critical, it is also essential that all bad actors who illegally made their way into the U.S. are removed. The next America First Administration must prioritize the removal of all known and suspected terrorists and Special Interest Aliens (SIAs), while not exempting whole classes or categories of illegal aliens from potential deportation. If necessary, the government must apply visa sanctions under Section 243(d) of the Immigration and Nationality Act to compel foreign countries to take back their nationals.

Finally, the next America First administration must increase screening and vetting of all illegal aliens, both at the border and for those attempting to utilize the legal immigration system. This could include suspending the refugee resettlement program for a period of time, as was done during the Trump Administration. Unlike most of the world, the United States classifies migrants seeking humanitarian relief from outside our borders as refugees and those inside our country as asylees—even though the legal standard is the same. When properly viewing the refugee and asylum systems collectively as humanitarian relief, a convincing case can be made that it is of higher urgency for the U.S. to resolve the cases of the millions of unvetted, so-called asylum seekers on U.S. soil before dedicating resources to bringing in refugees who have already fled persecution and have other options for placement.

COUNTERING TERRORISM AND TARGETED VIOLENCE

When most Americans think about terrorism, they understandably think of a threat abroad. This makes sense because terrorist hotbeds flourish in the Middle East and foreign aggressors take steps that challenge American principles of freedom and democracy. Countering terrorism is not limited to foreign policy or the Department of Defense apparatus, however. In fact, Congress established DHS as the unifying force between the intelligence and security agencies to prevent a future repeat of the communication failures that led to the 9/11 attacks. Specifically, the Office of the Director of National Intelligence and the DHS Office of Intelligence and Analysis were set up to fully integrate the intelligence Community and refine the global threat landscape as it changes over time.

From an immigration perspective, the Trump Administration used its authority under Section 212(f) of the Immigration and Nationality Act to impose visa restrictions on countries whose governments failed to provide the U.S. with sufficient information to vet their nationals. The rationale for this move was clear: it is detrimental to the interests of the United States if we cannot sufficiently screen and vet aliens seeking admission into our country. President Trump used similar authority to temporarily suspend the refugee resettlement program because of legitimate concerns that terrorists and other bad actors were exploiting this channel to gain entry into the United States.

This relatively new whole-of-government approach to countering terrorism and targeted violence has stopped plots against America and our strategic allies. Many of these examples are not known to the public, but those who have been privy to the threats and involved in the actions taken to thwart them can attest to this. However, there have been failures that the public is well aware of, including the 2013 Boston Marathon bombing[68] and the 2017 New York City subway bombing.[69]

America First Solutions to Countering Domestic Terrorism

Countering terrorism must include reinstating the Trump Administration's visa travel restrictions on all countries that refuse to provide sufficient and reliable data for the U.S. to properly vet their nationals. The America First approach to countering terrorism and targeted violence involves doubling down on the whole-of-government approach that the Biden Administration has de-emphasized. For example, National Security Presidential Memorandum 7[70] and National Security Presidential Memorandum 9,[71] both issued by the Trump Administration, empowered the Intelligence Community to streamline collaboration on review through the National Vetting Center. These two memoranda enabled real-time information sharing among intelligence agencies and greatly contributed to securing the homeland.

DHS and its law enforcement partners must also acknowledge the existence of violent extremist ideologies from Americans on our home soil that could lead to domestic terrorist attacks and be prepared to stop them. Americans deserve to feel secure in their houses of worship, schools, and public places, and the America First approach involves maintaining this level of security without infringing on their civil rights and civil liberties.

CYBERSECURITY AND CRITICAL INFRASTRUCTURE

The modern world, especially the United States, is highly integrated with internet and telecommunication connectivity. The prevalence of high-speed internet, email, phone, and text messages offer a host of benefits and efficiencies in our daily lives. They also create opportunities for nation-state actors, hackers, and terrorists to exploit cyber capabilities to seek economic, military, and political advantages over us.

It is not hyperbole to say that our adversaries are weaponizing the internet before our eyes. In 2023 alone, Chinese hackers infiltrated about 24 critical U.S. infrastructure systems, including a water utility in Hawaii. They also attempted to hack the Texas power grid.[72] The U.S. government has repeatedly alerted the public to Russian cyberattackers exploiting vulnerabilities in our sensitive electronic networks.[73] In December 2022, over $20 million in COVID-19 relief funds were stolen by hackers affiliated with the Chinese Communist Party.

The CCP represents the most persistent nation-state threat to the U.S. in the cyber realm. From 2020-2023, nearly half of known Chinese espionage incidents in the U.S. involved cyber spying.[74] The CCP has been pursuing a long-term "whole of nation" effort to threaten and undermine our economic vitality, national security, and international standing through strategic hacks and posting deceptive or incorrect information online. While the CCP is the biggest threat to U.S. cybersecurity, it is not America's only cyber adversary. Other cyber antagonists include Russia, North Korea, Iran, and other countries looking to undermine the United States. All of them are pursuing this goal through cyber espionage, coercive activities like blackmail to disrupt our economic prosperity, and negatively impact our intellectual horsepower.

America First Solutions to Defend America Against Cyberwarfare

To bolster our cybersecurity systems and critical infrastructure, Washington must require all cyber and tech entities from U.S. adversaries, especially from China, operating in the United States to comply with an enhanced vetting system to demonstrate that they will not collect sensitive information about our country or our citizens. Chinese nationals in particular should be banned from owning or acquiring property within a 50-mile radius of any U.S. government property. States such as Montana, Virginia, and North Dakota are already leading the way in this effort, with many more considering whole or partial bans.[75] Another proactive step is to ban Chinese technology firms from the state procurement process because the CCP is known to have exploited embedded electronic backdoors in systems to attack our critical infrastructure.

COUNTERING MALIGN INFLUENCE

Homeland threats to the southern border, terrorism, and cyber-attacks are well-defined issues that require whole-of-government approaches to defeat. A more opaque threat is the malign influence effort of nation-state adversaries around the globe. The threat from the Chinese Communist Party is the most prevalent because for decades it has aggressively expanded its focus on shaping information to advance pro-Chinese Communist Party propaganda. The substantial investment in third world countries, namely throughout Africa, is a clear example of the CCP buying influence to exploit these countries. China's Belt and Road Initiative, its global program of loans to finance infrastructure projects, may appear benign, but the reality is far more sinister. The CCP is using these strategic investments to make countries dependent on China for their future development, and the CCP expects loyalty when called upon on the global stage. The CCP expects loyalty when called upon on the global stage and is using these strategic investments to make countries dependent on China for their future development and expand its sphere of coercive influence.

In recent years, the CCP has directly engaged its malign influence campaign in the United States by exploiting the legal immigration system. It is well understood that no Chinese national departs the country for an international trip without the consent of the CCP, yet current screening and vetting procedures involved in the visa issuance process fail to flush out CCP loyalties. As a result, the F-1 (foreign student) visa and B-2 (tourist) visa are the avenues used by the CCP to lawfully infiltrate the U.S. Moreover, as U.S. states have tightened their financial belts and reduced funding for universities, they have routinely turned to foreign students as a source of revenue for the higher tuition rates they pay, typically in cash. This perverse incentive structure has granted CCP-aligned students access to university research labs and other facilities of national importance. There are numerous examples of foreign students stealing our intellectual property and research, including the 2019 case of Chinese national Zaosong Zheng using his student visa to smuggle vials of research specimens from a medical center in Boston back to China.[76] The same is true for those who enter the U.S. posing as tourists. Too frequently, these trips to major tourist destinations like Disney World are secretly paired with reconnaissance missions to record details about critical infrastructure and reported back to the CCP.

Another avenue the CCP is using to promote its malign influence in the U.S. is through utilizing investment vehicles to gain influence. Beyond the land purchases previously discussed, CCP-associated businessmen are buying luxury real estate, both residential and commercial, technology companies, and other promising startups. Additionally, there is growing concern about how TikTok is being used to manipulate users, namely young Americans, through its algorithms and the mining of users' data for the CCP.

AMERICA FIRST SOLUTIONSTO COUNTERING FOREIGN MALIGN INFLUENCE IN THE UNITED STATES

To combat foreign malign influence, especially from the CCP, the America First approach recommends taking a direct, aggressive approach towards these nation-states. This includes reimposing sanctions that the Trump Administration applied to Iran, Venezuela, and other adversaries. The U.S. needs to remove all Confucius Institutes and other Chinese state-backed education programs for K-12 age-students and university campuses. Visa restrictions also should be reimposed on Chinese foreign students similar to those implemented during the Trump Administration.[77] All American universities that receive federal or state grants, public employee pension systems, and other state retirement funds should divest all Chinese equities and bonds held in these accounts. We also call on the next administration to protect American universities from undue foreign influence by enforcing U.S. laws requiring them to disclose foreign gifts and donations.[78]

We also must flush out members of the Iran Experts Initiative, an Iranian influence operation, from the U.S. government. The federal government should also expand the Financial Intelligence Unit's cooperation with our allies in the Gulf states, including the United Arab Emirates, Bahrain, Kuwait, and Oman. The purpose of this effort is to limit or eliminate Iran and Hezbollah's global money-laundering operations that allow these bad actors to flourish. Congress should ban research grants involving our adversaries to and from U.S. universities to counter the infiltration of classrooms with anti-U.S. teaching and rhetoric. The U.S. also should ban TikTok and other Chinese apps such as WeChat, Temurm, CapCut, and SHEIN because they pose real threats to data privacy and national intelligence. Finally, the United States needs to conduct an aggressive public relations campaign that exposes the evils of the Chinese Communist Party, Hamas, Hezbollah, and other bad actors that intend to undermine the American way of life.

CONCLUSION

The threats to the homeland today are very different than they were in the lead-up to the 9/11 terrorist attacks. The Department of Homeland Security has a broad mission with an overarching goal of protecting the homeland. It cannot be overlooked how border security and immigration impact national security and how the safety of the American people cannot be guaranteed if we do not know who is in our country. Fortunately, the tools exist to secure the border and thoroughly vet all aliens attempting to enter the United States, either legally or illegally. DHS also must remain vigilant about the domestic terrorist threats and the potential role of citizen recruitment by our adversaries to help orchestrate terrorist attacks in the U.S. Lastly, an America First administration that operates from a position of strength on the global stage will send a clear signal to adversaries that their malign influence will not prevail. Shoring up critical infrastructure and cybersecurity platforms will go a long way, as will rooting out efforts to spread anti-American sentiment through our universities, businesses, and other entities.

5.

America First, Russia, and Ukraine

By Lt General (Ret.) Keith Kellogg and Frod Floitz

T he war in Ukraine is an avoidable tragedy that resulted from President Biden's incompetence as a world leader and his chaotic foreign policy. The war has divided Americans and the conservative movement over what America's involvement in this conflict should be and how the Ukraine War affects European and global stability.

The Ukraine War is an exceptionally complex foreign policy question for the United States.

Advocates of aggressive U.S. support, including some who call for direct U.S. military involvement, view the war as a significant threat to American, European, and international security. They claim that without robust and limitless American military aid to Ukraine, Russia will move after conquering Ukraine to rebuild the former Soviet Union and invade other countries, including NATO members. Some of these advocates claim that a Russian victory in Ukraine would undermine democracy and security in other areas of the world and could encourage China to invade Taiwan. Those who hold this view, especially President Biden, have strongly criticized as pro-Russia, pro-Putin, anti-democracy, and isolationist anyone who has opposed or even expressed skepticism about American military aid to Ukraine.

Although some U.S. critics of military aid to Volodymyr Zelenskyy's government might indeed be isolationists, the vast majority are Americans worried about whether America's vital strategic interests are at stake in the Ukraine War, the potential of the involvement of U.S. military forces, and whether America is engaged in a proxy war with Russia that could escalate into a nuclear conflict. They also see the need

75

to establish a plan to end this war and not simply provide weapons for a conflict that appears to have become a long-term stalemate.

As stated in Chapter 1, a primary requirement for the America First approach to U.S. national security is first a competent and decisive commander-in-chief—a president who exercises strong leadership on the world stage, names exemplary national security officials, and implements a coherent and effective foreign policy to protect America from foreign threats and promote its interests abroad.

The America First approach also requires a strong military, the prudent use of U.S. military force, and keeping U.S. troops out of unnecessary and unending wars. It means working in alliances and with partners to promote regional security while requiring alliance members and allies to carry their full weight in defending security in the region.

Based on these principles, we believe the tragic failures of the Ukraine War exemplify why the America First approach to U.S. national security better addresses the challenges this type of conflict poses to U.S. national interests and how it could have been prevented. Most importantly, the America First approach to national security provides guidelines on how this war can be brought to an end.

HOW AN AMERICA FIRST FOREIGN POLICY REDUCED RISKS FROM RUSSIA DURING THE TRUMP ADMINISTRATION

We believe the most important way the America First approach to national security could have affected the Ukraine War was to prevent it. A strong and decisive president who stood up to Russian President Vladimir Putin with a tough and coherent U.S. foreign policy for Russia, Ukraine, and NATO could have prevented Putin from ordering the February 24, 2022 invasion of Ukraine. In our view, tough and coherent policies implemented by President Donald Trump are why Russia refrained from invading its neighbors during his presidency but felt no such constraints during the administrations of George W. Bush, Barack Obama, and Joe Biden.

Trump dissuaded Putin from invading neighboring states because his leadership and foreign policies promoted deterrence and peace through strength. Putin saw in Trump a strong and decisive president who was prepared to use all tools of American power—peaceful and coercive—to defend U.S. interests. Similar to other U.S. adversaries, Putin also viewed Trump as unpredictable and unconventional. In light of Trump's threat to destroy North Korea if it threatened U.S. allies in the Asia-Pacific, Trump's summits with North Korean leader Kim Jong Un, moving the U.S. embassy in Israel to Jerusalem, bombing Syria for using chemical weapons on civilians, dropping America's largest bunker buster bomb on an ISIS redoubt in Afghanistan, imposing strong economic sanctions on China while keeping dialogue open with Beijing, Putin could not be sure how Trump would respond to Russian belligerence. This unpredictability played an important role during the Trump presidency in impeding hostile actions by U.S. adversaries.

Trump also had a Russia policy that demonstrated American strength. For example, in 2018, after the Russian mercenary Wagner Group advanced on U.S. bases in Syria, they were met with immediate and decisive action when President Trump authorized punitive airstrikes against them. Those airstrikes set back Russia's operations and influence in the region. Russia never retaliated against the United States over that attack—which reportedly killed hundreds of Russian mercenaries—likely because Putin did not know how Trump would respond.

The Trump Administration strengthened Europe's deterrence posture toward Russia by revitalizing the NATO alliance to work for American interests by pushing NATO members to contribute fairly to the alliance and meet their NATO Article 3 and Wales Declaration defense spending targets. By reforming NATO to return it to its original intent to serve as a collective security arrangement, the burden of Russian deterrence no longer fell solely on the United States. The Europeans were pressed to step up to defend their regional security and return to being effective allies.

The Trump Administration imposed strong sanctions against the Nord Stream II Pipeline, built to transport Russian natural gas from Russia to Germany, to halt its completion. Trump officials also pressured European states to delink from the Russian energy supply, an effort that undermined Russia's ability to weaponize energy in the region—and one that Europe resisted until Russia invaded Ukraine.

This included Trump publicly criticizing Germany for making itself dependent on Russian gas imports. At a July 2018 NATO summit, Trump condemned Germany's support of the Nord Stream II pipeline, saying, "Germany, as far as I'm concerned, is captive to Russia because it's getting so much of its energy from Russia." Trump was even more critical of Germany for its dependency on Russian energy in his September 2018 speech to the U.N. General Assembly. "Germany will become totally dependent on Russian energy if it does not immediately change course," the president said. "Here in the Western Hemisphere, we are committed to maintaining our independence from the encroachment of expansionist foreign powers." It is ironic today to watch video of German diplomats in the General Assembly Hall at the time laughing at Trump's criticism.

During the Trump Administration, the United States no longer tolerated Russia's repeated nuclear treaty violations and withdrew from the Open Skies Treaty and the Intermediate-Range Nuclear Forces (INF) treaty. The Trump Administration also began the process of withdrawing from the New START nuclear arms reduction treaty with Russia in hopes of negotiating a stronger and more effective treaty that also would include China's nuclear arsenal.

On Ukraine, the Trump Administration promoted a strong deterrent approach by authorizing the first-ever lethal military aid package to Ukraine, equipping its armed forces with advanced Javelin anti-armor missiles, naval vessels, and Mark VI patrol boats. This was a major break from the Obama Administration, which agreed only to provide nonlethal military assistance despite passionate appeals by Ukrainian officials for U.S. arms to fight pro-Russian separatist rebels in the Donbas.[79] President Obama refused to send weapons to Ukraine because he feared it would provoke Putin. President Trump disagreed and sent weapons to Ukraine as a sign of American strength and support for a friendly state.

At the same time, Trump was open to cooperation with Russia and dialogue with Putin. Trump expressed respect for Putin as a world leader and did not demonize him in public statements. Trump's political opponents criticized him for this, but Trump's approach was no different from how multiple U.S. presidents dealt with Soviet leaders during the Cold War. This was a transactional approach to U.S.-Russia relations in which Trump used his experience as a dealmaker to find ways to coexist and lower tensions with Putin while standing firm on American security interests. Trump spoke with Putin many times during his presidency, including at least five times in person and over 17 phone calls.

HOW BIDEN'S NATIONAL SECURITY INCOMPETENCE RESULTED IN DISASTER FOR UKRAINE

President Biden's poor leadership as commander in chief, a weak national security team and national security policies, combined with a complete misunderstanding of Russia, Putin, Ukraine, and NATO, established conditions that led Putin to order the February 2022 invasion of Ukraine and conduct an overt war of aggression in defiance of the United States and the international community.

Biden began his presidency by portraying himself as an anti-Trump president who would reverse all of his predecessor's policies. This meant reverting to naïve and failed foreign policies, mostly from the Obama Administration. Because of Biden's intense dislike of Trump, he attempted to reverse even Trump's successful policies and refused to give Trump credit for his foreign policy successes.

And yet Biden's foreign policies have been unserious and incoherent. Early in his administration, Biden designated climate change as the main threat to U.S. national security. Biden's orders led to the precipitous U.S. withdrawal from Afghanistan, an epic foreign policy disaster that did enormous damage to American credibility and global security. The president needlessly antagonized and alienated important U.S. allies, especially Israel and Saudi Arabia, and resumed President Obama's foolhardy efforts to appease Iran in the absurd hope of making it a U.S. partner for peace in the Middle East.

Biden's policy toward China has been weak and confusing. He did nothing to hold Beijing accountable for the origin and spread of the COVID-19 virus. He weakened the readiness of the U.S. armed services and military recruitment with ill-advised COVID vaccine mandates and by imposing diversity, equity, and inclusion indoctrination on personnel. Biden also has deliberately refused to secure America's southern border, which has led to a huge influx of illegal migrants.

In May 2021, nine months before Russia invaded Ukraine, the Biden Administration waived U.S. sanctions on the construction of the Russian Nord Stream II pipeline, a decision that garnered bipartisan opposition. Biden officials claimed at the time that the reason for this decision was to mend U.S. relations with Germany, which they alleged were strained over Trump Administration policies, such as challenging Germany's reliance on Russian energy and its failure to meet its NATO defense spending contributions.

Former Secretary of Defense Robert Gates wrote in his 2014 memoir, *Duty*, "I think [Biden] has been wrong on nearly every major foreign policy and national security issue over the past four decades." Gates wrote those words six years before Biden assumed the Oval Office and was talking about his foreign policy competency when he was a younger man. Today, Biden's signs of mental decline, frequent erroneous foreign policy statements that his aides quickly walk back, and his amateurish senior national security officials have added to a global perception that this is the weakest and most incompetent U.S. administration on foreign policy in history.

Biden's demonstrable lack of strategic skill increased the chances of Russia invading Ukraine by undermining the perception of American-led deterrence. More importantly, Biden's foreign policy incompetence led to critical U.S. policy errors that needlessly antagonized Putin and emboldened him to order Russian troops to invade Ukraine.

Biden Misjudged Putin Before He Ordered Russian Troops to Invade Ukraine

Ukraine's potential admission to NATO was a sensitive issue for Vladimir Putin even before Joe Biden took the oath of office in January 2021. Although Putin was momentarily open to the idea in the early 2000s, he began to speak out against it after the 2008 NATO Bucharest Summit, which confirmed that NATO one day planned to admit Ukraine as a member.

Putin has long argued that Ukraine could never leave Russia's sphere of influence by claiming Russians and Ukrainians are one people, denying that Ukrainians are a separate people, and opposing the idea of an independent Ukrainian state. During a one-on-one meeting with President George W. Bush in 2008, Putin said, "You have to understand, George. Ukraine is not even a country."[80] During a visit to Kyiv in 2013, Putin said, "God wanted the two countries to be together," and their union was based upon "the authority of the Lord," unalterable by any earthly force.[81] Putin underscored and highlighted this idea in a July 2021 essay, "On the Historical Unity of Russians and Ukrainians," in which he argued Ukraine could only be sovereign in partnership with Russia and asserted that present-day Ukraine occupies historically Russian lands.[82]

During a February 2024 interview with Putin by journalist Tucker Carlson, Putin provided a long, nonsensical account of Russian and Ukrainian history in which he disputed Ukraine's nationality and history and repeated his ridiculous claims that Russia invaded Ukraine in part to fight Nazism in the country.[83]

The Biden Administration's approach to national security rejected Trump's transactional approach to Russia, under which Trump established a working relationship with a U.S. adversary. Biden replaced the Trump approach with a liberal internationalist one that promoted Western values, human rights, and democracy. Contrary to the Trump Administration's America First stance on national security, the Biden approach put the idealistic agendas of the global elite ahead of a working relationship with Russia. Biden was not interested in working with Putin. He wanted to lecture and isolate him.

Biden's hostile policy toward Russia not only needlessly made it an enemy of the United States, but it also drove Russia into the arms of China and led to the development of a new Russia-China-Iran-North Korea axis. China and Russia hope to use this axis to challenge the current U.S.-led world order and the U.S. dollar as the world's reserve currency. Russia has used this axis to obtain attack drones from Iran and missiles and artillery shells from North Korea for its invasion forces in Ukraine.

Biden's approach ignored Putin's fear of Ukraine moving closer to the West and joining NATO. Although Biden and his senior officials never explicitly called for Ukraine to join NATO, they dangled NATO membership before Ukraine and repeatedly said this decision was up to Ukraine. Biden further confused the situation by stating several times in 2021 that the United States and NATO would stand behind Ukraine's "sovereignty and territorial integrity," statements that sounded like Biden offered Ukraine security guarantees. In addition, during a June 2021 NATO Summit, NATO reaffirmed the commitment made at the 2008 NATO Bucharest Summit that Ukraine would one day become a member.

Given Ukrainian President Zelenskyy's stepped-up campaign for NATO membership in 2021, these statements and gestures appeared to be more than implicit endorsements of Ukraine's bid for NATO membership in the near future.

Putin's paranoia about Ukraine joining NATO grew in September 2021 when the Kremlin strongly objected to Ukraine joining joint military operations with NATO members and said the expansion of NATO military infrastructure in Ukraine would cross a Russian "red line."[84]

In December 2021, as tensions grew and there were growing signs that Russia was planning to invade, Putin presented a five-point ultimatum demanding legal guarantees that NATO would not admit new members, especially Ukraine and Georgia. Putin also issued demands that would have undermined NATO, including giving up military activity in Eastern Europe. The Biden Administration rejected the ultimatum, threatened Russia with sanctions, and said America would "respond decisively" if Russia invaded Ukraine.

Biden confused the situation further in a January 18, 2022 press conference when he said Russia will "move in" to Ukraine but that the United States and its allies might be divided on how to respond if a Russian invasion was a "minor incursion." This gaffe shocked Ukrainian officials since it seemed to indicate Biden might tolerate Russia invading Ukrainian territory to some degree. More importantly, the gaffe telegraphed to Putin Biden's fear of escalation and lack of resolve just as he was about to order the invasion.

As Russia prepared to invade Ukraine, the Biden Administration scolded Putin and threatened "unprecedented" sanctions. Instead of using negotiations to de-escalate tensions, Biden reiterated to Putin and

Zelenskyy that NATO membership for Ukraine was still in Ukraine's hands. The Biden Administration also declassified intelligence on Russia's war planning in the misguided belief that it would somehow deter an invasion. As Russian tanks moved toward the Ukrainian border and an invasion appeared days away, Biden Administration officials stepped up their condemnations of Putin and threats of sanctions and isolation.

An America First approach could have prevented the invasion.

First, it was in America's best interests to maintain peace with Putin and not provoke and alienate him with aggressive globalist human rights and pro-democracy campaigns or an effort to promote Ukrainian membership in NATO. It made no sense even to allude to supporting eventual NATO membership for Ukraine, as this would require a unanimous vote of NATO members, which at the time was highly unlikely. Ukraine also needed to meet stiff membership requirements, including democratic and military reforms that included aligning the Ukrainian military with NATO equipment. (At the June 2023 NATO Summit in Vilnius, NATO members pledged to admit Ukraine once they agreed "conditions are met," and dropped the membership requirements. This was understood to mean NATO would consider admitting Ukraine after the war ends.)

Second, it was in America's interest to make a deal with Putin on Ukraine joining NATO, especially by January 2022 when there were signs that a Russian invasion was imminent. This was the time when the Biden Administration should have dropped its obsession with publicly criticizing Putin and worked toward a compromise. A U.S. offer to delay Ukraine's admission into NATO for a decade might have been enough to convince Putin to call off the invasion, but Biden Administration officials refused to make such an offer.

Third, the United States and its allies should have sent substantial lethal aid to Ukraine in the fall of 2021 to deter a Russian invasion. Instead, as an invasion appeared likely in December 2021, Biden ignored urgent appeals from Zelenskyy for military aid—especially anti-tank Javelins and anti-air Stingers—and warned Putin that the United States would send lethal aid to Ukraine *if* Russia invaded. Biden's message conveyed U.S. weakness to Putin, implying he could use military intimidation to manipulate U.S. policy toward Ukraine.

Biden's Errors at the Start of the War Doomed Ukraine

Russia reportedly began its February 2022 assault against Ukraine with a plan of invading over a 10-day period, quickly taking Kyiv, and annexing the country by August. It didn't turn out that way.

Ukraine's military learned from Russia's 2014 invasions and was much better prepared. Ukraine's army was well trained and had amassed billions of dollars in advanced weaponry from the West, including Javelin anti-tank missiles unblocked by President Trump that inflicted huge losses on Russian forces. Russia's army performed poorly due to inadequate leadership and planning, deficient equipment, poor logistics, and ill-trained troops. The Russian military was also unprepared to defend against state-of-the-art advanced missiles and attack drones.

Nevertheless, Ukraine's counteroffensive against Russia ran out of steam by the fall of 2022 because the United States and its allies failed to provide the country with the weapons it needed to continue the fight to reclaim its territory.

There were limits to how involved the United States could be involved in the conflict. To this day, America lacks a defense treaty with Ukraine and it is not a NATO ally. Intervening in the war in Ukraine lacked a clear, vital U.S. national interest. Moreover, there was a risk of nuclear escalation if NATO troops faced Russian forces in this conflict. This meant, as heinous as the Russian invasion was, the West, led by the United States, was unprepared for a response.

Like other NATO leaders, Biden correctly kept U.S. troops out of the conflict directly. Biden failed to recognize until it was too late, however, that it was in America's interests and the interests of global security for the United States to do everything possible short of direct U.S. military involvement to help Ukraine. To promote American interests and values, President Biden should have provided Ukraine with the weapons it needed to expel Russian forces early in the war and used all forms of statecraft to end the war, including sanctions, diplomatic isolation of Russia, and, ultimately, negotiations.

The main objective of military assistance to Ukraine, short of direct U.S. military involvement, was to prevent the precedent of an aggressor state seizing territory by force and defending the rules-based international order. It also was in America's interests to ensure that Russia lost this war because, due to Putin's decision to make Russia an aggressor state, a defeated and diminished Russia was the best outcome for U.S. and global security. Some believed this would prevent Russia from invading other states, including NATO members, after it conquered Ukraine. It also was likely that a devastated Russian military would allow the United States to direct its defenses against China, a far more serious threat to its national security.

Biden was prepared to give up on Ukraine after the February 2022 invasion and offered to evacuate Zelenskyy from Kyiv. Zelenskyy rejected the offer, famously replying: "The fight is here; I need ammunition, not a ride." Although Russian forces seized a significant amount of Ukrainian territory in the first few weeks of the war and got close to Kyiv, they were pushed back over the following six months when the Ukrainian army seized the initiative. Bolstered by years of training and an arsenal of advanced weapons, the Ukrainians surprised the world by dealing devastating losses to the Russian army.

By October 2022, Ukrainian counteroffensives had pushed Russia out of northern and central Ukraine. By November, they had recaptured 54 percent of the land Russia seized since the beginning of the war. This left Russia occupying an area of eastern Ukraine mostly comprised of the Donbas region plus Crimea, which Russia seized in 2014.

The United States and other NATO members limited their military aid to Ukraine in 2022 out of fear of escalating the conflict. In the early phases of the war, the Biden Administration delayed the provision of Army Tactical Missiles (ATACMS), altered the range capability of High Mobility Artillery Rocket System (HIMARS) missiles to prevent long-range strikes, and denied Poland's request to send MiG-29 fighter aircraft to Ukraine. As a result, Ukraine's arsenal ran low by October 2022, which gave Russian forces a chance to regroup. Ukraine would never again reclaim a strategic advantage in the war and the conflict became a stalemate by late 2022.

The *Wall Street Journal* discussed how the Ukraine War came to this outcome in a November 2023 article:

> *A growing number of Ukraine's backers in Europe and the U.S. say Kyiv likely would be in a stronger position today if the Biden Administration had more quickly delivered valuable equipment such as tanks, long-range rockets and jet fighters. Protracted debates about the armaments, which have been provided or are being prepared for delivery to Ukraine, meant Kyiv lost valuable time early this year when it could have pressed gains achieved against Russia late last year.[85]*

There were hopes that a new influx of advanced weapons from the United States and NATO members would help Ukraine turn the tide of the war in a spring 2023 counteroffensive. It didn't happen. Weapons arrived late and in insufficient numbers. For example, the Biden Administration failed to provide Ukraine with fighter aircraft and sent only 31 Abrams Tanks — equivalent to only a battalion. Ukraine also began to run out of 155 mm artillery shells by July 2023.[86]

Biden agreed in May 2023 to send F-16s to Ukraine. Not only were these fighters not available for the 2023 spring offensive, but as of this writing, they still have not arrived and are not expected to be deployed and combat-ready until mid-summer 2024 at the earliest. When the fighters arrive this summer, as few as six of the 45 planes promised will be delivered due to a lack of trained Ukrainian pilots, according to the *New York Times*.[87]

Ukraine's spring 2023 counteroffensive also failed because Russian forces had time to establish defenses in depth in eastern Ukraine that proved more formidable than Ukrainian officials had anticipated.

Biden Promotes a Proxy War with Russia

As the Ukraine War shifted to a new phase of stalemate and attrition in late 2022, the Biden Administration continued to lack a coherent strategy to help Ukraine win the conflict or end it. It provided greater numbers of advanced weapons but not enough to shift the war in Ukraine's favor. There was no U.S. strategy to achieve a ceasefire or an end state for the conflict or to deal with the reality that Ukraine would likely lose a long-term war of attrition. The Biden Administration also spurned attempts to hold peace talks. President Biden instead demonized Putin, often calling him a war criminal.

In short, the Biden Administration began in late 2022 to use the Ukrainian military to fight a proxy war to promote U.S. policy goals of weakening the Putin regime at home and destroying its military. It was not a strategy, but a hope based on emotion. It was not a plan for success.

Biden's repeated statements that he was prepared to send arms to Ukraine "for as long as it takes" without providing a strategy for Ukraine to win the war or a plan to end the conflict epitomized the real intention of his policy to use the conflict as a U.S. proxy war against Russia. Biden, throughout his tenure, attempted to define the "as long as it takes" approach by claiming the war was about standing up to a tyrant and defending and promoting global democracy. [88] But Biden never explained how U.S. military support of Ukraine would accomplish his goals.

The Biden Administration's approach to Ukraine garnered criticism from many Americans who were hesitant about the direction of the war and the amount of military aid the U.S. has provided.

The U.S. has given Ukraine over $113 billion in roughly the first two years of conflict. In addition, Congress approved a $61 billion Ukraine aid package in April 2024 that included $52 billion in military assistance and $9 billion in economic assistance. National polls revealed the majority of the American public was opposed to sending more military aid to Ukraine amid the 2024 stalemate.[89] The vast sum of support depleted U.S. military stockpiles, strained our defense industrial base, and jeopardized America's military readiness.

For example, since the beginning of the conflict, the U.S. has sent over 2,000 Stinger anti-aircraft missiles to Ukraine.[90] Yet at the current rate of production, it will take the United States 13 years to backfill and replenish this munition stockpile.[91] The U.S. has also sent Ukraine more than 2 million 155mm artillery rounds, but the U.S. currently produces only 14,000 rounds of 155mm ammunition per month.[92] The Pentagon has noted that 14,000 rounds are often depleted by the Ukrainian army within 48 hours of direct fighting between Ukrainians and Russians.[93]

As a result, Pentagon officials announced in December 2023 that U.S. aid to Ukraine has drained the Department of Defense's draw-down account to the extent that the U.S. will have to make "tough choices," either supporting America's own military readiness or continuing to "support Ukraine in the way they need to be supported on the battlefield."[94]

Former President Trump proposed in February 2024 to add some accountability to the Biden Administration's seemingly endless aid requests for Ukraine by making these payments a loan that Ukraine would repay after the war. This idea attracted bipartisan support and was being seriously considered by White House and congressional leaders when this book went to print.

Administration officials credit President Biden with successful leadership that provided Ukraine with the military assistance it needed to push back Russian forces. In their view, Biden helped save Ukraine by uniting and strengthening the NATO alliance. The truth is that NATO members stepped up to help Ukraine because it was in their security interests. It had nothing to do with the Biden Administration's diplomatic efforts. In many cases, such as when NATO members wanted to send F-16s and MiG fighters to Ukraine, Biden blocked or delayed those weapons. In other cases, European states provided weapons to Ukraine that the United States refused to send. Until October 2023, for example, the United States refused to send Kyiv a crucial long-range missile system, the ATACMS. Prior to that time, Ukraine had to rely on similar missiles from the French and British (SCALPs and Storm Shadows missiles).[95]

At the same time, the Biden Administration's flawed approach to the Ukraine War has strained NATO's defense industrial base so heavily that many are unable to backfill military equipment at the rate at which they are sending weapons to Ukraine. Admiral Robert Bauer, chairman of NATO's military committee, told the 2023 Warsaw Security Forum that "the bottom of the barrel is now visible" in terms of NATO allies' military stockpiles.[96] As a result, several of America's European allies have begun to prioritize their national defense over sending military aid to Ukraine.

For example, Poland has been a leading and consistent supplier of weapons to Ukraine, accounting for 17 percent of Ukraine's total imports of major arms, artillery, and weapons systems in 2022.[97] This provision of military equipment to Ukraine, however, has depleted Poland's military equipment stockpiles by approximately one-third and has challenged Poland's ability to provide for both its own military and Ukraine's military.[98] Despite increasing its military expenditure budget from 3 percent to 4 percent of its GDP in 2023, Poland's defense industrial base has faced challenges in backfilling its military stockpiles at the rate at which it is sending materials to Ukraine. As a result, Poland's military aid to Ukraine has resulted in "temporary gaps in the Polish military's capacities." In 2022, Poland sent MiG-29 fighter jets to Ukraine before the country received its procurement order for FA-50 aircraft from South Korea for its own military.[99]

The war in Ukraine and Ukraine's dependency on Western nations for military equipment has thus given rise to Ukraine fatigue among the Europeans, threatening to leave the United States, once again, as the primary defense contributor to Europe and further straining America's ability to maintain its own critical defense stockpiles.

Sparring Over Peace Talks

Biden's preference for using the Ukraine conflict as a proxy war to hurt Russia rather than help Ukraine win the war is also why the United States has done nothing to promote a cease-fire or a peace agreement. In some cases, the United States and some of its European allies have blocked attempts to pause or end the war. Under an America First approach to the Ukraine conflict, once it became a stalemate and a war of attrition, it was in the best interests of Ukraine, America, and the world to seek a ceasefire and negotiate a peace agreement with Russia.

Peace talks and a cease-fire to end the war are a complicated matter, obviously. The Ukrainian government understandably is resistant to any settlement that would reward Russian aggression and not restore all of its territory. Zelenskyy does not trust Putin to abide by a peace agreement or cease-fire. He signed a decree in October 2022 stating that Ukraine would refuse to negotiate with Putin.

Zelenskyy put forward a 10-point peace plan at a G-20 summit in November 2022. The plan's call for restoring Ukraine's territorial integrity and a Russian affirmation in accord with the U.N. Charter, withdrawal of Russian troops, and a special tribunal to prosecute Russian war crimes were ambitious and just. Since there was no way to force Russia to agree to such terms, however, Zelenskyy's plan went nowhere.

The Biden Administration's approach to negotiations has been devoid of strategy and presidential leadership. Biden and his team have consistently opposed any cease-fire or peace agreement that does not include a complete Russian withdrawal from all Ukrainian territory. Biden officials also have said they will not force Ukraine to agree to a peace agreement or join peace talks.

Former British Prime Minister Boris Johnson in April 2022 reportedly discouraged Zelenskyy from a possible cease-fire agreement, although the Ukrainian leader might have backed out of the proposed agreement on his own. Russian officials claimed the United States was behind Johnson's pressure to scuttle a peace agreement. [100] Biden Administration officials denied this. However, given its consistent opposition to a cease-fire and peace talks, we believe it is possible that Biden officials discouraged the Ukrainian government from striking a peace agreement with the Russians at the time.

In November 2022, General Mark Milley, then-chairman of the Joint Chiefs of Staff, voiced disagreement in internal administration meetings with the position of other Biden officials on Ukraine negotiating a settlement with Russia. Milley reportedly argued that the Ukrainian military had achieved as much as it could hope for at the time and urged Ukrainian officials to cement their gains in negotiations.[101] The Biden Administration did not adopt Milley's position.

Secretary of State Antony Blinken said in June 2023 that the United States would not support a cease-fire or peace talks until Kyiv gained strength so it could negotiate on its own terms. Blinken also claimed that giving in to pressure from Russia and China for negotiations would result in a false "Potemkin peace." [102] This remains the Biden Administration's position.

In lieu of establishing direct talks between Russia and Ukraine, President Biden has eroded the diplomatic channels necessary to reach a negotiated end-state to the war. Biden has repeatedly demonized Putin by calling him a war criminal and a dictator and even alluding to supporting regime change in Russia.[103] After the deadly October 7 Hamas terrorist attack on Israel, Biden likened Putin to Hamas.[104] Moreover, the president has yet to have a single phone call or meeting with Putin since the war began.

European states, especially France, have generally taken a position similar to Biden's "as long as it takes" approach to arming Ukraine but have been open to peace talks. France, the UK, and Germany appeared to break somewhat with the Biden Administration in February 2023 when the *Wall Street Journal* reported these countries wanted to promote stronger ties between Ukraine and NATO to promote peace talks because of their growing doubts that Ukraine could expel Russia from Ukrainian territory and because Western support for Ukraine could not continue indefinitely.[105]

There was a break between the foreign policy establishment and the Biden Administration on Ukraine in 2023 when Council on Foreign Relations President Richard Haass and Georgetown University Professor Charles Kupchan argued in an April 2023 *Foreign Affairs* article that the West needs a new strategy to get from the battlefield to the negotiating table in the Ukraine War because "the most likely outcome of the conflict is not a complete Ukrainian victory but a bloody stalemate." Their recommendation was for the Biden Administration to prioritize ending the Ukraine war by pressing for a cease-fire and peace talks.[106]

Haass reiterated this position on MSNBC's "Morning Joe" program, reportedly a favorite show of President Biden, on November 21, 2023 when he said the war is unwinnable and called for Ukraine to change its strategy to protect and save the 80 percent of the territory it controls and pursue a cease-fire with Russia. The host, Joe Scarborough, agreed with Haass' assessment.[107]

The late Henry Kissinger took a similar view in a spring 2023 interview with the *Economist* in which he said it was essential to end the war as soon as possible. A peace agreement, in Kissinger's view, would require territorial concessions by both sides. Because this would result in instability that could spark new wars, he called for a rapprochement between Europe and Russia to secure Europe's eastern border. Kissinger also changed his position in early 2023 to favor NATO membership for Ukraine.[108]

There were some reports in late 2023 that positions were shifting on talks to end the war. Putin signaled to European officials last fall that he was open to a cease-fire along the current battle lines. *Politico* reported in December 2023 that the Biden Administration and European officials were shifting their positions from total victory by Ukraine to improving its position in eventual peace talks to end the war. However, it appears the Biden Administration did not adopt this approach. Moreover, neither American nor Ukrainian officials showed interest in Putin's alleged peace offer, and U.S. officials reportedly formally rejected Putin's suggestion of a ceasefire in mid-February 2024.[109]

TIME TO STOP THE KILLING

Asked during a May 2023 CNN town hall whether he wanted Ukraine to win, President Trump answered, "I want everybody to stop dying. They're dying. Russians and Ukrainians. I want them to stop dying." Trump added: "I don't think in terms of winning and losing. I think in terms of getting it settled so we can stop killing all those people."

When the former president was asked if he thought Putin was a war criminal, he replied, "This should be discussed later, and if you say he's a war criminal, it's going to be a lot harder to make a deal later to get this thing stopped."

In a February 17, 2024 tweet, national security expert and retired Army Colonel Kurt Schlichter observed: "Ukraine is not losing because America hasn't given it enough shells. Ukraine is losing because there aren't enough Ukrainians. And I'm on the side of the Ukrainians. I helped train them."[110]

We agree with President Trump and Colonel Schlichter. America needs a new approach and a comprehensive strategy for the Ukraine War.

According to Ukrainian intelligence, an estimated 400,000 Russian soldiers are currently deployed in Ukraine and control much of Ukraine's eastern provinces of Zaporizhzhia, Donetsk, Luhansk, and Kherson as well as Crimea.[111] Russian forces have hardened their defenses along the 600-mile-long front line and have saturated an estimated 30 percent of Ukrainian territory with landmines.[112]

Schlichter is right about Ukraine facing a demographic crisis and running out of soldiers. About 200,000 Russian troops have been killed in the war, and 240,000 wounded. The Ukrainian army has suffered about 100,000 dead and up to 120,000 wounded. But Ukraine's population is much smaller than Russia's. The population of Ukraine today is estimated at 36.7 million, a significant drop from its February 2022 population of 45 million. Many Ukrainians have fled the conflict. The total population of free Ukraine may be as low as 20 million. On the other hand, Russia's population is 144 million.[113]

Reflecting these developments, CNN reported in November 2023 that training and recruiting Ukrainian troops had become a serious challenge, and the military was facing problems with enforcing mobilization rules.[114] On April 2, 2024, Zelenskyy signed a law to address the troop shortage by lowering the country's minimum conscription age for men from 27 to 25. The Ukrainian leader also signed new laws to do away with some draft exemptions and create an online registry for recruits.[115]

To add to these challenges, prospects for Ukraine's army in 2024 are not promising. After failing to move the battlelines during its 2023 counteroffensive, Ukrainian forces appeared to be losing ground in early 2024 because of battle fatigue, arms shortages, and what appears to be a new Russian offensive strategy. Although the $61 billion aid package that Congress approved in April 2024 and military aid from the EU might help Ukraine maintain the current battlelines this year, it will do so at the cost of the lives of thousands more Ukrainian soldiers and billions of dollars of military aid. There is little prospect that paying these high costs will allow Ukraine to regain its territory from Russia.

Moreover, given the Ukrainian army's manpower problems and the likelihood of growing opposition in the United States and Europe to providing huge amounts of military aid, the Ukrainian army probably will begin to lose ground over time.

Objections to continuing U.S. logistical support for the Ukraine War are also driven by other factors. The war is drawing down America's stockpile of advanced weapons, such as HIMARS missiles, that may be needed in other conflicts, especially if China invades Taiwan. Many members of Congress believe the Biden Administration should place a higher priority on stopping the huge influx of illegal immigrants crossing the U.S. southern border, the fentanyl crisis plaguing American communities, and the deterioration of our military instead of spending tens of billions of dollars on weapons for the war in Ukraine.

A prolonged war in Ukraine also risks deepening the alliance between Russia, China, Iran, and North Korea, which has been strengthened by the conflict. Iran and North Korea continue to supply Russia with the weaponry it needs to wage this war, while China remains a financial partner to Russia to deepen the two nations' "no limits partnership."

Many supporters of Biden's "as long as it takes" approach on the right and left in the United States as well as in Europe contend it is crucial to continue to arm Ukraine because Putin's invasion is a threat to global stability and democracy. Many claim other rogue states, such as Iran and China, will be emboldened by any outcome of the war that allows Russia to keep Ukrainian territory and does not hold Putin accountable. The trouble with these arguments is that it is too late to avoid the possible consequences of Russia's invasion of Ukraine. Sending weapons to an endless stalemate for these reasons is expensive virtue signaling and not a constructive policy to promote peace and global stability.

America First is not isolationist, nor is it a call to retreat America from engagement in the world. An America First approach to national security is, however, characteristically distinct from a foreign policy establishment that often keeps the United States mired in endless wars to the detriment of the country by putting idealistic principles ahead of the interests of the American people. There is a pathway forward in Ukraine in which America can keep its own interests prioritized while also playing a role in bringing the largest war in Europe since World

War II to an end. That role must be through decisive, America First leadership where bold diplomacy paves the way to an end-state for this conflict. What we should not continue to do is to send arms to a stalemate that Ukraine will eventually find difficult to win.

This should start with a formal U.S. policy to bring the war to a conclusion.

Specifically, it would mean a formal U.S. policy to seek a cease-fire and negotiated settlement of the Ukraine conflict. The United States would continue to arm Ukraine and strengthen its defenses to ensure Russia will make no further advances and will not attack again after a cease-fire or peace agreement. Future American military aid, however, will require Ukraine to participate in peace talks with Russia.

To convince Putin to join peace talks, President Biden and other NATO leaders should offer to put off NATO membership for Ukraine for an extended period in exchange for a comprehensive and verifiable peace deal with security guarantees.

In their April 2023 *Foreign Affairs* article, Richard Haass and Charles Kupchan proposed that in exchange for abiding by a cease-fire, a demilitarized zone, and participating in peace talks, Russia could be offered some limited sanctions relief. Ukraine would not be asked to relinquish the goal of regaining all its territory, but it would agree to use diplomacy, not force, with the understanding that this would require a future diplomatic breakthrough which probably will not occur before Putin leaves office. Until that happens, the United States and its allies would pledge to only fully lift sanctions against Russia and normalize relations after it signs a peace agreement acceptable to Ukraine.[116] We also call for placing levies on Russian energy sales to pay for Ukrainian reconstruction.

By enabling Ukraine to negotiate from a position of strength while also communicating to Russia the consequences if it fails to abide by future peace talk conditions, the United States could implement a negotiated end-state with terms aligned with U.S. and Ukrainian interests. Part of this negotiated end-state should include provisions in which we establish a long-term security architecture for Ukraine's defense that focuses on bilateral security defense. Including this in a Russia-Ukraine peace deal offers a path toward long-term peace in the region and a means of preventing future hostilities between the two nations.

Regrettably, we see no prospect that the Biden Administration will do anything to end the Ukraine War and may implement policies to make the conflict worse.

Nevertheless, the above are a few creative ideas for an America First approach to end the war and allow Ukraine to rebuild. President Donald Trump also has a strategy to end the war that he has not fully revealed. We are hopeful there will be a new president in January 2025 to implement these American First ideas to end this devastating conflict.

The Ukrainian government and the Ukrainian people will have trouble accepting a negotiated peace that does not give back all of their territory or, at least for now, hold Russia responsible for the carnage it inflicted on Ukraine. Their supporters will also. But as Donald Trump said at the CNN town hall in 2023, "I want everyone to stop dying." That's our view, too. It is a good first step.

6.

Communist China: A Singular Threat and a Comprehensive Challenge for America First Security Policy

By Stephen Yates and Adam Savit

T he Chinese Communist Party (CCP) represents the most comprehensive threat to our national security since the fall of the Soviet Union three decades ago. The essential difference is that the CCP is far stronger economically and culturally and is embedded into nearly every aspect of American life.

The emergence of China's military might, evident in the expansion of its navy, air force, and nuclear arsenal, which it has used to threaten Taiwan with invasion, menace its neighbors, and assert control over large swaths of sea and land in East Asia, has been enabled and sustained largely by leveraging the engine of U.S. economic productivity over the past four decades. Meanwhile, China's penetration into key strategic features of U.S. civil and economic life has been spurred by the passivity and lack of imagination of our political and business leaders.

Under the Trump Administration, the United States reversed decades of self-destructive policy that subordinated American economic and security interests to a globalist vision that would ostensibly transform China into a responsible partner. An America First China policy builds on those efforts to defeat China's malign influences, striving to make CCP policies largely irrelevant to American life.

The America First view of China policy distinguishes itself in identifying the primacy of concerns historically framed as economic or domestic as instead constituting the first crucial layer of our national security defenses that also factor directly into "hot war" contingencies in East Asia. We contend that these vulnerabilities must be successfully addressed through policies that embrace the inherent strength of the American people and the American system to preclude the need for a disastrous military confrontation. Fundamentally, the path to American success lies in our own economic prosperity, secure supply chains, energy independence, cultural resilience, and military deterrence to neutralize the threat from China while avoiding war.

A guiding principle of this mission is **reciprocity**. The CCP and anyone tied to it should not have access to land, infrastructure, intellectual property, educational opportunities, social media applications, and many other facets of civil society in the United States beyond that which Americans have access to in China. The CCP is exploiting its non-reciprocal access to the United States to undermine the U.S. economy and national security.

U.S. OPENS THE DOOR, AIDING CHINA'S EVOLUTION FROM ECONOMIC BACKWATER TO WORKSHOP OF THE WORLD

A CCP-dominated China emerged when the collapse of Japanese occupation in 1945 enabled the conclusion of a brutal civil war that saw the victorious Communists under Mao Zedong expel the Nationalists under Chiang Kai-shek to the island of Taiwan in 1949. The economic experiments of Mao's totalitarian regime led to the deaths of tens of millions of Chinese and kept China's economy agrarian and backward.

Initially allied with the Soviet Union, by the early 1960s Mao found the post-Stalin USSR not sufficiently Marxist and too conciliatory with the West. In the 1970s, President Richard Nixon and his National Security Advisor Henry Kissinger initiated diplomatic overtures to exploit the Sino-Soviet split, leading to increasing economic engagement.

By the late 1970s, the CCP had shifted its economy from central planning to a mercantilist system that used nominally independent businesses to adapt quickly to market demands. China became the world's export titan, earning the nickname the "Workshop of the World." Its gross domestic product (GDP) exploded from $232 billion in

1970 to nearly $16 trillion in 2019, averaging nearly 10 percent annual GDP growth between 1978 and 2018.[117]

The economic rise of China paralleled the rise of globalism, and with it, the promise of political liberalization blossomed naturally alongside economic growth and exposure to global markets. The creation of the World Trade Organization and the granting of permanent "most favored nation" status to China marked the ascendancy of this presumption among Washington policymakers.

Regrettably, improving economic conditions for millions of Chinese— mostly urbanites and recent internal migrants to China's booming coastal cities—did not lead to political liberalization. Instead, the most authoritarian and doctrinaire dictator since Mao appeared in 2012 in the person of CCP General Secretary Xi Jinping.

AMERICAN TRADE AND INVESTMENT FUEL CHINESE ECONOMIC GROWTH AND TECHNOLOGICAL PROGRESS

China's economic rise generally corresponds with trends in American investment and consumption, with wealth and industrial capacity flowing in one direction to our primary adversary. The trade imbalance of the past few decades is dangerous not only economically but also for national security, as it provides the very capital China needs for its unprecedented military buildup. Manufacturing has been offshored wholesale to China for lower labor costs with cheaper goods, then reimported to the United States for a vast consumer market. Chinese exports to the U.S. reached $583 billion in 2022, dominated by electronics and machinery.[118] This massive inflow of capital provides fuel for Chinese endeavors across government and civil society, including military expansion.

Recognizing this self-destructive interdependence, the Trump Administration singlehandedly shifted the window on politically acceptable trade policy toward China and initiated the still-evolving process of "strategic decoupling." Under the vision of former U.S. Trade Representative Robert Lighthizer, a series of tariffs with both strategic and punitive features were applied to $370 billion of Chinese imports, with a strong focus on the high-tech sector. These included tariffs levied under Section 301 of the Trade Act of 1974, which allows penalties against countries using unfair trade practices, and Section 232 of the Trade Expansion Act, which permits trade restrictions over national security concerns. This leverage brought the Chinese to the table to sign the Phase One trade deal, signed on January 15, 2020 and which took effect on February 14, 2020 and required Beijing to make important reforms in the areas of intellectual property theft, forced technology transfer, agriculture, services, and currency manipulation.

Most Americans are unaware that their mutual funds are also fueling CCP economic growth. A 2022 report by the Coalition for a Prosperous America (CPA) found that the Thrift Savings Plan (TSP), a retirement plan for 6.5 million civil service and military employees with more than $827.2 billion under management, had broad exposure to CCP companies. TSP's investment board admitted publicly that its new Mutual Fund Window had not conducted due diligence regarding whether these funds included Chinese-owned entities that might pose national security risks or fund CCP-tied companies engaged in human rights abuses. CPA found that within the mix of the 5,000 different funds on offer, at least 22 were China-only funds. Former Chairman of the U.S.-China Economic and Security Review Commission Roger W. Robinson, Jr. stated that these 22 and potentially hundreds of other funds, including Chinese companies, have undergone no diligence or material risk disclosure.[119] In November 2023, the TSP board removed China and Hong Kong stocks from its international fund. However, TSP officials reportedly said the decision was made not for national security or political reasons but because Chinese stocks are increasingly risky investments.

In addition, targeted outbound direct investment from U.S. firms has provided crucial liquidity to CCP high-tech projects, which are then used to strengthen military-civil fusion, fortifying the People's Liberation Army (PLA) and the CCP security state. A February 2024 report by the House Select Committee on Strategic Competition between the United States and the Chinese Communist Party studied a sample of five venture capital funds that had invested over $3 billion into critical technology companies in China.[120] This included $1.6 billion for artificial intelligence companies linked to human rights abuses and surveillance technologies, $1.2 billion to Chinese state-owned and partnered semiconductor companies, and $350 million to AI companies linked to the PLA.[121]

In August 2023, the Biden Administration announced an executive order that would empower the Department of the Treasury to prohibit or mandate notifications of foreign direct investment into the quantum technology, AI, and semiconductor sectors in China.[122] This step is to be commended, but the "small yard tall fence" approach and potential difficulties in enforcement will need improvements.

CHINA'S UNPRECEDENTED MILITARY BUILDUP

China has leveraged its stupendous economic growth, enabled by its unequal economic relationship with the United States, to build a world-class military in just a few decades. An annual 7.2 percent increase in China's defense spending in 2023 marked the second year in a row that it exceeded 7 percent, outstripping Beijing's reported 2023 GDP growth of 5.2 percent. By some measures, it has been the most rapid military buildup in history. The PLA includes a navy with the most ships, a huge air force including over 1,000 fighters and dozens of heavy strategic bombers, a massive array of missiles with the capability to hit and sink U.S. carriers and warships in the region, and a nuclear arsenal growing in size and complexity.

While the U.S. Navy is still technologically superior and boasts more tonnage, China only needs to outnumber and overwhelm U.S. forces in its immediate vicinity, while the United States has security responsibilities across the globe. China's navy surpassed the U.S. Navy as the world's largest naval force in 2020 with about 340 ships, compared to under 300 for the U.S. China plans to have 400 ships by the end of 2024, while the U.S. hopes to have 350 by 2045. China's third aircraft carrier is expected to enter service next year, and most worryingly, As Robert Wilkie noted in Chapter 3, China's shipbuilding capacity is estimated to be 232 times greater than that of the United States.[123]

China also continues to expand and modernize its nuclear and missile forces, aiming to have all three legs of the nuclear triad—intercontinental ballistic missiles (ICBMs), strategic bombers, and nuclear-armed submarines—in place soon. The Pentagon believes China has more than 400 operational nuclear warheads in its stockpile and could have about 1,500 warheads by 2035. The Pentagon reported to Congress in February 2023 that China has more land-based intercontinental-range missile launchers than the U.S.

The U.S. still has far more nuclear warheads than China, as well as air and naval delivery platforms, which give it a larger nuclear delivery capability. However, the growth of China's ICBM program indicates Beijing's determination to increase the size and capabilities of its nuclear arsenal, free from the bilateral agreements and understandings that governed the size and disposition of U.S. and Soviet, and now U.S. and Russian arsenals.

China also has recently deployed several advanced missiles, including hypersonic missiles, an air-launched ballistic missile, and a next-generation submarine-launched ballistic missile. China's substantial investments in space warfare are intended to undermine U.S. global leadership in space and to jam, hack, and destroy civilian and military satellites.

PROTECTING TAIWAN AGAINST POSSIBLE CHINESE MILITARY ACTION

This increased military spending underlines Xi Jinping's strategic prioritization of modernizing the Chinese military so it can project power in the region and specifically to ensure the PLA's ability to assemble a force with the capacity to invade, seize, and hold the independent island of Taiwan.

Taiwan is the key issue for U.S. military deterrence against the Chinese Communist Party in terms of strategy and symbolism. According to America First principles, the island must be defended. Taiwan sits as the keystone to the First Island Chain, which stretches from the northern islands of Japan through the Philippines and touches the north of Indonesia. This string of islands provides a natural barrier and creates chokepoints that effectively prevent China from projecting naval power into the open Pacific Ocean. Despite China's protests, the United States and other navies regularly transit the Taiwan Strait to reaffirm that it is an international waterway.

Preserving Taiwan's security is in the purely transactional economic interests of the United States, as it produces nearly 90 percent of the world's most advanced semiconductor chips. In addition, the Taiwan Strait is a major global shipping corridor, with 44 percent of the world's container fleet moving through it in 2022. In January 2024, Bloomberg estimated that a Taiwan conflict would cost the global economy $10 trillion or 10 percent of global GDP.

On January 1, 1979, the U.S. officially recognized the People's Republic of China with its capital in Beijing, simultaneously withdrawing recognition of the Republic of China based in Taipei. However, the 1979 Taiwan Relations Act also commits the U.S. to providing for the defense of Taiwan and maintaining de facto diplomatic relations with Taipei. The U.S. maintains that Taiwan's status is unresolved and must be resolved peacefully.

For decades, U.S. policy has maintained "strategic ambiguity" about a possible conflict between China and Taiwan, keeping Beijing uncertain by not clarifying how the U.S. would respond to maintain deterrence. On four separate occasions, President Joe Biden promised publicly that the U.S. would go to war with China over an invasion of Taiwan, undermining long-established protocol. Some liberal commentators have pointed to this as proof of Biden's "toughness" on China. Yet White House, State Department, and Pentagon officials quickly walked back Biden's statements each time since they flagrantly violated U.S. policy. Conversely, former President Trump, as recently as January 2024, refused to reveal his Taiwan strategy, saying it would "put me in a very bad negotiating position," therefore fortifying the proven policy of "strategic ambiguity."

Far from reassuring our Taiwanese allies and discouraging Beijing, the Biden Administration's mixed signals on "strategic ambiguity," along with other confusing and incoherent statements from the president, have undermined deterrence. In the larger global context, Biden's disastrous pullout from Afghanistan and appeasement of Iran have undermined the administration's credibility and America's global leadership.

As the value of the U.S. military deterrent has deteriorated, the power vacuum has been exploited by Russian President Vladimir Putin in

Ukraine and Iranian proxies in Gaza, Yemen, and Lebanon. Wasting our national security resources is exactly the kind of vulnerability that could motivate the CCP to invade Taiwan, perhaps before a possible second Trump term.

The deterioration of U.S.-China relations over the past three years, coupled with stepped-up and provocative Chinese military maneuvers around Taiwan, has led many U.S. experts to assess that an invasion could be imminent.

Even though Chinese plans officially aim to take over Taiwan by 2049, in March 2021, U.S. Admiral Philip Davidson warned that China might invade much sooner, within six years. In February 2023, CIA Director William Burns also stated that Xi Jinping wants his military prepared for a "successful invasion" of Taiwan by 2027.[124]

Elsewhere in the region, China has accelerated its efforts in recent years to enforce its sovereignty claims to the entire South China Sea by building military bases and airstrips on tiny islands and shoals. The Philippines, Vietnam, and Taiwan also claim some of these islands. China has used military threats and air and naval confrontations to bully regional states and the U.S. into recognizing its territorial claims. This has included several incidents involving Chinese Air Force jets flying dangerously close to U.S. Navy aircraft. There have also been several reckless maneuvers by Chinese ships in the South China Sea, such as ramming Vietnamese and Philippine ships and sailing too close to U.S. Navy ships.

The Arunachal Pradesh region on China's border with India, a remote territory in the Himalayas, has long been a flashpoint between the two countries. Chinese maps show the region as part of China. Chinese and Indian troops have engaged in several skirmishes since 2020 at the disputed line of control. Experts believe China has been conducting probing attacks in this region over the last few years to test the capabilities of the Indian military for a possible major land grab in the future. China also appears to be preparing for this contingency by building infrastructure and roads in the area. India has responded in kind with its own infrastructure projects.

AMERICA FIRST CANNOT BE AMERICA ALONE IN ASIA

Good faith allies of the United States who share risks and costs and contribute to collective deterrence against adversaries are at the heart of America First foreign policy. The U.S. military's power is the main guarantor of peace in the Indo-Pacific. The strength of our alliances there enhances its ability to confront the CCP with military, economic, or diplomatic measures. Unlike NATO's collective approach, the U.S. has individual "hub-and-spoke" agreements with Australia, Japan, the Philippines, South Korea, and Thailand. These alliances weakened after the Cold War but have grown stronger because of Xi's assertive nationalism and the revival of Maoist ideas in China, prompting several allies to boost their military readiness.

The U.S.-Japan alliance sets the standard for successful America First foreign policy. Over the past two decades, Japan has built itself into the diplomatic and military cornerstone of the American-led alliance system in Asia. Both the United States and Japan view CCP aggression in East Asia as their most important geopolitical challenge, with the prospect of a CCP conquest of Taiwan imperiling the 80 percent of Japanese energy and other imports that transit the South China Sea. Japan has promised to increase its defense spending from 1 percent to 2 percent of its GDP. The Japanese are acquiring hundreds of "stand-off" missiles capable of hitting mainland China, and they have fortified their Senkaku Islands (which are claimed by China), some of which are less than 100 miles from Taiwan.

With the Korean Peninsula frozen in conflict since 1953, nearly 30,000 U.S. troops are stationed in the South alongside a formidable South Korean military that stands to deter the nuclear-armed North. These forces are crucial to deterring China's likely attempts to goad Kim Jong Un's regime into mounting a Korean front in the event of a general conflict, but this would likely leave them unable to intervene directly in the vicinity of Taiwan.

While the United States pulled out of its huge Subic Bay naval base in the Philippines in 1991, a 2014 defense pact secured access to nine strategic sites across the country. The agreement does not establish permanent U.S. bases, but it does give the U.S. military a larger presence that could be crucial if a conflict were to break out in Taiwan or the nearby South China Sea.

Meanwhile, multilateral efforts meant to creatively pool resources against the rising tide of China have also coalesced. This includes the Quadrilateral Security Dialogue (the Quad). While some Western critics have dismissed it, the Quad has triggered China's insecurities, as *Bloomberg* reported in May 2023:

> *China has lambasted the Quad as a mechanism to contain its global rise. China's Foreign Ministry has accused the group of being dedicated to undermining China's interests. In April, ministry spokesperson Wang Wenbin said the group "is steeped in the obsolete Cold War and zero-sum mentality and reeks of military confrontation," adding that it "runs counter to the trend of the times and is doomed to be rejected."[125]*

An important feature of the Quad is that it brings India into the strategic picture as a counterweight with a massive population, growing military, and economic heft on China's western frontier. The Quad is discussed in greater detail in Chapter 8.

Incorporating Anglosphere nations with important interests in the Indo-Pacific, AUKUS is a trilateral security partnership among Australia, the United Kingdom, and the United States. The partnership's first pillar includes U.S. and British aid for Australia to acquire nuclear-powered submarines with conventional weapons, while the second pillar involves joint efforts on advanced military technology and abilities among the three countries. See Chapter 8 for more details on the Quad.

Meanwhile, China retains only one formal alliance with North Korea. Its informal partnerships are mostly with pariah states that are unimportant or unreliable.

China and Russia are united in trying to harm the U.S. geopolitically but have their own long-standing tensions over border disputes and control of resources in Russia's Far East. At a February 2022 summit in Beijing ahead of Russia's invasion of Ukraine, Xi and Vladimir Putin announced a "friendship without limits." Russia is the junior partner in the relationship, with one-tenth the population and one-tenth the economy of China. Xi likely regards this leverage over Putin as useful for strategic depth, Russia's veto power in the United Nations Security Council, and for generally making trouble for America. China has been indirectly supporting Russia's war effort by increasing energy purchases, selling Russia microchips for advanced weapons and aircraft parts, allowing Russia to bypass U.S. sanctions by purchasing goods from China in yuan, and providing various forms of lethal aid. In 2022, Russia was China's second-largest supplier of crude oil, coal, and pipeline gas and its fourth-largest supplier of liquefied natural gas.

North Korea provides a buffer between China and a Western-aligned South Korea, but Kim Jong Un's erratic behavior, illicit nuclear program, and the brittleness of his hereditary dictatorial regime also make the North a strategic liability. Iran, another sanctioned pariah in the West, has been a convenient geopolitical foil to U.S. dominance in the Middle East, as well as a source of fossil fuels and a trading partner. China is a major source of weapons for Iran and its terrorist proxies.

In Latin America, China has invested heavily in impoverished socialist Venezuela and hosted dictator Nicolás Maduro. Chinese naval navy ships have made many port calls in the country. Meanwhile, China maintains electronic eavesdropping facilities in Communist Cuba to spy on the United States.

CHINA'S USE OF ECONOMIC TOOLS TO ADVANCE XI'S AGENDA

Needless to say, the CCP has used its economic power to advance an aggressive global agenda. China is a major player in international finance and trade and is the largest trading partner for most of the world's countries. Beijing uses its economic power to steal trade and defense secrets and intimidate nations that disagree with or criticize China.

China is attempting to build its worldwide influence and secure access to energy and mineral resources through investment in the developing world. Much of this has been done through the Belt and Road Initiative (BRI), a massive infrastructure project to connect Asia, Europe, Africa, Latin America, and the Caribbean through a network of roads, railways, and ports. Mainly through the BRI, China has loaned more than $1.5 trillion to developing countries since 2000 and $104 billion since 2019, making it the world's largest bilateral creditor. China has been criticized for loaning more funds than creditor states can repay and for making loans to states that are bad credit risks. China has not hesitated to make BRI loans to brutal dictatorships and states with poor human rights records.

A prime example of China's "debt trap diplomacy" is the 70 percent CCP-owned China-Laos Railway, which helped boost Laotian public debt to $14.5 billion, half of which is owed to China.[126] In 2021, China was accused of trying to engineer the seizure of Uganda's sole international airport if the country defaulted on a $200 million Chinese loan to expand the facility. Chinese officials denied this allegation, and the airport is still controlled by the Ugandan government.[127]

BRI projects often double as military assets. China loaned Sri Lanka $1 billion to build the massive Hambantota port, but Sri Lanka defaulted in 2017, and China seized control of the port with a 99-year lease. In August 2022, a Chinese "survey ship," identified by security experts as a PLA intelligence ship, docked there, alarming nearby India and its allies.[128]

The *Economist* notes, however, that grandiose visions of the BRI have given way to hard economic and geopolitical realities:

> *China's faltering economy has made lavish spending abroad less popular among ordinary citizens. Other countries have also grown more wary of cozying up to China as its global rivalry with America heats up. The EU has tightened rules around foreign investments in critical infrastructure, citing national-security concerns.*[129]

China is committed to the "de-dollarization" of global trade. It has worked with the BRICS group—Brazil, Russia, India, China, and South Africa—to counter the Western-led global financial system and the U.S. dollar as the world's reserve currency. In 2017, China and the other BRICS nations launched the Shanghai-based New Development Bank, often called the "BRICS Bank," as an alternative to the Western-dominated World Bank. The BRICS has broadened its scope, adding

Egypt, Ethiopia, Iran, Saudia Arabia, and the United Arab Emirates (UAE) in 2024.

China also negotiated agreements to build an oil refinery in Saudi Arabia and to buy some Saudi oil in Chinese currency, the yuan, instead of the U.S. dollar. In March 2023, China signed an agreement with Brazil to drop the U.S. dollar in favor of their own currencies in trade transactions.

Recently, China has engaged in much more extensive use of diplomacy to advance its interests. This has included exploiting the Biden Administration's foreign policy missteps in the Middle East to build stronger Chinese economic and trade relationships with Saudi Arabia and other Persian Gulf states. Xi mediated an agreement in March 2023 to normalize relations between Iran and Saudi Arabia.

DEPENDENCE ON CHINESE SUPPLY CHAINS UNDERMINES NATIONAL SECURITY

The CCP's dominance over certain sectors of global supply chains, from minerals and chemicals to pharmaceuticals and medical devices to lithium batteries and solar cells, has allowed Beijing to manipulate geopolitics and advance its coercive foreign policy. Decoupling from these dangerous dependencies by reshoring, "nearshoring," or "friendshoring" critical supply chains is essential to an America First vision of national independence and sustainability.

China dominates important aspects of civil energy supply chains, with its share of manufacturing solar panels exceeding 80 percent (more than double China's share of global demand). China also accounts for more than 70 percent of the global total for battery manufacturing. Relatedly, the Chinese have shot to first place in the global electric vehicle market, increasing sales by 82 percent in 2022. This accounted for 60 percent of global purchases and outranked the traditional automotive production leaders, Japan and Germany.[130]

China's growing manufacturing prowess poses a danger to key American defense supply chains that now depend on Chinese producers. Late last year, for instance, the CEO of Raytheon, one of the largest U.S. defense contractors, said that it was impractical for the company to move its supply chains out of China.[131] A 2024 study by Govini, a data analytics firm, found that the CCP remains embedded in Pentagon supply chains across a dozen critical technologies. [132] Another independent study found that 41 percent of U.S. military platforms use Chinese-made semiconductors.[133]

Perhaps the clearest example of the strategic disaster of ceding critical supply chains to foreign adversaries is China's domination of the global capacity of mining (70 percent) and refining (85 percent) of rare earth elements. REEs play a critical role in American economic prosperity, energy independence, and national security. REEs are elements that are dispersed across the earth and, therefore, difficult to find in concentrations suitable for profitable mining. Many advanced technologies require components made from REEs, including magnets, batteries, and many of our most sensitive and critical military technologies. REEs that China dominates are used in electric motors in Zumwalt destroyers, sonar in nuclear submarines, and the stealth capabilities of F-22s. (See discussion of REEs in Chapter 10).

On August 1, 2023, China announced new export restrictions for foreign purchases of gallium and geranium, which are used to manufacture everything from microchips and fiber optics to satellites, "to safeguard national security." Clearly, China is willing to use its dominance of the mineral trade to undermine sensitive U.S. supply chains. Local sellers now must acquire a license for new and continuing exports, report the details of foreign buyers, and outline the end-use of the minerals, which will, in effect, restrict supply to the United States.

China's REE dominance is built into the Belt and Road Initiative, the heart of which includes building a global infrastructure network in mostly developing countries to secure access to valuable natural resources, fortifying its supply chains and trade routes in the process. BRI investments in the metals and mining sector rose from $6.8 billion in 2022 to $10.5 billion in 2023. These focused on Africa and Latin America, with the top destinations including Bolivia, Tanzania, Namibia, and Eritrea.

THE CCP THREAT TO STRATEGIC LAND, CRITICAL INFRASTRUCTURE, AND MILITARY INSTALLATIONS

Strategic Chinese acquisitions also extend the United States homeland, involving real property, including agricultural and ranch land, and land adjacent to military installations and critical infrastructure. Critical infrastructure is any asset that, if incapacitated, would have a debilitating impact on national security, economic security, or public health. Examples include gas and oil pipelines, electrical power grids, military installations, telecommunications facilities, and public transportation systems.

The CCP footprint is significant. According to U.S. Department of Agriculture reports, Chinese investors' holdings of U.S. agricultural land surged from 13,720 acres in 2010 to 352,140 acres in 2020—a stunning 5,300 percent increase. In total, this land is worth approximately $1.9 billion, and its acquisition was legal and largely unrestricted until recently.[134]

The National Governors Association in 2022 urged states to protect critical infrastructure. The NGA's report warned of foreign actors "directly target[ing] company insiders to gain access" and "physical attacks on the transmission and distribution of assets" to disrupt or destroy critical infrastructure.[135] A March 2021 report by the National Counterintelligence and Security Center concluded, "It is imperative that critical infrastructure entities prioritize and dedicate resources to preempt and/or mitigate insider threats." The report warned of the risk of debilitating critical infrastructure, including providing adversaries the ability to "influence or coerce U.S. decision makers in a time of crisis by holding critical infrastructure at risk."[136]

Meanwhile, land near military bases could be used for Chinese espionage, including intercepting military communications between unmanned air systems and space-based assets, according to U.S. Air Force Major Jeremy Fox, who called such data collection "a costly national security risk causing grave damage to United States' strategic advantages."

The Committee on Foreign Investment in the United States (CFIUS) regulates purchases by foreign governments that may impact national security, but its current mandate and purview prevent it from screening many dangerous purchases by the CCP, including the two most prominent and concerning cases.

In 2019, Chinese billionaire Sun Guangxin, invested an estimated $110 million in Texas farmland near Laughlin Air Force Base, along some of its training flight paths. He planned to build a wind turbine farm on a 15,000-acre Val Verde County parcel that would also give him access to the Texas electricity grid. CFIUS signed off on the proposal in December 2020, but a combination of state and local action deterred the development of the wind farm.

In 2022, Chinese food manufacturer FuFeng Group bought land near an important U.S. military base in North Dakota—a facility CFIUS failed to include in existing federal regulations as a designated military installation, and a transaction that CFIUS claimed it had no jurisdiction over, despite its proximity. Media exposure and local pressure defeated the proposed development, but CFIUS's unwillingness or inability to act exposed a major gap in land security.

Previously, U.S. laws and actions by federal and state governments have targeted the purchase of farmland to protect food supplies. Now they are also trying to control the sale of property to foreign adversaries to prevent spying or gathering intelligence near key U.S. locations. For example, H.R. 4577, the Protecting U.S. Farmland and Sensitive Sites From Foreign Adversaries Act, introduced by Representative Mike Gallagher (R-Wis.), would give CFIUS jurisdiction over all land purchases, establish a "presumption of non-resolvability" regarding national security concerns before CFIUS, introduce mandatory filings for adversary entities and expand the list of sensitive national security sites designated for CFIUS review.[137] In Kansas, H.B. 2766 would prevent "countries of concern," including China, from purchasing real property within 150 miles of a military installation.[138] The governor of Missouri issued an executive order banning "foreign adversary" entities from owning farmland within 10 miles of all military facilities in the state.[139]

The Chinese spy balloon that traversed the continental United States in early 2023 was a wake-up call for average Americans about the vulnerability of our airspace to Chinese surveillance penetration. Chinese acquisitions of our land constitute potential "permanent spy balloons" in our midst.

FORTIFYING AMERICAN INTELLECTUAL AND CULTURAL SECURITY

America First recognizes the benefits of free and open exchange needed for our academic and business environments to thrive, but also that limits must be placed on adversary countries and their citizens to protect our intellectual property and campus communities.

The U.S. higher education system admits hundreds of thousands of students from China who are sometimes under direct pressure from their government to commit espionage, undermining national security and compromising academic integrity. Under former President Trump, the United States had protocols and programs in place to counter this type of espionage, including the Department of Justice's China Initiative, which was disbanded by the Biden Administration following allegations of discrimination. A student visa policy based on America First principles means denying America's adversaries unchecked access to our educational and research institutions.

The CCP seeks to control American campus culture and enforce political alignment among foreign Chinese students. China uses student organizations to monitor and control Chinese students on campus and appropriates "woke" trends to gain political traction. It also exploits accusations of "racism" and "intolerance" to de-platform anti-CCP speakers and dissidents.

Starting in 2004, the CCP began sponsoring Confucius Institutes to export Chinese soft power to America, using the promotion of traditional Chinese culture to mask the transmission of CCP ideology and leveraging academic partnerships to influence university campus culture and counteract activities, events, or programs that would criticize the CCP. China's Propaganda Minister Liu Yunshan spoke of using "overseas cultural centers and Confucius Institutes (CIs)" to carry out propaganda battles. Confucius Classrooms extended this same mission into secondary schools.

As discussed in Chapter 4, Confucius Institutes in the United States have now largely closed following heightened public scrutiny but renewed CCP propaganda and recruitment activity has emerged in the form of the savvier and student-oriented Chinese Student and Scholar Associations (CSSAs), groups that keep Chinese foreign students immersed in Chinese culture and Chinese Communist doctrine while they study abroad.

The CCP also subverts U.S. higher education to fuel their technological and military progress. CCP partnerships with universities and their recruitment of individual researchers through their talent programs create an environment of "nontraditional collectors" of intelligence and intellectual property in the academic space. China has explicitly called for educational initiatives, direct funding of programs and faculty on U.S. campuses, and the placement of students in advanced graduate programs to advance its espionage and theft of intellectual property.

These educational partnerships are used by Chinese students to acquire specialized education and knowledge, which are then leveraged by China through formal state programs. China's military-civil fusion means that American universities are indirectly subsidizing the technological innovation of China and the People's Liberation Army.

This is part of a larger coordinated effort to force intellectual property transfers to Chinese entities that have undercut entire American industrial sectors. The U.S. Intelligence Community estimates the value of stolen American technology to be between $200 billion and $600 billion annually.

TikTok

China uses the mobile phone app TikTok to surveil and influence the American public, both through the data we produce and the information we share and consume. The CCP controls TikTok through its Chinese parent company, ByteDance, and has leveraged it as a data-harvesting weapon disguised as a social media platform that has become a dominant force in American youth culture.

TikTok is not merely a danger to the data integrity of individual citizens but also a significant threat to U.S. national security because the CCP has ultimate control over the data collected. The CCP could use embarrassing data gleaned from keystrokes to blackmail politicians, military leaders, or judges to influence their conduct. They could also use GPS data to track personnel movements on military bases, identifying times and spaces most optimal for sabotage efforts.

The CCP would gain from using TikTok to propagate videos that support CCP-friendly U.S. politicians, undermine American foreign policy, or exacerbate discord in American society. In the immediate aftermath of the October 7 terrorist attack in Israel and the war in Gaza, TikTok played a decisive role in supercharging existing anti-Israel sentiment among American youth to support Hamas' cause. They would presumably elevate anti-American propaganda in the case of a conflict over Taiwan to undermine our war effort.

Widespread and increasingly bipartisan recognition that TikTok is a clear and present security threat in need of remedy has resulted in a blizzard of policy solutions, from executive action on the federal and state levels to legislation and regulatory remedies, but all have fallen short. An effective solution must involve a blanket ban on the app or a forced sale of all ownership to an American company that controls the curation algorithm.

As of the publication of this book, the most successful legislative effort to date, the Protecting Americans from Foreign Adversary Controlled Applications Act, has passed the U.S. House of Representatives and was set to reach the Senate shortly after the time of this writing. This bill would prohibit social media applications such as TikTok from operating in the United States as long as they retain ties to foreign adversary governments, defined as China, Russia, Iran, and North Korea. If the application is controlled by a foreign adversary, the application would have to divest completely or face a prohibition on app store availability and web hosting services in the United States. If successful, the act would neutralize the threat of CCP exploitation while still preserving the ability of TikTok to operate under American ownership.

Underlining Beijing's hypocritical and nonreciprocal practices, it should be noted that most U.S. social media platforms, including Facebook, Instagram, Google, YouTube, and WhatsApp, have been banned in China.

Fentanyl as a Weapon of War

Fentanyl, the deadliest drug in U.S. history, is causing widespread harm and is a key part of China's harmful impact on Americans and their society. In 2022, synthetic opioids like fentanyl caused 73,654 deaths, threatening U.S. public health, economy, and society. In 2020, the DEA found that China was the source of the ingredients for almost all fentanyl entering the U.S. China's government is either involved in this or ignoring it.

While China inflicts this crisis upon the United States without moral qualms, drug dealers in China are subject to the death penalty. This policy echoes the cynical stance of the CCP in the early months of the COVID-19 pandemic, when it banned travel from Wuhan to the rest of China but deliberately allowed international flights to leave the country, spreading the disease across the world. China also told the world that the disease was not readily transmissible when authorities knew it was.

China places perverse incentives on many companies that manufacture fentanyl precursors as part of their business activities by labeling them "New and High Technology Enterprises." This qualifies them for financial rewards so that they pursue innovation and improve China's STEM fields.

Fentanyl precursors are increasingly shipped from China to Mexico, where the product is synthesized and then smuggled across the border. As Drug Enforcement Agency (DEA) Administrator Anne Milgram noted, "The only limit on how much fentanyl they can make is the amount of precursor chemicals they can get." In this way, the CCP provides the first essential link in the supply chain that brings fentanyl to American homes and communities.

RECOMMENDATIONS AND SOLUTIONS

Accelerate Strategic Decoupling

An America First China policy systematically detaches the CCP from the American engine of prosperity that fuels its government and military, starting with the most sensitive sectors and working down.

President Trump's Section 301 and Section 232 tariffs must be sustained to protect American jobs and manufacturing capacity, and the Phase One trade agreement must be strengthened and fully enforced. Wherever possible, we should develop supply chains that rely solely on American workers, our allies, or our friendly neighbors in the Americas.

U.S. outbound investment into China also strengthens the CCP economically and militarily. Mechanisms must be implemented to screen outbound investment into sensitive military-civil fusion sectors in China, including AI, quantum computing, and semiconductors. Instead, we must invest in American innovation and strategic sectors and build technological partnerships with key friends and allies.

We must also revoke China's permanent normal trade relations privileges.

Protect the American People by Strengthening our Military Deterrent and Infrastructure

America requires a robust military presence in the Western Pacific to maintain its strength and independence amid the China threat. A credible deterrent and peace through strength are the only proven strategies for avoiding war.

The United States requires a defense budget large enough to ensure supremacy in the naval, air, space, nuclear, and cyber domains, with an urgent focus on rebuilding the U.S. Navy and a credible nuclear deterrent. Essential to this is a comprehensive build-out of shipyards and increased training of engineers and technicians to build the ships needed for this dangerous era. We must also put priority on building stocks of ammunition and attending to deferred maintenance on critical weapons systems.

Defend Taiwan's Independence

Taiwan is the only democracy with no formal U.S. diplomatic relations. We should encourage diplomatic, cultural, and economic ties with Taiwan and educate the American public about the importance of supporting Taiwan as a small and successful democracy under threat from its giant Communist neighbor. We must support the acceleration of Taiwan's integration into the free world and global economy while strategically safe-shoring critical supply chains.

The United States must honor its stated commitments under the Taiwan Relations Act to fortify Taiwan's self defense and remove restrictions that prevent it from acquiring the military equipment and training it deems necessary to defend itself from CCP aggression.

Cultivate Strong Alliances with Regional Allies

Japan would be our most important partner in a Taiwan contingency outside of Taiwan itself. We should establish closer bilateral relations and encourage the re-arming of the Japan Self-Defense Forces, and vigorously support and equip our other regional allies and partners with advanced military capabilities to counter China's rise in East Asia and the South China Sea. As part of this, we must strengthen the multilateral AUKUS partnership and encourage the closer military integration of the informal Quad arrangement.

Stop CCP Theft of Intellectual Property and Harmful Activity at U.S. Universities and Research Institutions

An America First policy maintains our open and thriving business and academic environments and the freedom of movement that enables them while fortifying them against CCP exploitation. We must end the forced intellectual property transfers to Chinese entities that have cost hundreds of billions of dollars and enact and enforce strict punishments for violators.

Chinese partnerships with universities, and their recruitment of individual researchers through their talent programs, create an environment of "nontraditional collectors" of intelligence and intellectual property. Schools should require students and faculty to disclose and terminate their participation in programs designed to steal intellectual property, including the Thousand Talents Program, a Chinese government program discontinued in 2018 that offered large grants, mostly to leading Chinese scientists living abroad, to bring their research back to China.

Ban Confucius Institutes, Confucius Classrooms, Chinese Student and Scholars Associations

Because the CCP has used different names and configurations for their campus operations to avoid scrutiny successfully, Confucius Institutes, Chinese Student and Scholar Associations, and all similar groups must be banned so they cannot play these shell games in the future. Confucius Campuses must be banned from U.S. high schools.

We must establish restrictions and regulations on foreign donations and endowments from foreign governments or nationals to state universities and local school systems. We must also enhance scrutiny of foreign students coming from countries with adversarial governments attending American universities and imposing visa sanctions or travel bans if necessary. We must reinstate the China Initiative, a Justice Department program targeting Chinese infiltration of American civilian institutions, to protect the homeland.

Reshore Supply Chains of Rare Earth Element Mining and Manufacturing

The United States can establish secure and dependable supply chains for essential minerals by implementing comprehensive reforms to make the permitting process for domestic mining more efficient. We should also reduce reliance by ending federal subsidies for critical minerals from countries without strong political or security ties to the United States. Additionally, it is important to collaborate with allied countries to find new mineral sources, especially when we lack those resources domestically.

Protect Agricultural Land, Critical Infrastructure, and Military Bases from CCP Surveillance and Sabotage

The U.S. military has designated agricultural assets near military bases and critical infrastructure as potential perches for surveillance and sabotage. This encroachment provoked a flurry of state and national legislation regarding foreign adversary access to agricultural land. In 2023, states including Arkansas, Florida, Montana, North Dakota, Tennessee, Utah, and Virginia, passed measures to prevent the CCP from acquiring agricultural land within their borders. In 2024, many states are pursuing similar measures or bills preventing the acquisition of land within a designated radius of state military installations.

At the federal level, we must mandate that all land purchases made by foreign adversaries be publicly disclosed, that the Committee on Foreign Investment in the United States is given jurisdiction over all land purchases, and that the Secretary of Agriculture is added to the CFIUS board. To avoid a repeat of the FuFeng incident, we must overhaul the list of CFIUS "sensitive sites" to include a comprehensive list of military installations, including training routes, declared Intelligence Community sites and science and technology labs, as well as key infrastructure like our nation's telecommunications nodes, power plants, maritime ports, and airports.

Ban TikTok from All Devices and App Stores Nationwide

TikTok, a subsidiary of Beijing-based ByteDance, Ltd., is a CCP-controlled app that serves as an ingenious data-harvesting weapon. In the disguise of a social media platform, it has become a dominant force in American youth culture. An effective solution must involve a blanket ban on the app or a forced sale of all ownership to an American company that controls the curation algorithm. Impose Penalties on China for Transporting Fentanyl Precursors to Mexico

The U.S. is experiencing a critical public health crisis caused by fentanyl which results in tens of thousands of fatal overdoses annually. Fentanyl trafficked in the U.S. frequently originates in China. We must end the supply of fentanyl precursors from China to Mexico through tariffs and sanctions.

7.

America First, Israel, and the Middle East

By Ellie Cohanim

T his chapter unfolds against a backdrop of chaos and turmoil in the Middle East. Iran has ignited a series of provocations across the region, sparked by Hamas' depraved assault on Israel on October 7, 2023, followed by more than 160 attacks on U.S. personnel and assets by Iran-backed proxies.[140] This onslaught reverberated across Iraq, Syria, and Jordan, compounded by Hezbollah's missile strikes from Lebanon and assaults by Yemen's Houthi rebels on international naval and commercial vessels in the Red Sea. In an unprecedented escalation, the Iranian regime attacked Israel directly from Iranian soil on April 13, 2024, firing approximately 300 drones, cruise missiles, and ballistic missiles at Israel.

The worsening security situation in the Middle East is part of a broader deterioration of global security since 2021 because of President Biden's weak leadership, his unserious foreign policy, and a series of major foreign policy failures, especially the disastrous U.S. withdrawal from Afghanistan in 2021. This consequently weakened U.S.-led deterrence worldwide. President Biden and his administration's policies on Iran, Israel, and the broader Middle East, in just three tumultuous years, have left the region teetering on the brink of a regional conflict and perhaps a nuclear confrontation.

By contrast, the Trump Administration prioritized building a close relationship with America's allies in the region, especially Israel and Saudi Arabia. President Trump realized that it is in America's interests to ensure that its principal allies in the region are strong and secure, both economically and militarily, because a secure Middle East keeps the United States out of new and endless wars in the region. President Trump also recognized that many U.S. policies in place for decades concerning the Middle East and Israel had failed and that it was time to implement some new and revolutionary approaches.

President Trump set the stage for American leadership in the Middle East and new relationships with Arab and Muslim states by taking his first foreign trip to Saudi Arabia in May 2017, where he met with 50 Arab and Muslim leaders. Under President Trump's America First approach to U.S. national security, he reestablished U.S. credibility and deterrence in the region without involving the United States in new wars. He gave the U.S. military the green light to use the force necessary to destroy the Islamic State's control of territory in Iraq and Syria. The president also ordered the bombing of Syria in 2018 for using chemical weapons on civilians.

Although President Trump strived to keep the United States out of a new war with Iran, he indicated his willingness to use U.S. military force in response to Iranian provocations. In response to Iranian-backed attacks on U.S. bases in Iraq in late 2019 that killed an American contractor and Iraqi personnel, Trump ordered a drone strike that killed Iranian General Qasem Soleimani in Iraq in January 2020. In April 2020, President Trump also threatened to have the U.S. Navy destroy Iranian gunboats if they continued to harass Navy ships in the Persian Gulf. The Iranian ships stopped harassing American naval vessels after Trump's warning.

STANDING WITH ISRAEL

The United States was the first country to recognize Israel as an independent state. Following Israel's proclamation of independence on May 14, 1948, President Harry Truman swiftly issued a statement of recognition for the Jewish state.[141] Israel has remained America's closest partner in the Middle East, bound by mutual interests, economic ties, and shared historic and cultural touchstones. The enduring cornerstone of U.S. policy toward Israel firmly acknowledges Israel's legitimacy as a nation-state and affirms unwavering support for it as a crucial ally in the region.

An America First policy on Israel honors America's historical commitment to the Jewish State and is premised on the understanding that Israel *is* our leading ally in the region, one that the U.S. relies on for intelligence sharing, defense, and other technology co-development—and most importantly—for preserving America's interests in the region. As a result, President Trump is regarded as one of the most pro-Israel presidents in American history.

As explained in earlier chapters, a central principle of the America First approach to U.S. national security is putting the interests of our country first and not deferring to the demands and beliefs of the foreign policy establishment. Concerning Israel, the America First movement has put American and Israeli security concerns ahead of longtime and failed positions of the establishment. Using this approach, President Trump broke with the foreign policy establishment and State Department careerists by moving the U.S. Embassy to Israel to Jerusalem and recognizing Israeli sovereignty over the Golan Heights, an area that has been Israeli territory since 1967.

Many U.S. presidential candidates, Republican and Democratic, promised during their campaigns to move the U.S. embassy from Tel Aviv to Jerusalem but were later talked out of this by career State Department officials and foreign policy experts who claimed such a move would be too provocative and undermine the Middle East peace process. For example, before he left office, Secretary of State John Kerry warned President Trump in January 2017 that moving the U.S. embassy to Jerusalem would cause an explosion in the region and be detrimental to Israel's relationships with Jordan and Egypt.[142] President Trump didn't believe these warnings and ordered the U.S. embassy to be moved to Jerusalem in 2018. Kerry's doom and gloom predictions never materialized, and the embassy move had no effect on Israel's relationship with Egypt and Jordan.

The Trump Administration also put practical solutions to Middle East security ahead of the failed idealistic proposals of the past. For example, the Trump Administration put forward an innovative Middle East peace plan in early 2020, nicknamed the "deal of the century," that would have provided $50 billion in investment to the Palestinians, including $28 billion to Gaza.[143] After Palestinian leaders rejected this deal, the Trump

Administration officials struck another unprecedented agreement, the Abraham Accords, which normalized Israel's relations with the United Arab Emirates, Bahrain, and Morocco and is premised on two foundational understandings.

One was removing the Palestinian "veto" on any peace agreement between Israel and her Arab neighbors, a policy that the United States must fastidiously continue. No longer must regional stability, peace, and prosperity under the U.S.-led order be held hostage to attempts at first resolving the Israel-Palestinian conflict.

Second, the Trump Administration acknowledged the threat that Iran poses to our regional allies. By constraining Iran, the Trump White House regained the trust of our regional partners, paving the way for peace. The Trump Administration continued to pursue dialogue toward additional normalization agreements between Israel and other Arab states. The Abraham Accords also improved relations between Israel and Saudi Arabia and opened the door to a future normalization agreement between the two states.

The genius of the Abraham Accords was recognizing that Middle East states desired productive economic and security relationships with Israel and were tired of allowing the Palestinian leadership, with its corruption and association with terrorism and instability, to continue to block such arrangements. The Trump Administration also made clear that if the Palestinian Authority refused to drop its association with the terrorist group Hamas, it would not receive aid from the United States. As a result, the Trump Administration cut off more than $200 million in U.S. assistance to the Palestinian Authority, much of which was to go through the United Nations Relief and Works Agency (UNRWA). UNRWA has been criticized for decades for funding Hamas and promoting hateful anti-Semitic and anti-Israel propaganda. (UNRWA is discussed in greater detail later in this chapter.)

The Trump Administration also moved to incorporate Israel into the U.S. Central Command (CENTCOM), a historic first that has proven to be remarkably successful. Since this integration, there have been several joint military exercises involving Israel, the U.S., and Gulf allies like the UAE and Bahrain. Looking ahead, it is crucial that CENTCOM continue fostering these regional military collaborations while preserving Israel's

Qualitative Military Edge (QME) over its neighbors. Notably, the existing memorandum of understanding (MOU) governing U.S. foreign defense aid to Israel will expire in 2028, offering an opportunity for the next administration to reaffirm its commitment to upholding Israel's dominant defense capabilities. Moreover, following the October 7 Hamas terrorist attack and its aftermath, Israel must be granted access to a greater quantity and faster delivery of munitions and weapons systems during times of war.

These were America First policies that promoted the interests of the United States and its close ally Israel and abandoned failed U.S. policies of the past.

COUNTERING IRAN

Acknowledging and standing up to the threat of Iran as a state sponsor of terror attempting to acquire nuclear weapons was a central focus of President Trump's America First Middle East policy. Trump's "maximum pressure" campaign reversed the appeasement of Iran by the Obama Administration and was designed to rein in Iran's malign activities to destabilize the region primarily through economic and political pressure. As explained earlier, Trump's Iran policy also relied on a perception of American deterrence and the president's willingness to use military force against Iran if necessary to defend American interests.

A principal part of President Trump's Iran policy was withdrawing the United States from the 2015 nuclear deal with Iran, the Joint Comprehensive Plan of Action (JCPOA), on May 8, 2018. Trump referred to this agreement as the "worst deal ever" and vowed as a candidate to either fix or withdraw from the agreement. The JCPOA was a controversial agreement negotiated with Iran by Secretary of State John Kerry and was criticized for its weakness and concessions to Iran. Although Congress was unable to block the agreement, a majority of House and Senate members voted against it in disapproval votes in September 2015. In addition, the U.S. agreed to the JCPOA despite opposition to the deal by Israel and Saudi Arabia.

Like many other of President Trump's foreign policy decisions, the decision to withdraw from the JCPOA was strongly resisted by the foreign policy establishment, European leaders, and U.S. government careerists. It also was opposed by several of President Trump's political appointees, such as National Security Adviser H.R. McMaster and Secretary of State Rex Tillerson.

As he did with much of his national security policies, President Trump defied this pressure and withdrew from the JCPOA on May 8, 2018. This decision put the interests of the United States and allies in the Middle East ahead of the policies of the foreign policy establishment elites.

BIDEN RETURNED TO THE FAILED U.S. MIDDLE EAST POLICIES OF THE OBAMA ADMINISTRATION

The surge and instability and violence in the Middle East since Joe Biden became president is a direct result of his administration abandoning President Trump's America First Middle East policies and reverting to the failed Middle East policies of President Obama. Instead of continuing President Trump's successful transactional relationships with key Middle East states, President Biden snubbed Saudi officials at the start of his presidency, even refusing to speak with Saudi Arabia's de facto ruler, Crown Prince Mohammed bin Salman on the phone. The Biden Administration also put U.S. arms sales to Saudi Arabia on hold and issued travel bans against Saudi citizens in response to the 2018 killing of journalist Jamal Khashoggi, a matter that the Trump Administration had largely resolved. The Biden Administration also initially tried to sideline Egypt over its human rights record.

The Biden Administration caused tension with Israel by resuming payments to the Palestinian Authority, providing it with an estimated $1 billion as of October 2023, even though Biden officials knew some of these funds would be provided to Hamas.[144] The Biden Administration also pressed for a two-state solution peace plan and often lectured Israeli officials over West Bank settlements and other internal Israeli political matters, such as a 2023 Knesset bill to overhaul Israel's Supreme Court.

The Biden Administration initially tried to ignore the Abraham Accords and not use this title for the agreement because it did not want to give the Trump Administration credit for this deal. Biden officials later relented, agreeing to use the Trump Administration's title for the agreement and expressed support for expanding it to Saudi Arabia in March 2023. The Biden Administration did not reverse the move of the U.S. embassy to Jerusalem or the Trump Administration's recognition of Israeli sovereignty over the Golan Heights, probably due to strong support for these moves by pro-Israel Americans. However, Biden officials irritated the Israeli government by attempting to reopen the American consulate for Palestine in Jerusalem, which the Trump Administration closed in 2019. When the Israeli government refused to allow this, the Biden Administration upgraded the Palestinian affairs office in the American Embassy in Jerusalem to a virtual U.S. consulate for Palestine.

As bad as the Obama Administration's appeasement policies of Iran were, the Biden Administration's have been even worse. President Biden entered office determined that the U.S. rejoin the JCPOA and improve the agreement. Talks began among JCPOA parties in Vienna in the spring of 2021. However, these were indirect talks because Iran refused to participate in negotiations in the same room with American diplomats. Despite generous concessions made by the United States during 18 months of these talks, an agreement to revive or improve the JCPOA was never reached. So desperate were Biden officials to get a new nuclear deal with Iran that, at one point, it floated rationalizations for taking Iran's Revolutionary Guard Corps (IRGC) off the U.S. list of foreign terrorist organizations.[145] Concessions offered to Iran by the Biden Administration in the talks were so extreme that they caused three members of the U.S. negotiating team to resign in late 2022.[146]

Despite President Biden's desire to constrain Iran's nuclear program by reviving and fixing the JCPOA, Iran's nuclear program surged to new levels during his administration. Iran significantly increased uranium enrichment and the number of its advanced uranium centrifuges starting in 2021, which increased the number of nuclear weapons it could construct. In April 2021, Iran began enriching uranium for the first time to 60% uranium-235, a level just below weapons-grade. As a result, American physicist and nuclear expert David Albright stated in a January 2024 report that Iran "would need only about a week to produce enough for its first nuclear weapon. It could have enough weapon-grade uranium for six weapons in one month, and after five months of producing weapon-grade uranium, it could have enough for twelve."[147]

Iranian revenue also surged during the Biden Administration, mostly because the U.S. ended President Trump's Maximum Pressure sanctions on Iran and has failed to enforce oil sanctions. According to a Heritage Foundation report, Iran has received approximately $71.02 billion more in revenue as of October 2023 under Biden than it would have received under Trump. Much of this revenue was Iranian oil sold to China.[148]

After failed U.S. and European attempts in early 2023 to restart nuclear talks, there were multiple press reports that the Biden Administration negotiated a partial nuclear deal with Iran in the spring of 2023 through indirect talks mediated by Oman.[149] This agreement reportedly was negotiated as a secret, oral, and unwritten deal. Biden Administration critics claimed this was done to evade oversight of the agreement by Congress.

The deal was described as an interim agreement with major U.S. concessions. These reportedly included freezing Iran's enrichment of uranium at 60% uranium-235. Iran also was allowed to keep its nuclear infrastructure, including advanced uranium centrifuges, and permitted to continue to develop this technology.

Iran reportedly agreed under the deal to stop its proxy groups from attacking U.S. forces in Syria and Iraq and to cooperate with IAEA investigations of its nuclear program. Iran never abided by either of these provisions.

In exchange for agreeing to the above requirements, Iran was to receive more than $20 billion in sanctions relief. The U.S. also reportedly agreed not to impose new sanctions on Iran.

The agreement also included a U.S.-Iran prisoner swap in exchange for a payment to Iran of $6 billion, a payment that Biden critics have justly described as ransom to free innocent Americans imprisoned in Iran.

AMERICAN WEAKNESS CAUSES INSTABILITY AND OPPORTUNITIES FOR U.S. ADVERSARIES

There have been many signs that President Biden's weak national security policies resulted from resuming Obama-era approaches to U.S. national security and rejecting the Trump Administration's America First approach. These included the disastrous U.S. withdrawal from Afghanistan, the Biden Administration designating climate change as the top threat to U.S. national security, the Russian invasion of Ukraine, significantly increased Chinese threats to Taiwan, and a surge in North Korean missile threats. These developments, coupled with the above examples of Biden's policy missteps in the Middle East, resulted in other troubling developments that undermined U.S. interests and the likelihood of increased instability in the future.

On the global stage, a seismic shift is underway as China, America's foremost adversary, maneuvered to exploit U.S. weakness under the Biden Administration to assert its dominance and reshape the unipolar international order into a "multilateral world order."[150] In the Middle East, a formidable alliance between China, Russia, and Iran is coalescing, complete with joint military exercises, a shared weapons supply chain, and cooperation to circumvent multilateral energy sanctions and anti-terrorist finance schemes. China's ascent to superpower status is underscored by its mediation of a peace deal between Saudi Arabia and Iran, a bid to construct a nuclear plant in Saudi Arabia,[151] and heavily discounted purchases of oil from Iran.[152]

Meanwhile, Russia and Iran have cemented a symbiotic relationship, with growing volumes of trade across sea, rail, and road.[153] Through its military intervention in Syria, Russia provided crucial protection to the Iran-backed regime of Bashar al-Assad, ensuring its survival amid a protracted and brutal civil war.[154] In return for this support, Iran has reciprocated with large shipments of drones,[155] missiles,[156] and UAVs (Unmanned Aerial Vehicles) to Russia, bolstering its military arsenal in its ongoing war in Ukraine. In doing so, Russia and Iran have not only solidified their partnership but also furthered each other's military interests, shaping the dynamic of conflicts beyond the borders of both nations.

THE OCTOBER 7, 2023, HAMAS ATTACK AND THE SURGE IN VIOLENCE BY OTHER IRANIAN PROXIES

On October 7, 2023, 3,000 Hamas terrorists crossed into Israel from Gaza and killed over 1,200 Israelis and foreign nationals. Hundreds were beaten, mutilated, and raped by the terrorists. An estimated 253 Israelis and foreigners were taken hostage and brought back to Gaza. This brutal attack was accompanied by a surprise air, land, and sea attack by Hamas on Israel; and was followed by a surge in attacks by other Iranian proxies, including missile and drone attacks by Yemen's Houthi rebels against Red Sea shipping and Israel; over 120 attacks against U.S. bases in Syria and Iraq by Iran-backed militias; a surge in cross border attacks against northern Israel from Lebanon by Hezbollah, another Iranian terrorist proxy.

The brutal October 7 Hamas terrorist attack was the deadliest day against the Jewish people since the Holocaust. Many experts believe this attack and the surge in attacks by other Iranian proxies was a direct result of the Biden Administration's failed Middle East policies. This included a significant deterioration in American deterrence in the region and a significant growth of Hamas and Iranian coffers because of Biden Administration policies. There also was a perception of divisions between the United States and Israel because of political squabbling and public criticism of the Netanyahu government by Biden Administration officials.

This was the opposite of the successful America First policies of the Trump Administration of standing with Israel, one of America's closest and most important allies, and promoting American and global security with peace through strength.

President Biden's initial response to the horrific October 7 terrorist attacks was commendable and included declaring America's "rock solid" support for Israel, military aid, sending two aircraft carriers to the eastern Mediterranean as a sign of American support and deterrence, and traveling to Israel on October 18 to personally express his support for the Israeli people.

Regrettably, the Biden Administration's overall policy toward Israel after the Hamas attack became increasingly hostile and openly critical. Biden officials have publicly criticized how Israel has conducted the war against Hamas, blamed the Israeli government for the humanitarian crisis in Gaza, and demanded that Israeli officials agree to a two-state solution peace plan and an immediate end to the war prior to Israel's military defeat of Hamas. Such public criticism of a close U.S. ally, especially an ally at war, is obviously highly inappropriate. The Biden Administration has persisted in pushing proposals to create a new Palestinian state, despite adamant opposition to them by Israeli officials who believe such an arrangement would reward Hamas' genocidal October 7 massacre.

Prime Minister Netanyahu and other Israeli officials have made clear that the notion of a Palestinian state is dead for Israel until the Palestinians can be de-radicalized. In their view, Israel can no longer agree to a long-term peace agreement that gives a separate state to an enemy that is sworn to destroy the State of Israel and kill Jews. As I will explain below, no such agreement is possible before a comprehensive deradicalization program is completed.

Incredibly, Senate Majority Leader Chuck Schumer, the most senior Jewish member in the Senate, condemned Israeli Prime Minister Netanyahu in a March 14 speech from the Senate floor as "an obstacle to peace" and called for new elections in Israel. Schumer also condemned how the Netanyahu government has conducted the war against Hamas and for its opposition to a two-state solution peace plan, which Schumer said will make Israel a "pariah."

What makes the Biden Administration's current policy toward the Israel-Hamas War even more reprehensible is that Biden officials and Senate Democrats such as Chuck Schumer are attacking Netanyahu and the Israeli government because the Israel-Hamas war is highly unpopular with progressive Democrats, especially younger Democrats and Muslim voters in Michigan and Wisconsin. The Biden Administration and its allies want Israel to end the war as soon as possible because they fear it will lead to Biden's defeat in the November presidential election. They thus decided to throw Netanyahu under the bus and gut U.S.-Israel relations to gain political advantage in a U.S. presidential election.

Moreover, the Biden Administration's purported contemplation of unilaterally "declaring a Palestinian state"[157] following the conclusion of the conflict reflects a concerning disregard for the Israeli public's ongoing sacrifices in fighting a war against those responsible for the deadliest attack on Jews since the Holocaust. Moreover, American unilateral declaration of a Palestinian state may contravene the terms of the Oslo Accords, thereby rendering them null and void. In such a scenario, Israel would be compelled to reassess its options, potentially hindering progress toward an end to the conflict.

U.S. policy should be anchored in the belief that only Israelis and Palestinians can determine the terms for coexistence as neighbors. While the U.S. can serve as an impartial mediator in facilitating such discussions, the current Biden Administration is being driven by domestic political considerations, hindering its ability to navigate this complex issue effectively.

April 2024 Iranian Drone and Missile Attack Against Israel Reflected Weakened U.S. Deterrence

On April 13, 2024, Iran fired more than 300 drones and missiles against Israel. This attack was the first Iranian attack against Israel from Iranian soil, marking an unprecedented and significant escalation in the tensions between the two countries. It also was an attack likely caused by weakened U.S. deterrence.

Iran claimed the missile and drone attack was retaliation for Israel's bombing and destroying a supposed Iranian consulate in Damascus, Syria that killed at least seven Iranian officials including Mohammed Reza Zahedi, a top commander in Iran's elite Revolutionary Guards, and senior commander Mohammad Hadi Haji Rahimi.

Iran condemned the bombing in Damascus as an attack against Iranian diplomats at an embassy facility. The *Wall Street Journal* dismissed this claim in an April 1, 2024 editorial:

> *The attack was carried out with precision on a building next to Iran's embassy that reportedly served as the IRGC military headquarters. Much hemming and hawing will turn on whether this building was a diplomatic or military site. The IRGC and its Quds Force are U.S.-designated terrorist organizations that plot and execute Iran's*

strategy of regional subversion and expansion. These are men with rivers of blood on their hands.[158]

Worried that Iran might attack U.S. troops in Iraq or Syria in retaliation for the Israeli attack in Damascus, the Biden Administration informed Iran that it had nothing to do with the bombing and did not know about it in advance. Iran replied by warning the U.S. not to get involved in the fight between Israel and Iran. In response, Iran offered not to target U.S. facilities when it retaliated.

This was another feckless response by the Biden Administration to a Middle East crisis. The Biden Administration should have supported Israel's attack on the IRGC facility in Damascus and made clear to Iran that it would not tolerate any retaliation against Israel.

Many pundits claimed the April 13 Iranian drone and missile attack against Israel was symbolic and not a serious threat to Israel because the missiles and drone launched in the attack were easy for Israel to shoot down and there was no damage or injuries in Israel except for one child who was injured by falling shrapnel. 99% of the drones and missiles were intercepted by Israel, the U.S., and Jordan.

Other experts raised concerns that the Iranian attack against Israel may have been a test to probe Israeli missile defenses for a future Iranian attack using a larger number of more dangerous missiles. There also were concerns about the precedent of Iran attacking Israel directly from Iranian soil. For these reasons, there were calls in Israel and the U.S. for Israel to retaliate by attacking targets in Iran.

The Biden Administration leaked to the press that President Biden told Prime Minister Netanyahu in a phone call during the Iranian attack that the U.S. would not participate in or support any Israeli counterattack against Iran.[159]

This statement by Biden to Netanyahu – and the Biden White House leaking it to the press – were more instances of the president needlessly disrespecting a close U.S. ally. This statement also was unfortunate because the U.S. effectively took options to deal with Iran off the table and communicated more disagreements between Washington and Jerusalem. Such public disagreements probably emboldened Iran to launch the April 13 missile and drone attack.

The Israelis surprised the international community, and most importantly, Iran itself, when on April 19 Israel struck the Russian-made S-300 air defense battery system at the Isfahan airport deployed to provide defensive cover for nuclear facilities in Isfahan and the nearby Natanz underground nuclear site. The Israeli strike was limited and extremely precise. Later reports would detail that due to pressure exerted by President Biden on Prime Minister Netanyahu, Israel shifted from its original plan to conduct a broader, and more exacting strike on multiple military targets in Iran. Still, the Israeli attack on Iran's most advanced air defense system used to protect its secretive nuclear site certainly communicated a strong message to Iran of Israeli capabilities—specifically the option to strike nuclear sites had Israel chosen to--while being limited enough to allow Tehran to "save face" and avoid the need for further retaliation.

POLICY RECOMMENDATIONS

Profound U.S. policy changes are urgently needed to undo the damage done to Middle East stability by incompetent Biden Administration policies and to restore the security interests in the region of the United States and its allies. This means reinstituting an America First approach to promote American strength, stand solidly with the State of Israel, and recognize Iran as a U.S. adversary and state-sponsor of terrorism.

Countering President Biden's weakness with a strong and decisive president who reestablishes American deterrence will be the most important way to reverse the deterioration of security in the Middle East since 2021. Having a U.S. president in office once again whom our enemies fear and who they believe could employ massive U.S. military power if necessary to counter their provocations will go a long way toward stopping the recent surge of attacks by Iran and its proxy groups and prevent another deadly attack like October 7.

American strength and credibility in the Middle East will not just promote stability but will counter the current efforts by China and Russia to expand their influence with regional states at America's expense due to the Biden Administration's incompetent policies. The new administration must demonstrate to states like Saudi Arabia that the United States is a credible and reliable ally who will treat them respectfully and not pursue policies counter to their interests, such as trying to revive the JCPOA. America must make it clear to its friends and allies in the Middle East that it is in their best interests to forge closer diplomatic, economic, and military relationships with the United States rather than with China and Russia.

The U.S. Must Stand With Israel Once Again

The world also must know once again that there is no daylight between the United States and Israel in its friendship and on security issues. The Biden Administration's bickering with the Israeli government and its failure to veto UNSC Resolution 2728 on March 25, 2024 (a resolution that demanded an immediate cease-fire in Gaza without requiring that Hamas release hostages) has undermined regional security and helped to isolate the Jewish state. The majority of the American people do not share the hostility of the global elite and American progressives toward the state of Israel and will strongly support efforts by a future administration to reverse the Biden Administration's craven hostility toward it.

In a future Republican administration, policymakers should explore the possibility of establishing a more extended memorandum of understanding with Israel. This agreement could go beyond conventional defense aid or foreign military financing (FMF) and include specific allocations for funding various military assets, such as F-15s, F-35s, bunker-buster bombs, and KC-46A aerial refueling aircraft, which may prove vital for defensive actions against Iranian facilities. Given the ongoing conflicts involving Iranian proxies in Gaza and Lebanon, along with escalating tensions with a potentially nuclear-enabled Iran, there is a pressing need for the United States to accelerate the procurement of advanced fighters and combat helicopters. The evolving defense ties between Russia and Iran further demonstrate the urgency of bolstering the F-15 fleet. With the possibility of Moscow supplying S-400 air defense systems to Iran for safeguarding its nuclear installations, Israel's F-15s become indispensable not only for potential operations against Iranian targets but also for swiftly countering the threat posed by precision missile launches from Hezbollah in Lebanon. Hence, it is imperative to expedite the delivery of an additional squadron composed of 25 Lockheed Martin F-35s, one squadron of Boeing's F-15 EX, and a squadron of Apache E attack helicopters. The Israeli Air Force's request for the simultaneous upgrade of its existing 25 F-15Is to match the avionic configuration of the F-15 EX should also be prioritized.[160]

It is crucial that the memorandum of understanding (MOU) revisit the policy regarding Israel's ability to convert a portion of U.S. aid into shekels, restoring the prerogative that was in place before the Obama Administration. This adjustment would enable Israel to procure necessary goods and services to support equipment acquired from the U.S. for offshore procurement (OSP) purposes. The ongoing conflict in Ukraine has prompted a significant shortage of Western munitions and weapons systems.[161] In light of these circumstances, it becomes increasingly evident that permitting Israel to manufacture at least some of its munitions domestically would be mutually advantageous for both the U.S. and Israel. This approach would not only enhance Israel's self-reliance in meeting its defense needs but also strengthen its capacity to swiftly respond to emerging security threats in the region. Moreover, accelerating domestic production would contribute to the long-term sustainability of Israel's defense infrastructure, reducing dependence on external suppliers during times of global instability and regional unrest.[162]

The next administration also must prioritize expanding the Abraham Accords to include more of Israel's Arab neighbors, especially the Kingdom of Saudi Arabia. Saudi Crown Prince Mohammed Bin Salman has indicated the Kingdom's tacit acceptance of a Jewish state in the region.[163] Much of the Saudi Normalization talks center on security guarantees, which the Kingdom is seeking from the United States. Given that Saudi Arabia has been a historic and significant U.S. ally, these security and defense requests should be given serious consideration. Any U.S. security guarantees granted as part of a Normalization deal with Israel can be put forth to the U.S. Congress as a Treaty, making such guarantees irreversible by any future Democrat administration.

Support for Gaza Demilitarization and Palestinian Deradicalization

In the immediate post-October 7 war period, the U.S. should actively support Israel's strategy to demilitarize Gaza and undertake efforts to deradicalize religious, educational, and welfare institutions within the Strip. To sustain the demilitarization process, the U.S. should facilitate coordination between Israel and Egypt aimed at thwarting weapons and missile smuggling across the Egyptian border, particularly in the vicinity of the Rafah crossing. Crucially, the U.S. needs to encourage moderate Gulf states like Saudi Arabia and the UAE to contribute to their region's stability by assisting in financing the reconstruction of Gaza. Subsequently, the civilian administration of Gaza should be entrusted to reputable entities with no ties to terrorism or extremism, ensuring effective governance and promoting stability in the region.

Moreover, any financial assistance provided by the U.S. to the Palestinian Authority must be contingent upon its commitment to implementing deradicalization programs and in strict adherence to the principles outlined in the Taylor Force Act. This legislation serves as a critical tool in preventing the diversion of aid funds toward incentivizing terrorism. Moving forward, the United States must unequivocally assert its stance against any Palestinian governing entity that propagates, sanctions, or rewards acts of terror.

In the near term, donor nations should be prepared to redirect funding if necessary, and intelligence agencies must implement rigorous counterterrorism vetting processes. Plans for transitioning UNRWA operations should be developed, with a focus on ensuring that aid reaches those genuinely in need and promoting accountability in the use of funds.

In dismantling UNRWA, the U.S. should finally call into question the criteria UNRWA used in counting the number of Palestinian "refugees." By any other standard, descendants of 1948 Arab refugees born abroad, and often with citizenship in second countries, cannot claim refugee status. To be clear, these people are fully resettled without any support from UNRWA. UNRWA has used this inflated count to advocate for increased funding and, as a result, has extended the Israel-Palestinian conflict's reach into third countries.

Reinstitute Maximum Pressure Against Iran

A new America First administration must immediately cease the Biden Administration's misguided effort to treat Iran as a partner for peace in the Middle East and to revive the deeply flawed JCPOA nuclear deal. This new administration must recognize Iran for what it is: an American adversary and the world's leading sponsor of terrorism. This new administration will not seek war with Iran, will be open to negotiations, and will use tools of statecraft possible short of war to de-escalate tensions with Tehran. However, the new president will make it clear that he is prepared to use military force against Iran if necessary to protect American interests.

To build on the maximum pressure campaign of the Trump Administration, the U.S. should cut off Iran's access to its frozen assets in other countries. In addition to imposing sanctions on key regime entities that wish to harm Americans, the future administration should also cut Iran's financial ties to other countries and rigorously enforce existing sanctions.

Despite the Iranian government's theocratic nature, the Iranian people's continued resilience against this oppressive regime signifies their unwavering determination for change. Maximum Pressure on Iran thus must be coupled with support for the people of Iran. The application of Maximum Pressure on Iran inherently aids the Iranian people by weakening the oppressive regime, thereby bolstering the populace. Conversely, Maximum Support for the Iranian people places pressure on the regime by empowering citizens and fostering a burgeoning organic movement. Therefore, the forthcoming U.S. administration should actively engage with the secular democratic Iranian opposition. This engagement should prioritize capacity-building initiatives for civic activists within Iran, revitalize funding efforts through the State Department for civil society, and commence strategic planning for supporting a democratic transition within the nation.

Recognizing the gravity of Iranian actions and their implications for regional stability and nuclear proliferation, U.S. policymakers ought to keep all options on the table—even acknowledging that a decisive military strike might become necessary to deter further aggression and safeguard U.S. national security interests. In the short term, this should include a more aggressive targeted killing campaign against Iranian and proxy operatives in Iraq, Syria, and Lebanon.

As a long-term strategy, however, merely targeting Iran-backed militias in Iraq and Syria in response to the killing of U.S. soldiers and nuclear proliferation will be insufficient and ineffective to deter Iran. To establish credible deterrence, the U.S. must firmly convey that the killing of American soldiers and the regime's access to nuclear weapons are red lines that will result in strikes within Iran's borders.

Such action would reaffirm the U.S. commitment to safeguarding American lives, both domestically and abroad, while also sending a clear message to adversaries regarding our boundaries. Taken as a whole, a Maximum Pressure/Maximum Support approach would demonstrate the next administration's dedication to exhausting all available options in addressing the Iranian threat while showcasing its determination to confront challenges to international peace and security.

CONCLUSION

The People's Republic of China has successfully created an anti-American axis in partnership with Russia and Iran, which threatens the U.S.-led world order, all as a direct result of President Biden's incompetent national security policies. While each member of the axis—China, Russia, and Iran—poses distinct challenges to U.S. interests in their respective regions, the overarching threat they collectively represent demands a comprehensive strategic response from the United States. Democrat administrations have opted to relinquish spheres of U.S. influence and power to China and Russia, deliberately weakening America's position on the global stage.

It is urgent that a new president in January 2025 take steps to immediately restore America's unparalleled global standing, reassert America's status as THE global superpower, and protect the U.S.-led international order by bolstering and supporting allies while containing and confronting adversaries. In the Middle East, the U.S. must bring security and stability to the region with decisive America First national security policies that re-establish America's relationship with Israel and counter Iran's malign influence with a Maximum Pressure/Maximum Support strategy. The elusive peace in the Middle East, which has been sought by the foreign policy elites, will be achieved only through reasserting American strength.

8.

America First, NATO, and U.S Alliances: Why America First is Not Isolationism

By Morgan Ortagus

An America First foreign policy, often misconstrued as isolationism, stands apart from the past 30 years of foreign policy by Republican and Democratic presidents. It promotes the interests of Americans while actively engaging with the international community through strong alliances. America First foreign policy views international organizations and alliances as a way to leverage cooperation and enhance America's position in the world.

At the same time, international organizations and alliances need robust accountability and transparency to ensure they are not undermining American sovereignty or promoting globalist agendas that undercut Americans' economic well-being and security. America should not give in to the European elite to join radical globalist agreements such as the Paris Climate Accords.

Although the United States will work with allies and international organizations to promote global and U.S. national security, America also must not give up its sovereign right to take action to defend itself. Europe and the United Nations do not and must not have vetoes over national security decisions made by our president.[164]

Legendary Pentagon advisor Andrew Marshall provided helpful guidance in 2018 on how America should devise its strategic participation in international organizations: we should view China as the primary threat, and everything else falls secondary.[165] Given China's pervasive presence and abuse of international organizations, preventing the Chinese Communist Party from taking over multilateral organizations is critical, and it will require America once again to take a leadership position. This echoes and amplifies President Trump's commitment to promoting sovereignty and defending the interests of the American people.

NATO AND AMERICA'S EUROPEAN ALLIES

The North Atlantic Treaty Organization (NATO) stands as a bedrock of transatlantic security, keeping the peace through the collective defense commitments of its member states. For centuries, European countries fought wars among themselves, but since NATO's founding in 1949, that has largely halted.

NATO has pivoted from its singular focus on the Soviet Union and Russia to the fight against radical Islamic terrorism. In addition, President Trump led the NATO allies to recognize the increasing hostility of China, and he focused on the need to unite in efforts to curb its predatory tactics and deter China's ability to infiltrate the communications systems of our allies. Amid this backdrop, the Trump Administration embarked on a mission to revitalize and strengthen NATO, reaffirming America's commitment to its allies while advancing a vision of security rooted in the principles of the America First policy. [166]

Today, America's relationship with NATO and our European allies is in trouble. Despite pressure from multiple U.S. presidents — especially President Trump — to convince NATO members to meet their treaty obligations of spending at least 2 percent of their GDP on defense, as of February 2024, only 18 of NATO's 31 members had met this goal.[167]

According to a Heritage Foundation study, the European defense spending picture is even worse. The report notes that the British army is at its smallest since 1710, and would struggle to put a single division in the field. Germany had 5,000 battle tanks during the Cold War but has only 300 today. France has only 222 tanks and 19 large surface warships, according to the report.[168]

Many European states also have come under criticism for not contributing enough to support Ukraine in its war against Russia. According to the same Heritage report, although three Western European states — the UK, Netherlands, and Norway — have exceeded U.S. aid to Ukraine as a percentage of GDP (0.37 percent), several other

Western European states have given far less. Germany has provided only 0.2 percent of GDP in aid to Ukraine; France, 0.06 percent; and Italy, 0.06 percent. (Six East European states have given more aid to Ukraine than the United States as a percentage of GDP.)[169]

The failure of major European states to pay a fair share of their collective defense and aid to Ukraine has become a growing concern among many in Congress in light of the over $113 billion in humanitarian, financial, and military aid the United States has provided to Ukraine since February 2022 and another $61 billion approved by Congress in April 2024. (Please see Chapter 5 for a detailed discussion of America First and the war in Ukraine.)

These developments raise questions about America's defense relationships with NATO and its European allies. Under an America First approach, these relationships should be partnerships in which all members carry their weight and fairly contribute to our collective defense. Moreover, European conflicts like the war in Ukraine should be the primary responsibility of European states. It makes little sense for the United States to spend a greater percentage of its GDP on the war than France, Italy, and Germany. The American taxpayer should not bear a larger burden of this war than European taxpayers.

A future America First president must put strong pressure on European states to spend their fair share on collective defense and assume greater responsibility for defending their regional interests. With 13 NATO members currently falling short of their 2 percent spending obligation, accountability is key.

The United States should also push NATO to appoint a new secretary general from an Eastern European country closer to the Russian threat. It is worth noting that NATO's Eastern European members have contributed far above their 2 percent obligations.

Rectifying defense spending deficiencies is not just about finances. It is about reaffirming NATO's solidarity against evolving threats, such as China's growing influence and aggression. America must be able to depend on NATO for any confrontation with the Chinese Communist Party. For nearly eight decades, the United States has defended Europe from Russian aggression. Now, the United States needs to be certain that NATO will have its back regarding China.

How President Trump Held NATO Accountable

One of the Trump Administration's most important foreign policy achievements was significant progress in rebalancing financial contributions among NATO member states. For years, the United States complained that the American taxpayer shouldered a disproportionate burden in funding NATO's operations and capabilities.[170] But until President Trump arrived, those complaints resulted in no action.

President Trump's effective push for member nations to fulfill their financial commitments not only strengthened the alliance but also reiterated the strategic advantage of U.S. leadership in defending democratic principles worldwide. By the end of 2020, NATO allies committed to increasing defense spending by $130 billion, a testament to the administration's efforts to ensure fair burden-sharing within the alliance.[171] President Trump's insistence that all NATO partners contribute adequately to defense expenditures underscored a key principle: NATO should be supported financially by all members, not primarily the United States.[172] While only three NATO members met the two percent GDP spending threshold when President Trump took office, an additional five countries joined that cohort in 2019, resulting in a collective investment increase of $130 billion.

The Trump Administration's work to make NATO stronger will have lasting effects. It shows how important it is for countries to work together toward mutual defense. Marshall Billingslea, a former Treasury Department assistant secretary who worked on stopping terrorism financing, says NATO countries need to share defense costs more fairly. Even though Germany has started to spend more on defense, Billingslea points out it will take more than a year to make up for past shortfalls. Billingslea believes it is crucial that NATO members meet their defense spending commitments so the alliance can address new threats, known and unknown.[173]

Beyond financial contributions, the Trump Administration also stepped up efforts to promote defense investment and modernization within the alliance. Recognizing the need to adapt to evolving security threats, the administration advocated for increased investments in critical capabilities and technologies to enhance NATO's deterrence posture.[174]

NATO countries agreed to spend $400 billion more on their militaries by 2024. This money will go toward better equipment and facilities.[175] This significant investment in defense modernization signaled NATO's readiness to confront emerging threats and maintain a credible deterrent posture in an increasingly complex security environment.

The Trump Administration also pushed for a stronger NATO role in Eastern Europe to confront a resurgent Russian aggression. The administration conducted more military exercises and increased the presence of troops in NATO members closest to Russia. Trump also urged NATO to do more about terrorism and immigration challenges. By pushing for NATO's increased involvement in non-traditional security areas, the Trump Administration sought to adapt the alliance's mandate to reflect contemporary challenges, enhancing its relevance and effectiveness in safeguarding transatlantic security.[176]

Asian Alliances and American Interests

America's strong alliance with Japan and South Korea and its large military presence in the Asia-Pacific region have kept the peace and promoted stability in this region since the end of World War II. Out of the ashes of that terrible war, Japan has become one of America's closest and most trusted allies.

America's relationship with South Korea is just as strong and has ensured deterrence along the Korean DMZ for the past 70 years. America's strong support of Taiwan, coupled with its policy of "strategic ambiguity," has prevented war with Communist China and helped safeguard the island republic's freedom and security.

In recent years, the term "Asia-Pacific" has been replaced by some national security experts with the term "Indo-Pacific." This is because of the growing threat posed by China both to Asia-Pacific nations and to India. Growing Chinese aggression against Taiwan, in the South China Sea, and along the India-China border has led regional states to pursue joint strategies to defend against China, such as the Quadrilateral Security Dialogue (the Quad), discussed later in this chapter.

Maintaining and strengthening America's alliance with its Asian allies is crucial in light of growing threats in the region, not just from China but also from North Korea and Russia. Too often, American presidents become so distracted by conflicts in other areas of the world, especially the Middle East, that they neglect the security concerns of their Asian allies. This was true of the Obama Administration, which claimed it would "pivot to Asia" to deal with growing threats from Beijing. Instead, Obama and his team became obsessed with striking the disastrous 2015 nuclear deal with Iran.

The Biden Administration has continued along this dangerous path. Without question, President Biden's weak foreign policy and his disastrous withdrawal from Afghanistan emboldened China to step up its provocations against Taiwan and in the South China Sea. North Korea's significant expansion of its missile program since 2021, along with possible preparations for a seventh underground nuclear test, has seen no real policy response from the Biden Administration. This has been driven by the president naming a part-time North Korean special envoy and a failure of top Biden officials to attempt bilateral diplomacy with their North Korean counterparts.

The Biden Administration's weak Asian foreign policy has also led to joint Russia-Chinese naval and air exercises in the region and a new Russia-China axis that has been augmented by North Korea and Iran.

As part of this budding relationship, North Korean dictator Kim Jong Un met with Russian President Vladimir Putin in Vladivostok in 2023. During the visit, Kim reportedly agreed to provide Putin with additional weapons for the war in Ukraine. In turn, Putin reportedly offered Kim satellite and missile technologies.

On January 12, 2023, President Biden met with South Korea's President Yoon Suk Yeol and held a summit at Camp David in August 2023 with leaders from Japan and South Korea. The parties agreed to work closer together in response to concerns about China and instability in Asia. Although Biden deserves credit for these efforts, it is fair to say the meetings were a response to his administration's neglect toward our Asian allies and their worries about whether the United States would support them against China and North Korea.

President Yoon triggered the administration's alarm with his statement on January 12, 2023 about the possibility of South Korea developing its own nuclear weapons or asking the United States to redeploy tactical nuclear missiles to South Korea in response to North

Korea's threats. Yoon's comments caused panic in Biden's national security team and led to a crash program to repair U.S. relations with South Korea and Japan, culminating with the Biden-Yoon summit and the Camp David summit.

In September 2021, the leaders of Australia, the United Kingdom, and the United States announced the creation of an enhanced trilateral security partnership called "AUKUS." This new alliance is intended to assist Australia in acquiring nuclear powered submarines and establishing a new cooperation between the three states to counter increased threats from China in the region, especially in the South China Sea. The AUKUS agreement also includes cooperation in countering cyber warfare, threats from artificial intelligence, undersea capabilities, hypersonic and counter-hypersonic, electronic warfare, innovation. and information sharing.

The AUKUS agreement is one of the Biden Administration's few foreign policy achievements and should be continued and developed by future administrations. However, there was a pall over the launch of the new alliance because French officials protested getting blindsided by the agreement, which coincided with Australia cancelling a 50 billion euro deal to buy diesel-powered submarines from France.

After the AUKUS agreement was announced, French Foreign Minister Jean-Yves Le Drian said, "There was lying, there was duplicity, there was a major breach of trust." France also recalled its ambassadors to Canberra and Washington in response to the agreement.

The Biden Administration acknowledged its mistakes in how it handled the AUKUS agreement with France and began a process of "in-depth consultations to repair relations. Although U.S.-France relations recovered, the poor communication was an unforced error by the Biden national security team.

Building and maintaining strong security alliances is vital for an America First foreign policy. The Biden Administration's poor handling of security in Asia has made the United States and the world less safe. A successful policy would avoid war by working with allies to keep peace and avoid dragging U.S. troops into unnecessary conflicts. But weak, incompetent policies such as those of the Biden Administration in the

Asia-Pacific could lead to unwanted military conflicts involving U.S. forces. Peace through strength works. Ignoring allies does not.

How President Trump Revitalized America's Asian Alliances

In the Indo-Pacific region, the Trump Administration recognized the strategic importance of strong alliances in maintaining regional stability and deterring would-be adversaries. One of the cornerstones of the administration's strategy in Asia was deepening the U.S.-Japan alliance, a vital partnership for regional security and stability. Through a series of defense agreements and joint military exercises, the administration enhanced the interoperability and readiness of U.S. and Japanese forces, strengthening our deterrence against China's People's Liberation Army.[177]

President Trump set the stage for his America First approach to trade and America's relationship with Asian states in a 2017 speech to the Asia-Pacific Economic Co-operation (APEC). He said the United States would no longer tolerate "chronic trade abuses" and in trade relationships – he would put America first.

In his speech to APEC, Trump criticized the World Trade Organization for not enforcing trade rules and said trade imbalances with the U.S. had cost millions of American jobs. Trump said America was ready to make bilateral trade agreements with "any Indo-Pacific partner here who abides by fair reciprocal trade," but only "on a basis of mutual respect and mutual benefit."[178]

During Trump's tenure, Japan increased its defense spending, with commitments to enhance its defense capabilities through increased purchases of U.S.-made military equipment.[179] Japan pledged to invest over $240 billion in defense capabilities by 2024. This substantial boost in defense investment underscored Japan's commitment to enhancing its military capabilities and contributing more effectively to regional security efforts.[180]

Trump's approach was to encourage our Asian allies to assume a greater share of the burden in addressing common security challenges, including responses to North Korea's nuclear program and China's aggression in the South China Sea. Our allies pursued diplomatic engagement with Pyongyang and emphasized denuclearization, as well as pursuing the issue of abducted Japanese citizens. There also was close collaboration on North Korean policy.[181]

America was blessed to have now-Senator Bill Hagerty (R-TN) as ambassador to Japan from 2017-2019. He was a first-rate diplomat who negotiated one of the only bilateral free-trade agreements in the Trump Administration. Hagerty also renegotiated the U.S. military presence in Japan. The alliance and partnership with Japan should be at the top of the new administration's global priorities. The next ambassador to Japan will be a crucial appointment.

President Trump's North Korea policy, especially his personal diplomacy with Kim Jong Un, is a case study of how an America First foreign policy can work. The president was clear in 2017 that the United States would not tolerate growing missile and nuclear threats from North Korea. In a landmark speech to the U.N. General Assembly in September 2017, Trump said, "The United States has great strength and patience, but if it is forced to defend itself or its allies, we will have no choice but to totally destroy North Korea."

Trump's tough rhetoric, sanctions, and policies against North Korea in 2017 led Kim to agree to diplomacy with the United States, including a summit with the president in Singapore in June 2018. Although the United States worked closely with Japan and South Korea in its approach to North Korea, the Trump Administration did not give either state a veto over America's North Korea policy. Specifically, the United States listened to South Korean President Moon Jae-in but took a much harder line against Pyongyang than Moon wanted. The United States also deliberately excluded Moon from the Singapore Summit because he was too willing to make concessions to North Korea.

This is an America First foreign policy in action: American strength, presidential leadership, peace through strength, and working with allies with the caveat that the United States will sometimes act independently when it is in our Nation's interest.

The Trump Administration focused not only on security but also on building economic ties with Asia. U.S. negotiators made deals with Japan and South Korea to make trade fairer and more reciprocal.[182] In 2019, the United States and Japan signed two agreements. One was the U.S.-Japan Trade Agreement, which reduced tariffs on $7.2 billion of U.S.

farm products. The other was the U.S.-Japan Digital Trade Agreement, which set high standards for digital trade, such as allowing data to move freely across borders and ensuring privacy and security online. Both agreements started on January 1, 2020.[183]

Similarly, the U.S.-South Korea Free Trade Agreement was renegotiated to improve market access for American agricultural products and reduce non-tariff barriers to trade.[184]

The Trump Administration worked to boost investments between the United States and Asian nations, which led to more jobs and growth. It launched efforts like the Indo-Pacific Economic Vision to improve infrastructure, internet connections, and energy projects across the region. Investments from Japan and South Korea in the United States hit all-time highs, benefiting both countries' economies.[185]

President Trump's personal rapport with Japanese Prime Minister Shinzo Abe played a crucial role in strengthening bilateral relations and advancing shared strategic objectives. Abe served the Japanese people admirably before his tragic death in 2022 by an assassin's bullet. Through frequent meetings and high-level dialogues, the administration reaffirmed the U.S. commitment to its Asian allies and underscored the importance of the U.S.-Japan alliance for regional stability.[186] Active engagement with Japan, coupled with similar efforts across the region, demonstrated the administration's commitment to promoting U.S. interests while fostering greater security and prosperity in the Asia-Pacific.

By prioritizing security cooperation, economic engagement, and diplomatic leadership, the Trump Administration laid the groundwork for a more secure, prosperous, and interconnected Asia-Pacific region. As the United States continues to navigate the complex challenges and opportunities in Asia, the legacy of the Trump Administration's efforts to fortify alliances and deepen partnerships will endure, shaping the future of regional security and prosperity.

The Trump Administration helped revitalize the Quadrilateral Security Dialogue, known better as "the Quad," which is a partnership between the United States, Japan, Australia, and India. The four wanted to work more closely to address security concerns and keep the Indo-Pacific area stable and open.[187]

The truth is that President Trump's leadership resurrected the Quad, which had died during the Obama Administration. Countries saw a marked increase in diplomatic engagement and military cooperation during Trump's tenure. High-level meetings among Quad members became more frequent, signaling a commitment to better dialogue and coordination. In addition, joint military exercises, such as the Malabar naval exercises, saw increased participation and complexity, symbolizing a deepening of military collaboration within the Quad framework.[188]

Americans often take the status quo for granted. We assume goods can be freely transported on ships, fishing vessels can freely operate in international waters, and civilian aircraft can fly in international airspace without interference. China's nefarious plans and activities imperil each of these freedoms and could derail the entire global economy.

That is why the Quad's attention and strategy aims to uphold freedom of navigation, overflight, and adherence to international law in the region, countering China's maritime claims and activities.[189]

Moreover, China, through its Belt and Road Initiative, bribes and coaxes corrupt officials in the Asia-Pacific and other regions with deals that can be used to install Chinese military infrastructure and spyware within what appear to be civilian projects.[190] Worse, these countries are often unable to make the projects profitable, saddling them with debt that binds them to Beijing's whims. The United States should explore and advance alternatives to China's Belt and Road Initiative with transparent and sustainable infrastructure investments in the region. We do not need to give handouts to compete with China. Instead, we should leverage smart financing options so countries can remain free and independent.

At the same time, the Trump Administration focused on better intelligence sharing with the "Five Eyes" alliance, which includes the United States, UK, Canada, Australia, and New Zealand. The goal was to improve how these countries share intelligence to face new threats, especially in cyberspace and from terror-sponsoring countries such as Iran.

The Trump Administration also worked to bolster cybersecurity within the Five Eyes to guard against cyber attacks from other countries, terrorist groups, and the pernicious influence of Chinese technology.[191] Together, these initiatives reinforced the administration's commitment to strengthening Asian alliances and countering China and other transnational threats.[192] To that end, the Trump Administration led efforts to stymie the reach of Chinese tech companies, notably Huawei and ZTE, within Five Eyes countries. Recognizing the national security risks posed by those companies, the administration advocated restrictions on their participation in critical infrastructure projects, especially burgeoning 5G networks.[193] By prioritizing cybersecurity and countering Chinese technological influence, the Trump Administration reaffirmed its commitment to protecting American interests and safeguarding the integrity of the Five Eyes alliance.

Why Alliances and American Deterrence Are Crucial for Middle East Stability

America's strong alliances in the Middle East, including its longstanding partnership with Israel, have helped keep the region stable. Good relationships with countries like Saudi Arabia, Egypt, Jordan, Iraq, and the Gulf states are important for peace and for countering malign activities by Iran and radical Islamist terrorist groups. These alliances are also key in preventing China and Russia from gaining more influence in the Middle East at America's expense.

The Obama Administration bungled American Middle East policy by attempting to treat Iran as a potential partner for peace in the region and downplaying America's critical relationship with Israel. This led to the Joint Comprehensive Plan of Action (JCPOA)—better known as the Iran nuclear deal. This deal emboldened rather than hindered Iran's nuclear weapons and long-range missile programs, along with its meddling in other countries' affairs. (The JCPOA is discussed in great detail in Chapter 7.)

Biden's Middle East policy has been even worse. President Biden started his term snubbing Saudi Arabia and Egypt and downgrading America's relationship with Israel by attempting to upgrade the U.S. relationship with Iran and the Palestinians. The old Obama

Administration policy of appeasing Iran returned with a vengeance. This included almost 18 months of futile negotiations, during which Biden Administration diplomats offered increasingly generous concessions to Iran in their desperate efforts to revive the JCPOA that President Trump properly abandoned in 2018. Growing provocations from Hamas, Hezbollah, Houthi rebels in Yemen, and Shiite militias in Iraq and Syria—all Iranian proxies—are the direct result of Biden's policies to mollify Iran and weaken American deterrence in the region.

According to a Heritage Foundation study in October 2023, the Iranian government had accrued approximately $71 billion in additional revenue during the Biden Administration compared to the Trump Administration because Biden officials have refused to enforce sanctions.[194] Iranian oil sales to China account for much of that windfall. The Biden Administration has also sent more than $1 billion in aid to the Palestinians since 2021. This includes aid to the United Nations Relief and Works Agency (UNRWA), whose own employees overwhelmingly support Hamas.[195] These funds, combined with the erosion of American deterrence, helped make possible the deadly October 7, 2023, Hamas terrorist attack against Israel. (UNRWA is discussed in greater detail in Chapter 7.)

The Biden Administration's ineffective policies in the Middle East have handed opportunities to Russia and China to expand their influence at America's expense. China has been building economic ties with countries like Saudi Arabia and other Gulf states. Beijing now buys oil from Saudi Arabia using Chinese yuan. China also stunned the world in March 2023 when it announced it had brokered an agreement to restore diplomatic and economic ties between Saudi Arabia and Iran.

America needs strong allies in the Middle East and must work to maintain these relationships. This requires enlightened policies that reflect American interests and the interests of states in the region. Such relationships should promote America First goals by bolstering alliances and American deterrence and decreasing the chances of military conflicts that could involve the United States.

Sadly, the Biden Administration's approach to the Middle East has been the opposite of a responsible and enlightened America First approach. More ominously, the Biden Administration's incompetent

Middle East policies have increased the chances of a regional war and bolstered the influence of China, Russia, and Iran at the expense of the United States and our allies in the region, especially Israel.

HOW PRESIDENT TRUMP'S AMERICA FIRST POLICIES SUCCEEDED IN THE MIDDLE EAST

Under President Trump's leadership, the United States showcased unwavering support for the alliance with itself and Israel, leading to several landmark achievements. As noted in earlier chapters the United States recognized Jerusalem as Israel's capital in December 2017, a significant diplomatic milestone that sent a powerful signal: the U.S. stands with Israel unconditionally and unequivocally. [196] Pundits opposed the move, predicting war would break out in response, using that excuse to oppose the move. Yet there was no war. They were wrong every time. The result of the Trump Administration's principled stances was that friend and foe alike knew they could not separate the United States from its allies.

President Trump's first trip abroad to Saudi Arabia in May 2017 was no accident. He wanted to confirm the strong ties with the Saudis and speak to Arab and Muslim leaders about fighting terrorism. This important visit showed that Trump's transactional approach to his "America First" policy was about maintaining good ties with major countries for the benefit of Americans. Even though the United States and Saudi Arabia disagreed on subjects like human rights, Trump believed it was vital to maintain good overall relations with Arab countries. This also prevents losing influence to rivals like China.

A landmark success for the Trump Administration in the Middle East was brokering the Abraham Accords. Pursuant to this set of deals, Israel and several Arab countries, including the United Arab Emirates, Bahrain, Sudan, and Morocco, agreed to establish normal relations with each other.[197] These agreements changed the region's dynamic, as these countries previously had refused to recognize Israel. The deals were made possible because these Arab nations understood the closeness of the relationship between the United States and Israel.

The Abraham Accords under President Trump led to new diplomatic and economic ties between Israel and Arab nations. The deals with the

UAE and Bahrain are expected to bring in billions from investments, trade, and tourism. Trade between Israel and these countries has increased. For example, trade between Israel and the UAE rose to $222.3 million in October 2023. Peace in the Middle East is not just good for those countries; it provides major benefits to the United States. The agreement bolsters American security, narrows the areas where terrorists can hide, and ultimately could reduce how much U.S. taxpayers spend on global peace and stability. Again, supporting our allies is at the heart of an "America First" foreign policy when Americans benefit.

As discussed in Chapter 7, the Trump Administration's Middle East policy also included a Maximum Pressure campaign of strong sanctions and diplomatic efforts against Iran. President Trump often notes that as a result of these actions, Iran was left nearly bankrupt by the end of his term.

This included Trump's move in 2018 to leave the 2015 JCPOA nuclear deal, especially after evidence of Iran's secret nuclear activities was uncovered in 2018. While America's European allies and many in the media criticized the decision to abandon the deal, Israel, Saudi Arabia, and other Middle Eastern countries that were directly affected by the growing threat from Iran supported the move. Quite simply, Trump's decision strengthened ties between the United States and these key Middle Eastern allies.

President Trump's decision to withdraw from the JCPOA also reflected his belief that although the United States should work with and consult America's allies on important national security matters, Europe and the New York Times do not have a veto over U.S. foreign policy. America will do what it deems necessary to promote American and international security.

The Trump Administration built stronger relationships with Gulf Cooperation Council countries, leading to enhanced security cooperation and expanded joint military exercises. In the past, these countries had frequently bought weapons from other nations, including our adversaries. Under Trump, the United States started to take over as their main arms supplier. The Trump Administration approved arms sales worth more than $110 billion to Saudi Arabia and the UAE alone.[198] These sales were of U.S.-made weapons, supporting American businesses and jobs. The weapons helped these Arab countries fight terrorism themselves, saving U.S. dollars and lives. This was another America First win.

The Trump Administration worked with Middle Eastern countries to counter terrorism, especially the ISIS threat. ISIS had expanded in Syria and Iraq and radicalized scores of fighters. This led, during the Obama years, to attacks in Europe and the United States.

The United States led a global effort that took back 110,000 square kilometers from ISIS.[199] President Trump also authorized the strike that killed Abu Bakr Al-Baghdadi, the leader of ISIS. The Trump Administration defeated the physical caliphate and severely degraded the group's freedom to operate.[200] There remains the question of what to do with the many ISIS fighters and their families in camps in Syria and Iraq. The plan is to make their home countries take them back to ease the burden on Syria and Iraq and to prevent any new terror group from freeing these fighters.

The Trump Administration prioritized efforts to counter extremist ideologies, promoting tolerance and pluralism in the region. Initiatives such as the establishment of the Terrorist Financing Targeting Center in Riyadh fueled collaboration with Gulf partners. The Center works to disrupt terrorist financing networks, targeting countries and others that support groups like ISIS and al-Qaeda.[201] This is the kind of international organization that serves our interests and those of world security.

THE UNITED NATIONS

The brainchild of President Franklin D. Roosevelt and British Prime Minister Winston Churchill, the United Nations was founded after World War II to prevent another devastating world war and perhaps the end of humanity.

During the Cold War, the U.N. became dominated by the Soviet Union and radical Third World states. From time to time, however, the world body managed to promote international security and helped end conflicts, usually by sending peacekeepers to troubled areas of the world. The United States, on occasion, succeeded in persuading Russia and China, both veto members of the U.N. Security Council, to vote with the United States on resolutions addressing vital threats. For example, Russia and China voted to allow the use of force to expel Iraq from Kuwait in 1990 (China abstained). Both voted to condemn North Korea's first nuclear test in 2006. Russia and China also voted to sanction Iran from 2006 to 2011 for its covert nuclear program and uranium enrichment program. The Trump Administration succeeded in getting the Security Council to pass six resolutions condemning North Korea's nuclear program in 2017, often with Russian and Chinese abstentions.

While the U.N. has been useful to the United States at times, its perceived and actual corruption, along with bias against the United States and Israel, have alienated many Americans. Many members of the U.N. pursue a vision of global governance that does not always align with U.S. interests. The U.N. has been accused—rightly—of being unfairly critical of Israel, passing 140 resolutions against the Jewish State from 2015 to 2022, compared to 68 for other countries during the same period.[202] This imbalance has led to questions about the U.N.'s fairness and its dedication to real peace, security, and prosperity worldwide.

The U.N. and other international organizations also have justly earned a reputation for corruption and politicization. This includes wasteful international bureaucracies filled with incompetent officials. Spies obtain diplomatic visas and live in New York City under the auspices of the U.N. The United States has struggled with this problem for decades and attempted to combat it by restricting its contributions to international organizations and sometimes withdrawing from them.

China has effectively influenced international organizations to support its views. An example is the World Health Organization (WHO). WHO did not hold China accountable for the COVID-19 pandemic, very likely because of China's control over the organization and its leader, Tedros Adhanom Ghebreyesus. Because of this, President Trump decided to leave the WHO in 2020, but President Biden rejoined it on his first day in office. President Trump also withdrew from the notoriously corrupt, anti-American, and anti-Israel U.N. Educational, Scientific and

Cultural Organization (UNESCO) in 2017. President Biden reversed this decision and rejoined UNESCO in 2023.

The Biden Administration's approach to the U.N. has been as inept as its other foreign policies. It has proposed adding more members to the Security Council, which would reduce America's influence and diminish our veto power. Although Biden Administration officials have been understandably discouraged by Russia's frequent veto of resolutions condemning the war in Ukraine, they have been extremely shortsighted by trying to diminish the Security Council veto, which the United States has used successfully hundreds of times in the past to block anti-American and anti-Israel resolutions. In any event, any attempt to restructure and Security Council or change its veto system is likely to fail due to opposition from Russia and China. But this effort could harm America's reputation in the long run, giving our opponents a chance to criticize us whenever we use our veto in the future.

President Trump understood the U.N.'s uses and its limitations. He used his 2017 General Assembly speech as a platform to condemn growing threats from North Korea. His U.N. ambassadors successfully passed resolutions in the Security Council against North Korea. Trump saw the U.N. as a tool to advance American interests. He did not rely upon the U.N., but he successfully used it when it could advance his America First agenda.

CONCLUDING THOUGHTS

To maintain global leadership, the United States must focus on actions that advance our strategic interests and help rather than undermine our security. Following an America First approach, the United States should build strong relationships with allies and effectively oppose adversaries, leading to a future of strength and continued prosperity. Alliances remain a key part of this strategy, as they help the United States influence global matters peacefully and avoid wars. If war is thrust upon us, however, our greatest comparative advantage over our adversaries will be our network of alliances across the world.

9.

Bad Trade Policy Endangers American National Security

By Robert Lighthizer

America First foreign policy increasingly revolves around two key principles: mutual defense and balanced trade. The first principle, detailed extensively in prior chapters of this book, focuses on strengthening our alliances by investing in our own military and persuading our allies to pay their fair share towards their own military forces. The second principle concentrates on ensuring that our global trade relations are balanced and align with our national needs.

In the post-Cold War era, foreign policy professionals have largely ignored the importance of a balanced trade policy for American national security. Policymakers in Congress and successive administrations were willing to make economic concessions to allies in the hope of gaining goodwill and cooperation in security matters. This often resulted in a weaker U.S. economy, and, ironically, few significant changes in allies' security strategy. These same experts were also willing to make concessions to adversaries either in the mistaken belief that economic integration and trade, even trade that resulted in massive annual deficits, would lead those adversaries to freedom, democracy, and peace or in the hope that ignoring growing mercantilism and unfair practices would "stabilize" our relationship with our competitors.

In recent years, and particularly during the Trump Administration, national security experts have come to realize that transferring our wealth, jobs, and industrial capacity to our adversaries had the opposite effect. It made them richer and bolder. It supplied needed capital that paid for their military and helped develop their technology, including lethal military capabilities. Indeed, ignoring the economic war waged against American producers has made a hot war more likely, enabling the return of the very great power competition foreign policy professionals once thought to be over. All the while, our free trade posture towards the global economy eroded our own industrial capacity, weakening our ability to mobilize resources for war and lowering the credibility of our deterrent threats.

Today, it is increasingly clear that the best thing we can do for our own national security and for that of our allies is to not only have the finest military in the world but also to have the strongest economy powered by the most advanced technology. That requires an America First balanced trade policy which both ensures U.S. wealth and technology do not flow to our adversaries and promotes a robust defense industrial base.

ADJUSTING OUR ECONOMIC RELATIONSHIP WITH CHINA

The starting point for a balanced trade policy must be ensuring that our economic relations with adversarial nations like China, Russia, Iran, and North Korea do not aid their geopolitical ambitions at the expense of the United States. Fortunately, apart from the Obama Administration's failed Iran nuclear deal, for decades robust trade controls tightly restricted American wealth and technology from flowing to countries like Russia, Iran, and North Korea. Regrettably, however, the same kind of restrictive policies did not apply to China. Instead, American politicians believed open trade with China would change the nature of the Chinese political system and soften Chinese leaders' ambitions, so they imposed few restrictions on U.S. economic exchanges with China.

For decades, the Chinese government exploited this American free trade policy to advance the country's own industrial base, which fed into China's military modernization and grander geopolitical ambitions. Since the 1980s, official Chinese policies have intentionally aimed to steal American technology and displace American industrial capacity. To this end, the Chinese state employs joint venture mandates, technology transfer requirements, massive targeted industrial subsidies, widespread cyber theft, and industrial spying to achieve this end.[203] China also uses traditional mercantilist policies like currency manipulation, tariff barriers that protect their home market, and restrictive, discriminatory regulatory schemes to benefit domestic Chinese producers.[204] Through its use of this comprehensive suite of unfair practices, China has successfully built what is now by far the world's largest manufacturing economy.

One result of this policy imbalance is China's accumulation of massive trade surpluses both with the United States and the world economy at large. Our year-after-year trade deficits with China transfer trillions of dollars of American wealth to Chinese companies, and ultimately the Chinese Communist Party. In 2001, China's GDP stood at $1.3 trillion; 12% of America's GDP of $10.6 trillion. Twenty years later China's was $17.7 trillion, 78% of America's $23 trillion GDP. China is rapidly catching up. Over the same period, China's annual trade surplus with the United States grew from $80 billion to about $340 billion.[205] During a 20-year period, the United States imported over $6 trillion more in Chinese goods than it exported to it.[206] And these are just the official numbers. The likely real number of our annual wealth transfer to China is much higher, particularly if you factor in the value of stolen American technology (which the U.S. Intelligence Community estimates to be worth between $200 billion and $600 billion annually), the number of Chinese products transshipped through other countries, the value of undeclared Chinese goods that come into America through the de minimis loophole (which one estimate put at $188 billion per year), and the value of illicit fentanyl Chinese chemical companies send to drug cartels in Mexico.[207]

Thanks in large part to American wealth and technology, modern Chinese companies are dominant players across the global value chain. They are market leaders for strategic goods like nuclear power plants, commercial ships, lithium-ion batteries, critical minerals, steel, aluminum, and much more.[208] Chinese control of these industries feeds into the growing modernization of their military, which now leads the world across many crucial military capabilities, including air defense systems, cruise and ballistic missiles, and naval shipbuilding.[209] This military powers China's geopolitical assertiveness detailed elsewhere in this book.

Making matters worse, China's growing manufacturing dominance means that many key American supply chains now depend on Chinese producers. Late last year, for instance, the CEO of one of the largest U.S. defense contractors, Raytheon, said that it was impractical for the company to move supply chains out of China.[210] More recently, an independent study found that 41% of U.S. military platforms use Chinese-made semiconductors.[211]

If we want to become serious about combatting Chinese geopolitical aggression, we must start by changing our economic relationship. It makes no sense to prepare for a possible war with an adversary while at the same time both underwrite and depend on that adversary's industrial base. The only way to adequately reset our international economic relations with China is by enacting a policy of strategic decoupling from China.

Strategic decoupling does not mean that the United States should have no economic relationship with China. Instead, it means that we should adjust our economic relationship with Beijing so that it favors America and our allies. Such a policy would need to be clearly articulated and phased in over a period of years to minimize economic disruption for regular Americans.

As I detailed to Congress in congressional testimony in May 2023, a strategy of strategic decoupling must begin by withdrawing China's most-favored nation status and putting in place new, higher tariffs on their goods to bring about balanced trade and stop the transfer of U.S. wealth to China.[212] If China buys $150 billion in goods from the United States, we should only buy the same amount from it. We also must act to strengthen U.S. customs laws to ensure that Chinese companies cannot dodge higher tariffs by transshipping goods through countries like Vietnam or Mexico into the U.S. market. We should remove the de minimis loophole for non-market economies like China and lower the de minimis threshold for the rest of the world.

Strategic decoupling also requires disentangling our technology exchanges with China through export and import restrictions. We should develop new technology at home or with our allies and expand our export controls that restrict high-tech exports to China. Similarly, we also must enhance limits on inbound investment from China and outbound U.S. investment to China to assure that both are in our national interest.

All these policies – a trade regime designed to help us and our workers, not transferring wealth to an adversary, striving for technology independence, and regulating incoming and outgoing investment so that it benefits us – are essentially the policies that China has toward the United States. Their policies on trade, technology. and investment are all designed to help only the Chinese state. An American trade policy of strategic decoupling from China will be, at its core, a policy of reciprocity.

The process of strategic decoupling began in the Trump Administration when it put tariffs on $370 billion of Chinese imports, notably highest on Chinese high-tech exports. The tariffs have significantly reduced our dependence on Chinese suppliers of tariffed goods and forced our companies to shift some manufacturing home and other manufacturing to friendlier countries. At the same time, the Trump Administration ramped up export controls on Chinese companies to restrict the flow of high-tech goods to its defense industrial companies like Huawei, and the Trump Department of Justice started a China-focused unit dedicated to enforcing U.S. laws against Chinese economic espionage. The world did not end, despite the protestations by countless commentators. Companies adjusted, and our economic relations with China began to change.

Thanks to the long-term effect of these policies, U.S. economic integration with China is trending in the right direction. In 2023, our trade deficit with China was at the lowest level since 2010.[213] Still, many key supply chain dependencies on China remain and our trade deficit with China persists. It is time to take the next steps toward a wider strategic decoupling.

REBUILDING THE U.S. DEFENSE INDUSTRIAL BASE

A balanced trade policy, however, cannot stop at just ensuring that our wealth and technology is not supporting our adversaries. Resetting our trade posture also requires that we ensure that our trade flows with all nations – not just adversarial ones – do not weaken American defense industrial capacity. Unfortunately, our free trade policy eroded our industrial base, which left unchecked will make it harder for our military to mobilize domestic economic resources during wartime.

Statesmen, strategists, and scholars have long noted the important role that industrial capacity plays in supporting and augmenting a nation's military power. As Alexander Hamilton put it, the "independence and security of a Country appear to be materially connected with the prosperity of [its] manufactures."[214] The past few decades of American global supremacy allowed us to forget this important point. After all, industrial capacity mattered little in America's most recent wars, which we fought against adversaries with military and industrial power that paled in comparison to our own. A war with China would be different. It would pit the United States against another great power, in the kind of conflict our nation has not waged since World War II.

Most wars begin with notions of 'quick' victories. The Kaiser's generals had their Schlieffen Plan. Nazi Germany had its Blitzkriegs. Putin had his strategy. Wartime leaders always make the promise, "The troops will be home by Christmas." Yet, history tells us the harsh reality: wars between adversaries with similar military capabilities often are long wars of attrition. To win them, a nation needs to possess a stronger domestic industrial base that it can rely on to better re-supply its armed forces and provide for the needs of its civilian population in wartime.

"Powerful enemies," Franklin Roosevelt once noted, not only must be "outfought" but also must be "outproduced" so "overwhelmingly that there can be no question of our ability to provide a crushing superiority of equipment in any theater of ... war."[215] Outproducing an adversary requires more than just the defense industry. Every country goes to war with a defense industrial capacity that is limited by peacetime fiscal constraints on military procurement. As a result, from day one of a major war, the defense industry alone is unable to meet wartime production demands.

To fill that production gap, a nation must convert its defense-adjacent commercial industrial capacity. Commercial factories must be turned into defense plants. Factory workforces must be retrained to produce military platforms and equipment. The tanks that General Patton rode to victory in World War II, for example, were made in converted auto plants. This process takes time, but the nation with the more robust defense-adjacent commercial industry will do it quicker.

Aside from military preparations, an effective national security strategy also requires industrial preparations for war. Yet, for decades, our trade policy ignored that reality. As we took down our trade barriers, many nations across the world – including China – continued implementing mercantilist policies. They kept subsidizing advanced industries, protecting domestic manufacturers, and manipulating free market forces to their strategic advantage.

As a result, American manufacturers   unprotected at home and preyed upon abroad – decided to offshore their production capacity. America's share of global manufacturing rapidly fell from 25 percent in 1997 to 17 percent in 2019 (China's share is almost 30 percent).[216] Real growth in our manufacturing sector slowed from 4.9 percent in the 1990s to 1.4 percent in recent years, and our trade deficit in manufactured goods tripled, driven by declining American production of critical civilian and defense-related goods like auto parts, pharmaceuticals, machinery, metals, electrical equipment, semiconductors, and precision tools.[217] Today the official overall U.S. trade deficit in goods with the rest of the world is over $1.2 trillion a year.[218] Importantly, this deficit is not isolated to old lower-tech manufactured goods, it also includes the most advanced products. While the United States once was a net global exporter of advanced technology products, today we run an annual $244 billion deficit in these goods. [219]

This general industrial malaise has carried over to our defense and defense-adjacent industrial base. To take one example, America's once great shipbuilding sector now struggles to build more than two U.S. Navy destroyers a year.[220] China, meanwhile, is on track to build at least five.[221] The picture is no better in other parts of the defense industry. Over the past year, as the United States ramped up its efforts to supply munitions to Ukraine, American ordnance contractors that build precision-guided weapons have struggled to meet delivery timelines for our military.[222] We are not even fighting in this war, yet our defense industry is already reaching its breaking point.

It is not hard to imagine, then, what would happen if our defense industry went into a real war with China. War games performed by the Center for Strategic and International Studies indicate that the United States would run out of key munitions within one week of a conflict with

China.[223] We need to be clear-eyed: our defense industry alone cannot re-supply our armed forces during a major war, and we lack a sufficient defense-adjacent industrial base that could be converted quickly to defense production. Further, we would struggle to manage supply chain shortages for a variety of critical civilian goods. In short, our industry is not prepared for war. This very fact erodes the credibility of any threat to prosecute a long, drawn-out conflict with China and seriously undermines our deterrence posture.

What will fix this problem? First, we need to begin by understanding just how pervasive our supply chain dependencies are and where our industrial base weaknesses exist. To do that, we need to establish better supply chain coordination efforts at the White House. A recent bipartisan bill that would set up a White House office focused on economic resilience and supply chain security provides a great model on this front.[224] Then, we need to design a U.S. economic policy to fix our supply chain dependencies and restore our industrial base. To do this, we should rely on the kinds of conservative economic policies that have brought prosperity in the past, like a sensible pro-growth business tax regime, a much less costly regulatory system, appropriate subsidies, a fair and balanced trade policy, and robust worker training. We also should begin to deploy our tariff revenue to finance new advanced technology-related manufacturing projects. Our focus must be clear: it is time to start building things here again. Anything short of that invites future military disaster.

CONCLUDING THOUGHTS

As Washington begins to take the threat from China more seriously, the government must also make a serious change in our international trade policy that puts the economic and security interests of the American people first. We must stop the flow of our wealth to adversaries, better protect our technology, and stop incoming and outgoing investments that hurt our security. At the same time, we must move quickly to reinvigorate our own defense industrial base so we are better prepared for future wars. In short, an America First national security policy must be based on mutual defense and balanced trade.

10.

Energy Security is National Security: America First and the Importance of an American Energy Powerhouse

By Rick Perry and Sam Buchan

Energy security is essential to the American way of life. Energy independence, embraced and empowered under the Trump Administration, not only ensures robust economic growth, it also empowers the United States to advance its security interests and support America's allies and partners abroad - unimpeded by foreign dependencies. Energy security is not a novel concept derived from the ever-increasing complexities of our modern energy systems but rather a constant of global energy markets and a core value of the America First approach to U.S. national security.

This is a lesson forgotten time and again throughout history, much to the detriment and despair of nations. In 1913, Prime Minister Winston Churchill aptly described the energy supply situation of the day, observing that "[s]afety and certainty in oil lie in variety and variety alone." This principle is true for every available resource and commodity.

Concerns over energy security would later be one of the reasons that spurred Imperial Japan to launch its brazen surprise attack on the United States at Pearl Harbor in 1941 following a U.S.-imposed oil embargo. At the end of the 20th Century, energy was also an impetus, if not the leading factor, in a coalition-led effort to liberate energy-rich Kuwait from the grip of Saddam Hussein's regional ambitions of despotism. Later U.S. engagements in the Middle East and North Africa would also see energy feature prominently, directly or indirectly.

The lesson here is that times have changed very little despite the vast and myriad innovations made by private industry with much of the R&D coming from the crown jewels of the American scientific community – the Department of Energy's national laboratories.

Today, we see reminders of the importance of energy security. Every American, whether they recognize it or not, faces the realities of an increasingly interconnected energy network in their daily lives. From the cost of gasoline—a derivative of a complex global commodities trade and industrial mechanisms—to the cost of modern rooftop solar panels—a product of global mining and manufacturing operations—we are ceaselessly engaging in a system that is dominated by energy insecurities.

Today, hydrocarbons account for approximately 78 percent of total U.S. energy consumption (over 80 percent of global consumption). By 2050, they are forecast to account for 74 percent. Meanwhile, renewable energy over this period is expected to grow from 10 percent to 16 percent of consumption. These are factors that must be accounted for and done so from a position of measured optimism. Energy and climate policy development must remain grounded in realism and not become subordinate to climate ideology. Data must trump dogma.

That is not to say that we should abandon the pursuit of innovative technologies, whether wind, solar, battery storage, hydropower, geothermal, hydrogen, nuclear fission and fusion, or any number of advanced technologies yet to be developed. Quite the opposite: in light of the gravity of economic and national security considerations, energy security cannot simply rest upon an idealized future. A diversity of sources, supplies, and routes – the same principle promoted by Winton Churchill – are the most basic yet critical requirements for ensuring energy security and the related prosperity derived from it and why America First energy policies are firmly anchored in our support of all energy sources and technologies.

It is often challenging to discuss a 1:1 comparison of policies related to energy security without acknowledging the differences between national economic models and unique regional or national needs. For instance, the "Shale Revolution" in the early part of this century shows that America's success in achieving energy independence and becoming a dependable energy exporter to our allies primarily comes from innovations led by the private sector or those spurred by market signals. While this is often the case for much of the industrialized world, it is worth noting that state-owned entities are more the norm than the exception across the international energy landscape.

That being said, it has been the role of private industry in the past several decades that has led to major innovations with global implications—the vast majority of which come from the United States. Whether this is the new-found energy superpower status of the United States through the shale revolution, innovations in renewable energy technologies, or leaps and bounds in the development of advanced nuclear reactor technologies, the United States is leading the way. We are not just the world's energy superpower, we are the leading energy innovator.

These are the advancements that policymakers should always bear in mind when considering the next phase of energy security policy and whether it promotes or inhibits that innovation. The federal government's role best serves American energy security, and therefore, national security, when it functions as a responsible enabler of growth—growth that better ensures the diversification of sources, supplies, and routes for Americans and our allies and partners.

EARLY LESSONS IN ENERGY SECURITY

In the early years of World War II, the United States found itself in a position reminiscent of today's geopolitical circumstances. America's already significant natural resources were needed to mobilize the Allied war effort in Europe. In August 1942, the United States began construction on what were the longest oil and refined products pipelines to date—1,200 miles connecting production basins in Texas to the American eastern seaboard known as the 'Big Inch' and 'Little Big Inch' pipelines.

Beyond the historic scale of this federally-backed infrastructure project, perhaps its most astounding accomplishment was that construction of this pipeline was completed in less than one year.

169

Because of such public-private efforts, the liberation of Europe was possible. As historian Keith Miller put it, "[I]t cannot be stated too forcefully, American oil, which amounted to 6 billion barrels, out of a total of 7 billion barrels consumed by the Allies for the period of World War II, brought victory."

Some 20 years later, the United States again found itself confronting the challenges of energy security, this time in an altogether different global energy market—a "Golden Age" characterized by sustained economic growth and prosperity in North America and Europe. This period saw the United States shift from a net energy exporter to a net importer, driven largely by growth in transportation. Recognizing the market opportunity, the Organization of the Petroleum Exporting Countries (OPEC) was founded in 1960 and quickly mobilized to control as much as 50 percent of the global oil market. By 1960, oil represented 50 percent of global energy consumption—OPEC, therefore, controlled 25 percent.

OPEC's newfound stature would be leveraged to disastrous effect when, in reaction to U.S. and Western support for Israel during the Yom Kippur War of 1973, OPEC declared an oil embargo. The result sent shockwaves through Western markets, largely dominated by import-driven economies. In 1973, the price of a barrel of oil increased 301 percent from $2.90 per barrel to $11.65 per barrel, which in today's dollars would be the equivalent of an increase from $60 to $240 per barrel.

The policy response from the United States and many Western nations was equally dramatic. Price controls and fuel rationing were implemented, and legislation targeting energy security were introduced and ratified, including the development of the International Energy Agency in 1974—an international organization dedicated to the energy security of its import-dependent members, the development of the Strategic Petroleum Reserve (SPR) in 1975, and the creation of the U.S. Department of Energy in 1976. The lessons learned from this period of OPEC market dominance led to a cycle in which U.S. foreign policy was myopically focused on Middle East stability and regional relations, given the region's function as America's de facto gas station. Figure 1 demonstrates the frequency with which geopolitical conflicts in the Middle East translate to global supply disruptions.

Figure 1: Geopolitical Impacts on Global Oil Production and Supply, 1970-Present.

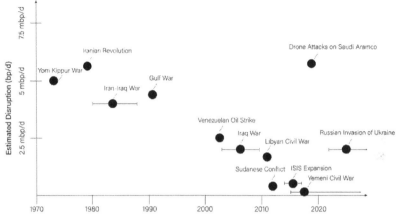

AFPI graphic, AFPI Center for Energy & Environment. U.S. Energy Information Administration data, March 2024.

While many policies enacted in response to the Arab Oil Embargo were momentarily impactful in addressing energy security concerns, including energy efficiency measures and energy system redundancies like the SPR, they were ultimately insufficient to cope with long-term U.S. economic growth and ambitions. Simply put, innovation and production did not keep pace with energy demand. There was also a new threat to energy security, one that had its footing in both the anti-nuclear movement of the 60s and 70s—the environmentalist movement.

While much of the underpinnings of this movement were warranted—largely unchecked industrial waste discharge, etc.—the fervor over the nuclear incidents at Three Mile Island in the U.S. and Chornobyl in the then-Soviet Union (present-day Ukraine) only served to further fuel the anxiety propagated by many environmentalists. Despite nuclear energy being the safest energy source, these incidents only stoked fears of environmental and human catastrophe. The alternative championed by the green movement, specifically environmental regulations and a push toward renewable energy, left much to be desired in terms of guaranteeing any semblance of energy security or prosperity.

While environmental regulation has a role, excessive or antiquated regulations demonstrably lead to inefficiencies, cost increases, and stifled innovation. This, in turn, can undermine the government's role of ensuring responsible market growth by limiting growth prospects altogether—a scenario known as the "regulatory paradox." The rapid expansion in the number of environmental regulations makes it unimaginable today to achieve the record deployment of energy infrastructure witnessed during World War II. It now takes an act of Congress just to complete critical energy infrastructure—this was demonstrated in the case of the Mountain Valley natural gas pipeline in June 2023.[225]

Renewable energy alone is incapable of meeting overall energy demand. The aggressive deployment of renewables, specifically wind and solar (absent significant advancement in battery storage), threatens to destabilize the U.S. power grid. This is a risk on several fronts, through the displacement of proven clean and reliable baseload power sources, such as natural gas or nuclear power, only to increase dependence on intermittent power generation. Taken together, the current application of environmental regulations and an aggressive renewable energy deployment strategy threatens the overall ability of the U.S. and our allies to adequately respond to future energy disruptions. Industrial capacity is also critical to national security. As in much of Europe, industrial capacity cannot be maintained by energy strategies that overly favor renewable energy. The result is likely to be continued deindustrialization or increased subsidization of industry carried on the shoulders of the taxpayer.

AMERICA'S ENERGY REVIVAL

Between the mid and late 2000s, technological innovations, namely hydraulic fracturing and horizontal drilling, generated new relief for American energy consumers and rebalanced the global energy landscape for the United States. The days of U.S. consumer subjugation to global instability, oil-producing cartels, and foreign energy-producing nations were sharply reduced. Case in point: the market dominance of OPEC was eroded from its height of approximately 50 percent to some 32 percent today.

This was the benefit of the Shale Revolution. Before this development, natural gas prices closely tracked the price of a barrel of oil despite divergent end-uses—a pricing relationship that carried implications for consumers, particularly given the historical trend of Western dependence on the volatile Middle East energy-producing region. However, the ensuing growth in American natural gas production shattered this price correlation.

Just in terms of natural gas, the White House Council of Economic Advisers estimated in 2019 that the growth in domestic supplies through the shale revolution saved the average American family about $2,500 per year in energy costs. Moreover, the false notion of "peak oil," which had dominated the mindset of policymakers for decades, was obliterated by 2010. Oil production between 2005 and 2023 increased by roughly 140 percent, while natural gas production during this same period increased by roughly 100 percent. This historic growth in U.S. production levels eventually led the Obama Administration to approve the first-ever liquified natural gas (LNG) export terminal and Congress to pass the legislation that lifted the ban on crude oil exports as part of the Consolidated Appropriations Act of 2016, paving the way for the surge in LNG exports that have revolutionized global energy markets and provided energy security for American allies and partners. It is also worth noting that the innovations that led to the shale revolution, specifically directional drilling, have led to significant growth prospects for leveraging America's geothermal potential.

Regarding foreign policy flexibility, America's energy revival and new-found position as an energy superpower enabled the United States to drastically engage areas of the world that it had previously needed to approach delicately. For instance, America was free to recognize Jerusalem as the rightful capital of Israel, pursue the historic Abraham Accords, and hold Venezuela and Iran accountable for human rights atrocities and state-sponsorship of terrorism, just to name a few, without fear of triggering catastrophic repercussions in global energy markets.

Similar benefits were extended to customers of American-sourced energy resources. For example, in European markets, important allies gained greater leverage in their contract negotiations with Russia, which regularly uses energy as a means of political coercion and extortion. Key examples include the elimination of 'take-or-pay' clauses and the destination clauses, which either forced consumers to pay for unneeded resources or prohibited the purchaser from reselling supplies to other countries (i.e., Ukraine). This latter measure was particularly effective in undermining Russia's destabilizing efforts in Ukraine in 2009 and in the aftermath of the 2014 Ukrainian Revolution of Dignity – in both instances, Russia attempted to literally freeze out the country over political disputes.

U.S. technological advances in hydrocarbon extraction were far from the only major advancement in U.S. energy production during this period. Significant developments in renewable energy technologies, including wind turbines, solar photovoltaic (PV) cells, and battery storage technology, all experienced innovations with profound implications for U.S. energy security. Former Under Secretary of Energy Paul Dabbar went further to outline the key differentiator of the U.S. energy landscape, stating, "the private capital markets flooded funding into the energy sector to take advantage of these new technologies and policies. For example, North American upstream capital investments went from approximately $50 billion annually in 2001 to $250 billion annually at its peak in 2014."

The ultimate result of the Shale Revolution is that the United States now possesses the coveted position of being a "swing producer," meaning that the United States can scale its oil and natural gas production levels relatively rapidly in response to market conditions, as well as non-market actions such as OPEC's price-setting efforts. The global balance of power has shifted away from OPEC toward market-oriented producers like the United States, as evidenced by OPEC's significantly diminished market share.

In recent years, the trend of American energy innovation has continued at pace. One technology, however, is increasingly proving to be a game changer in both global energy security and the desire to deploy clean and reliable energy, and it is one in which the United States maintains a comparative advantage—advanced nuclear reactor technologies. Small modular reactors, advanced reactors, and micro-reactors have all emerged as frontier technologies that will shape the energy systems of tomorrow. These technologies also have security enhancements and passive safety features that allow for automatic shutdown and cooling without human intervention. Within the context of global security concerns, these reactors also greatly reduce the risks of nuclear proliferation.

ENERGY SECURITY IN THE DEVELOPING WORLD

American energy security does not operate in a vacuum, nor do policy decisions by other nations fail to impact the American homeland. More often than not, the recent history of American foreign policy has been dominated by responses to foreign failures that create broader implications for America and its allies and partners. Key among such failures is the reality that many nations suffer from chronic energy poverty – the lack of access to abundant and reliable energy supplies. As a result, these nations are often characterized by economic underdevelopment, social instability, and limited capacity for governance, all of which can contribute to a heightened risk of civil and regional conflict.

Energy poverty exacerbates economic disparities, fueling tensions and competition over resources. Countries rich in energy resources may become targets for external aggression or internal conflict over control of those resources. Examples of this include the dispute over energy resources between Sudan and South Sudan following the partition of greater Sudan in 2011, as well as the ongoing civil war in Libya.

The mismanagement of energy resources is also a factor when considering energy poverty. In such instances, social unrest is often a response to real or perceived corruption within a nation that fails to adequately meet its people's needs. Examples include the mismanagement of natural resources in Venezuela, Lebanon, and Nigeria, which have perpetuated the cycle of energy poverty, political instability, and regional tensions.

As a supplement to the assertion that the advancement of global democracy is the primary means of ensuring peace and stability, effective energy policies can contribute to the success of nations by offering a viable path to alleviate of the root causes of instability. This also can provide reliable trading partners for nations with few alternatives and keep them out of debt-trap diplomacy schemes like China's Belt and Road Initiative.

In recent years, U.S. foreign energy policy has been pulled between a desire to impose climate-first energy systems (i.e., only renewable energy) on nations struggling with energy poverty on one hand, and a desire to promote regional stability through responsible energy production and trade in energy goods and services. To the chagrin of many nations, the result has often led to international support that seeks to impose energy systems on countries less tailored to the individual needs or resources of particular regions and more reflective of U.S. domestic political winds.

It is the height of hubris for developed nations to inflict their clean energy morals in this way on a developing world that often lacks many basic societal needs. Both the Obama and Biden Administration's efforts to restrict international financing away from more reliable hydrocarbon-based sources in favor of more costly and unreliable renewable energy have and will continue to prove insufficient in meeting the growth prospects of our global trading partners. The thinking here appears to be: better to be green and impoverished in the eyes of the United Nations than to prosper.

The dire consequences of this pull between climate-first and a realistic approach to energy security also hamper our ability to hold adversarial nations accountable. In the aftermath of Russia's invasion of Ukraine and the subsequent efforts by Western nations to sanction Russian energy sources (Russia is the world's third-largest producer of oil and largest producer of natural gas), a major fault line emerged between industrialized and developing economies. Many countries, including long-time U.S. partners such as India, prioritized policies that best ensured the energy security of their countries. That is, they chose to continue imports of Russian energy. In the absence of sufficient alternative energy sources (i.e., further growth from friendly and trustworthy sources like the United States), as well as the attractiveness of relatively low-cost energy, turning to Russian energy was not surprising. As Roger Pielke Jr. stated in his Iron Law of Climate Policy, "When policies focused on economic growth confront policies focused on emissions reductions, it is economic growth that will win out every time."

A more appropriate foreign energy policy would be to eliminate restrictions that disadvantage the financing, production, or export of energy goods and services capable of delivering scalable, reliable, and clean energy that truly meets the economic aspirations of developing or developed countries. This type of supply-side strategy, one embodied in the role of the United States as a swing producer, is one of those rare examples in which U.S. policies that adequately consider the needs of foreign countries offer a direct economic benefit for the United States and go further in reinforcing American interests abroad.

Moreover, engagement in responsible trade between U.S. industry and foreign nations carries the benefit of substantially improving the governance of natural resources and the mitigation of corruption. However, this also requires a significant overhaul of how the federal government views the world and America's role in it as an energy superpower. The alternative methodology, which makes American interests subordinate to international bodies, such as the United Nations, the International Energy Agency, and others that have strayed from the core responsibility of ensuring global energy security, only furthers the divide between industrialized and developing economies.

GARNERING ENERGY SECURITY IN SUPPORT OF AMERICAN INTERESTS

Beyond the chronic threat of energy poverty or the access to affordable and reliable energy sources, there is the immense challenge of what can be dubbed a "galloping troika of illicit energy trade" that undermines international efforts to counter adversarial nations or hold countries accountable for human rights violations, and state-sponsored terrorism, etc. For instance, the Chinese Communist Party's efforts to vitiate Western sanctions on Iran and Venezuela and, therefore, eliminate the influence of the United States saw exports from these two countries to China grow to about 324 million barrels in 2021.

At the same time, Western nations have sought, often in vain, to severely limit the ability of Russia to market its energy resources in response to the country's invasion of Ukraine. Iran's experience in evading Western sanctions, utilizing its so-called "ghost fleet" of oil tankers, is now deployed to support President Putin's efforts to translate oil sales into military spending. It is estimated that Russian revenue from the sale of oil and natural gas exports, despite falling some 24 percent in 2023, still generated the equivalent of $99.4 billion. The Russian government, largely due to the continued energy appetite of the developing world, specifically through rapidly expanding energy trade with China expects its revenue to recover to some $129.5 billion during 2024.

While the intention behind the G7's effort to impose a $60 per barrel price cap on Russian oil exports is certainly warranted, the overall effort was largely doomed from the beginning. This instance represents a classic example of the 'Prisoners' Dilemma,' in which one instance of a lack of solidarity with the proposal undermines the entirety of the effort. In effect, despite the efforts of the G7 to impose the price cap, the existence of a globally connected market makes this a near impossibility, particularly as much of the developing world continues to prioritize meeting domestic demand rather than adhering to G7 mandates. Since the imposition of the price cap in December 2022, the price of Russian Ural crude oil has repeatedly maintained a price above the $60 cap.

Turning back the pages of history showed us the immense role that U.S. energy resources and innovative capacity can play. A case in point is the U.S. response to Allied energy demand during World War II. However, much to the detriment of our allies and partners today, the United States is demonstrating reluctance to support global demand as global policymakers seek to impose their dogmatic approach to climate change and scuttle the global benefits of American energy.

Take, for instance, the ability of the United States to respond to the threefold challenge of a global pandemic, the re-emergence of war on the European continent, and the persistent blight of energy poverty. No commodity demonstrates what Joseph Sternberg labeled "a crisis of choice" better than the case of LNG. In stark contrast to the past ventures of U.S. public-private partnerships, a comparison of the first two years of the administrations of Presidents Donald Trump and Joseph Biden demonstrates the very regulatory paradox mentioned earlier. The Federal Energy Regulatory Commission (FERC) under President Trump's first two years issued permits for 44.6 billion cubic feet per day (bcf/d) of natural gas pipeline capacity, whereas FERC under the first two years of President Biden issued a mere 4.5 bcf/d. Without pipelines, the ability of the United States to respond to future crises is severely hampered—a far cry from the monumental resource mobilization during World War II.

There is another contrast in executing sound energy policy, which can be seen comparing LNG export authorizations and a debate that has been ongoing within U.S. energy policy circles since the growth in domestic production. Under President Trump, the U.S. Department of Energy extended LNG export authorization through 2050 to ensure greater market predictability and reassure American allies and trading partners that the U.S. was a reliable partner in guaranteeing their energy security.

The Biden Administration took the opposite course of action. In January 2024, the White House announced that the Department of Energy would be imposing a moratorium on all future LNG export authorizations pending further review. This moratorium, or "pause," is the equivalent of America taking a knee in the race to meet worldwide energy needs. Such short-sighted efforts amount to nothing less than the ceding of global market share to American competitors and adversaries and the near-abandonment of U.S. allies at a time when they require American energy most.

The debate over the value of LNG exports should have been a topic left to history, particularly following the very real benefits expressed by many U.S. allies, particularly those on the front line of energy insecurity. After all, the comparative advantage of the United States emerges as many European countries viewed U.S. supplies as reliable, flexible, and price competitive under long-term contracts. When framing U.S. supplies against Russia's historic use of energy as a geopolitical weapon, exporting "freedom gas" in the form of liquified natural gas becomes an attractive antidote. However, this is not the only casualty of the Biden

Administration's utilization of climate change to undercut America's role as a global energy superpower. Keep in mind that this is the U.S. government limiting the American private sector's ability to sell into the worldwide market. At the government-to-government relationship level, America's NATO allies like Poland and Germany and Indo-Pacific allies like Japan and South Korea are left questioning the reliability of the United States private sector as a guarantor of energy security and our government as a trusted ally.

ENERGY SECURITY AND CLEAN TECHNOLOGY

It has been said that "not since the transition from whale oil has any major economy undergone an energy transition." For instance, the world still uses significant amounts of wood (biomass) for energy, whether heat or power. Regardless of recent energy transitions (some would call them transformations), the world has been captivated by the notion of undertaking a transformational energy transition made urgent by the contentious science behind climate change. The Biden Administration has gone so far as to designate climate change as the top threat to U.S. national security. According to President Biden, "The only existential threat humanity faces, even more frightening than a nuclear war, is global warming."

Clean energy sources, or rather the limited interpretation of clean energy sources as defined by progressives and their special interest cohorts, have repeatedly been touted by Secretary of Energy Jennifer Granholm as the "best peace plan the world has ever known" or "energy sources that can't be weaponized." The reality, however, is that clean energy is just as susceptible, if not more so, to weaponization as any other resource – the evidence of this is present today and in the recent past.

In the mid-2010s, global commodity markets reeled as China orchestrated a mass market distortion by restricting exports of critical minerals, specifically rare earth elements (REEs). This had the effect of undermining the positions of many competitors seeking to capture market share. Moreover, as global policies advancing an energy transition continue to stress the role of renewable energy technology, there is a severe risk of undue dependence on China for renewable energy technology and essential materials. It is also critical to bear in mind that many of these same critical minerals are integral components of the American defense arsenal, whether in America's F-35 fighter bomber or missile guidance systems.

For example, China's share of global PV manufacturing exceeds 80 percent (more than double China's share of global PV demand), and China also accounts for over 70 percent of the global total for battery manufacturing. Moreover, China dominates the global supply of rare earth elements (85-90 percent), cobalt (68 percent), lithium (60-70 percent), and nickel (60 percent), just to name a few. The threats of such a severe dependence on Chinese supplies were used as a catalyst for Congress to enact the Inflation Reduction Act (IRA), which established significant incentives for the domestic production of these increasingly important commodities. However, there are significant deficits in America's strategy to mitigate China's outsized role. "Permitting" is first among them. Efforts like President Trump's Executive Order 13807 on "Establishing Discipline and Accountability in the Environmental Review and Permitting Process for Infrastructure" sought to improve many of the issues hindering the deployment of traditional and clean energy infrastructure capable of bolstering America's energy security and resilience. President Biden's subsequent reversal of this progress demonstrates the short-sighted and tragically ironic policy framework offered by climate activists. It should be apparent to all that longer infrastructure deployment timelines – or no deployment - translate directly to a prolonged reliance on Chinese imports of critical materials.

First and foremost, U.S. foreign policy should not return to a position of dependence for the sake of embarking on an energy transition, particularly one without a clear pathway for secure supplies of essential resources. This is a false choice. Often those advocating for such an energy transition brush past the complex issue of where to obtain the critical minerals and other resources required for this transition, particularly resources primarily under the control of China. Today's energy transition advocates also ignore the urgent challenge of regulatory reform and counter-NIMBY (not in my backyard) efforts that are required to propel sustainable growth in the clean energy sector, specifically mining. At present, the path to an energy transition that pursues the elimination of hydrocarbons proposes to exchange the geopolitical leverage granted by an abundance of natural resources (minerals, oil, natural gas, etc.) for the dependence on the resources of foreign adversaries - effectively eliminating the benefits of the Shale Revolution.

Specifically considering China, the America First approach to energy security asserts a more aggressive stance in countering China's efforts to monopolize the extraction, processing, and manufacturing of critical resources as well as China's rampant intellectual property theft. In this regard, reshoring and friend-shoring domestic manufacturing capacity is an opportunity that not only benefits the American economy but also adds much-needed resilience to global supply chains that have demonstrated extreme exposure to China. An America First approach is at odds with the Biden Administration's efforts to grant repeated waivers to Chinese-backed products that have been allowed to seize Western clean energy deployment ambitions, despite growing bipartisan agreement on the economic and military threat posed by China.

REBALANCING INTERNATIONAL COOPERATION TO PRIORITIZE ENERGY SECURITY

International cooperation is more essential than ever in guaranteeing energy security for future generations. Collaborating with allies and partners is essential to ensuring the stability of global energy markets and to address common challenges such as the resilience of global energy supply chains, infrastructure protection, and the ever-growing threats to physical infrastructure, such as cybersecurity. However, the tug-of-war between energy security and climate change continues to threaten the ability of the United States to execute a coherent foreign energy policy. In the absence of the U.S. government as a reliable partner dedicated to using its natural resources and innovative potential to advance the security and economic interests of the free world, it cannot be guaranteed that the developing world will continue to follow American leadership or engage in U.S.-led global financial structures. Rarely should the policy of one nation (i.e., climate-first) be a determinant for the internal deliberations of another. Rather, it is in

America's interests to serve as a reliable provider of critically needed energy goods, services, and innovations to a world in which demand will only continue to grow.

In a similar vein, the policies of the United States should not be dictated by the internal policy ambitions of any single nation, region, or international organization. This is precisely the lesson learned from America's past dependence on OPEC and Middle Eastern supplies of energy resources, and where the value of an America First approach to energy security comes into full force.

International organizations like the World Bank and the IEA – an organization that energy expert Robert McNally accurately describes as a "climate obsessed international organization" that has "strayed from its security mission" – only serve to widen the policy discrepancies between the industrialized and developing economies it seeks to represent equally. Case in point is the World Bank and IEA's advocacy for policies restricting future investment in hydrocarbon resources and infrastructure. These misguided policies seemingly proclaim some enlightened stature among the industrialized world as a *casus belli* against the very resources that propelled economic growth, energy security, and national security gains over the past century and a half.

Similarly, those pushing an extreme climate-driven net zero viewpoint are signaling an absurd ultimatum to developing countries that they must accept the abject poverty in which many of their citizens live and restrict themselves to a limited range of ineffective green strategies for economic growth. The result is that we have abandoned a desire to reach a common cause with the developing world, forcing them to seek alternatives to meet their ambitions. Sadly, these alternatives only further undermine American interests by driving would-be partners into the arms of Russia and China. Here we find the root of the problem that is leading to the growth of the so-called "non-aligned world" – a foreign energy policy that comes across for what it truly is: unfounded hypocrisy rooted in increasingly unsettled science.

That is not to say that pursuing clean energy deployment is antithetical to energy security. In fact, renewable energy can certainly play a role in reinforcing energy security, but it is far from the ultimate solution. Similarly, resources such as hydrogen, battery storage, and many other forms of clean energy offer significant opportunities for global energy security, but their associated risks, such as the water intensity of hydrogen and the dominance of China within battery supply chains, all demand viable solutions that do not sacrifice the integrity of any nation's energy security.

ENERGY SECURITY: A STRATEGIC IMPERATIVE

The United States is undoubtedly an energy superpower, but the question is whether or not this new-found status will be sustained in a policy environment increasingly defined by a myopic fixation on climate change as an existential national security threat. Innovation, technology-neutral policies, the world's most dynamic capital market, and an abundance of natural resources stand as the leading enablers of this growth. The federal government is not among those top factors. In fact, the federal government's repeated failure to reign in the regulatory paradox it has created is an instance in which the federal government actively and passively undermines the role of the United States as an energy superpower.

Energy security is too often taken for granted. America's new-found status as an energy superpower has largely liberated the American people from foreign energy dependence. American interests abroad have been transformed to allow for never-before-seen foreign policy flexibility. This flexibility reduces the chances for foreign conflict and the deployment of U.S. troops in new and possibly unending wars. It also provides an ability to offer viable energy alternatives and pathways to energy security for American allies and partners.

This status and the benefits it provides must be protected. It requires vigilance on the part of the American people, industry, and policymakers to ensure that our innovative and natural benefits are responsibly leveraged to the benefit of America and its allies and partners. America cannot afford to be a reluctant leader in global energy markets. Our leaders must ensure that U.S. energy security is equivalent to national security. The most impactful means of beginning this process is to empower industry to innovate, access, produce, transport, and export the vast energy potential of this great nation. This is the key to securing America's role as an energy superpower for decades to come and the only viable means of putting Americans and their interests first.

11.

The America First Approach to U.S. National Security Requires Fixing America's Intelligence Community

By Sam Faddis

The America First approach to government means responsible and ethical management that puts the American people and their interests first. This includes ensuring that tax dollars are spent prudently for government agencies that reflect American values.

The U.S. government spent almost $100 billion on America's 18-member Intelligence Community (IC) in 2023. Unfortunately, the management and operations of our intelligence agencies have fallen far short of America First standards. U.S. intelligence agencies are not focused on critical threats to national security. They have become vast, risk-averse bureaucracies whose priorities are to protect and expand their agencies. Intelligence has been politicized, and intelligence officers have meddled in politics, including by promoting fraudulent claims to influence the outcome of the 2016 and 2020 presidential elections. U.S. intelligence agencies waste time and money on social engineering, including indoctrination in the diversity, equity, and inclusion ideology.

The IC exists for one purpose: to keep Americans safe in their beds at night. It is failing in that mission. Worse yet, while floundering abroad, the IC is increasingly focused on domestic political matters in which it should never be involved. Americans are now being threatened by the very agencies that exist to serve them. U.S. intelligence agencies that spy on the American people and the staff of presidential campaigns are not just breaking the law, they are also putting their personal and political interests ahead of the security interests of their country.

Worst of all, America's intelligence agencies today act as if they are an independent branch of government that does not answer to the President of the United States.

THE URGENT NEED FOR INTELLIGENCE REFORM

To ensure the president has the intelligence he needs to protect America's security and freedom, substantial reforms must render the U.S. Intelligence Community nonpolitical, efficient, and, above all, competent. Unfortunately, all efforts at reform to date have failed and arguably made the situation much worse. Despite massive budgets and stunning technological capabilities, the IC continues to disappoint and problems compound. Doing more of the same will only guarantee continued frustration and endanger national security.

On September 11, 2001, members of al-Qaeda hijacked four airliners. They crashed three of them into their targets. The fourth was prevented from doing so only by the heroism of the brave Americans on board.

Al-Qaeda was not some unknown entity. It had been around for years. Osama bin Laden had threatened to attack Americans on our soil for years. Al-Qaeda had blown up two of our embassies in East Africa. Al-Qaeda had almost sunk the USS Cole in Yemen. Al-Qaeda had tried once before to destroy the World Trade Center.

And yet the United States had not a single source inside that organization capable of warning us of the 9/11 attacks that would kill almost 3,000 Americans. We were incapable of intercepting terrorist communications that would provide warning of an impending attack. All of our spy satellites and multi-billion-dollar signals intelligence systems proved useless.

On May 2, 2011, U.S. special operations personnel attacked a compound in Pakistan and killed Osama bin Laden. That operation in and of itself was clearly a success. The fact that it took almost ten years to find and kill the mastermind behind the 9/11 attacks is what should give us pause.

Bin Laden fully understood the technical capabilities of U.S. intelligence. After his escape from Afghanistan in December 2001, he established himself in a compound with no internet service. He had no cell phone. He communicated with his organization through a courier system and dealt with those couriers face-to-face. There were no emails, text messages, or phone calls to intercept.

All of our technical capabilities proved useless. Finding Bin Laden meant placing a source inside al-Qaeda at a high enough level to know his physical location. It took almost a full decade for the CIA, with all its resources, to acquire such a source, even when locating Bin Laden was probably the single highest priority for the agency.

In 2020, the world found itself in the midst of a pandemic that originated in China. Despite attempts to characterize COVID-19 as a natural outbreak of a disease found in bats, it has become abundantly clear that the virus was the product of gain-of-function research in a Chinese bio lab in Wuhan. Warning signs pointed to the risky work being done in Wuhan and startlingly lax laboratory practices.

Biological warfare threats are real and have been considered such for many years. Collection on both state and terrorist biowarfare programs is one of the IC's top priorities. The existence of the lab from which COVID-19 emerged was not a secret. Neither was the fact that the Chinese were working overtime to make coronaviruses more dangerous to humans.

And yet, we received no warning prior to the outbreak of the pandemic. When people began to get sick here and around the world, the IC could not provide useful information regarding the origins of the disease. Even now, years later, our intelligence agencies appear unable to tell us precisely how the pandemic began.

We had no sources inside the Wuhan Institute of Virology in 2019. We apparently have no sources there now. Our vaunted technical capabilities have proved useless. The Chinese could have created a virus much more lethal than COVID-19, turned it loose on us, and killed a significant portion of our population. We would never have seen it coming.

Why? Why is an intelligence apparatus staffed with highly talented people and provided with resources unparalleled anywhere else failing to perform its core functions?

Two reasons. Bureaucratization and politicization.

BUREAUCRATIZATION

Let's begin with bureaucratization, or what a CIA veteran once characterized as a "bureaucratic hardening of the arteries."[226]

The world of intelligence is one of shades of gray, ambiguity, and thinking "outside the box." It requires creative, flexible minds operating in a flat, nimble structure capable of acting quickly and exploiting fleeting moments of opportunity. On the street, it requires operators capable of adapting and moving decisively in foreign environments. At the analytical level, it demands smart, well-trained people who can think like our adversaries and put themselves in their shoes.

We spent decades perfecting our policy for the handling of in-air hijackings. It boiled down to presenting no resistance, doing whatever the hijackers wanted, and getting the plane to the ground where it could be reached by hostage rescue forces. Somebody somewhere should have been capable of understanding what this response would mean if the hijackers intended not to land the plane but to use it as a missile. No one did. They were all locked into seeing the problem through our eyes, not through the eyes of our enemies.

Intelligence officers talk about *tradecraft* for a reason. Intelligence is not a science. It is a craft. At times, it is an art. Not everyone can do it. Certainly, not everyone wants to do it. It can be a very tough business.

Intelligence operations require people who have impeccable gut instincts, can make decisions quickly and on the fly, can navigate through a maze of mirrors, and can tolerate extremely high degrees of ambiguity. When you are face to face with a dangerous person on the street in a slum in South Asia or a desert in the Middle East, you do not have time to deliberate. You can't phone home for guidance. Washington is 10,000 miles away and filled with bureaucrats. The only person who knows what to do is you, and you need to act *right now*.

Intelligence analysis requires individuals who will use all sources of information to produce crucial assessments to help the president keep our nation safe and free. Intelligence analysts understand and value the hard work that goes into intelligence collection and the risks of stealing secrets to inform U.S. policymakers. Intelligence analysts provide high-quality, reasoned, and truthful intelligence assessments, but they know intelligence is not truth and is often wrong. They also understand that they do not make policy, and presidents and other officials are not bound to accept or act on their analyses.

We have forgotten all of this. We have done our level best to turn the various components of the Intelligence Community into ordinary federal agencies. Recruiters no longer search for intangibles or focus on the key psychological traits critical to success in the world of spying or the best and brightest to serve as intelligence analysts. They increasingly focus on details such as skin color, sexual orientation, and support for liberal and progressive ideologies.

Training has been softened and has become increasingly formulaic. We act as if anyone can be taught to conduct espionage or write predictive analysis. We are now all fungible. This is no longer an arcane craft to be practiced by a select group of unique people. Instead, we send people to training for a few months and expect they will be fine.

We have buried operations and analysis under endless layers of middle management. The fact that we can move large quantities of information over vast distances somehow now compels us to do so. A case officer in the field may spend days completing the requisite paperwork for a single asset meeting. Every moment he or she is sitting behind a desk is a moment they are not meeting sources, recruiting new sources, or learning the environment around them. Analysts must comply with risk-averse and politically correct corporate lines in their assessments, are pressured to avoid controversial subjects, and must negotiate long chains of management review.

Back home, the intelligence operations bureaucracy is increasingly filled with individuals who have never demonstrated they can accomplish anything on the street. In many cases, they will only have left Northern Virginia for a handful of short trips abroad. They have laughed at the boss's jokes. They have demonstrated their fealty to the prevailing groupthink. They have moved paper, attended meetings, and climbed the corporate ladder.

In large measure, operations officers have no idea how to run an operation or recruit a source. They have no idea how terrorists think or how to put themselves in the shoes of Xi Jinping as he contemplates his next move on the world stage. They have no comprehension of the apocalyptic worldview of the Shia mullahs who rule in Tehran.

Practically everything the United States has done since 9/11 has made the problem of bureaucratization worse. We did not react to that disaster by clearing the decks and returning to basics. We didn't fire the people who allowed 9/11 to happen and replace them with action-oriented reformers. We reacted by adding massive new layers of bureaucracy and throwing money at the problem.

In response to a recommendation by the 9/11 Commission, Congress in 2005 established the Office of the Director of National Intelligence. Originally envisioned as a small coordinating staff to make the constituent players in the IC work together, share information, and be more effective, the ODNI has ballooned into a massive bureaucratic edifice that bogs down the entire system with paperwork and process and duplicates the functions of the agencies that existed before its founding. The ODNI has also gone far beyond its mandate to coordinate intelligence by becoming a major producer of intelligence.[227]

Somewhere in some Third World hellhole, the same six guys are trying desperately to gather intelligence on a terrorist threat to commercial airliners. Meanwhile, back in Washington, D.C., massive new office buildings filled with flat-screen computer monitors have been added to produce PowerPoint presentations and briefing memos for the endless rounds of meetings that occur each day. One of the largest of these is the massive ODNI headquarters in Tysons Corner, Virginia, located just six miles down the road from the CIA's large headquarters complex in Langley, Virginia.

Post-9/11, the Department of Defense decided it needed to move into the realm of strategic human intelligence in a big way. It established what amounts to its own CIA, the Defense Clandestine Service.[228] Legions of additional "case officers" were sent to training in new courses at Fort Huachuca in Arizona.[229] The National Security Agency also pumped money into yet more new "capabilities" designed to duplicate the existing functions of other agencies. Massive amounts of money were spent on these new enterprises.

All of this made about as much sense as telling the CIA to build aircraft carriers and duplicate the functions of the U.S. Navy. We spent huge amounts of money and diverted scarce resources from all sorts of other endeavors. There was no measure of effectiveness. Throwing money at our problems was taken as a substitute for solving them.

Throughout the entire IC today runs a mentality of timidity and risk aversion. Our Intelligence Community was meant to do what everyone else considers impossible. It was supposed to be run by people who wanted to steal the crown jewels and would do so if you told them to. Not anymore. Now it is run by people looking for operations with no possible downside and, therefore, have no particular upside, either.

We now cannot put a source inside a Chinese bio lab or the leadership structure of the Taliban or next to Vladimir Putin. Those kinds of operations, by definition, require the willingness to take risks and the ability to manage those risks. We don't have either anymore.

Our IC is supposed to provide the critical predictive analysis that allows us to stay at least two steps ahead of our adversaries. It does not. It provides watered-down assessments that tell us nothing of value or utility. When and if we are hit by another terrorist attack by al-Qaeda on our own soil, it will come as a surprise. When and if the Chinese impose a blockade of Taiwan, we will find out about it when news agencies broadcast the official CCP communique announcing the beginning of the operation.

POLITICIZATION

The steady bureaucratization of the IC has been underway for decades. Since the election of Barack Obama as president in 2008, however, we have added another major and even more serious problem: politicization. Agencies that should not come within 10 miles of American domestic politics have involved themselves directly in the democratic process.

On September 11, 2012, two American compounds in the Libyan city of Benghazi were attacked by a well-known Islamic militia with a history of strikes on Western targets. One of the compounds, occupied by the Department of State, was overrun. The American ambassador to Libya, who was visiting from Tripoli at the time, was killed.

The other compound was occupied by CIA personnel and was better prepared to resist. The personnel there held out long enough for an ad hoc relief force from the embassy in Tripoli to arrive, allowing for them to be evacuated. No American military relief force was sent by the Obama administration.

Throughout the attacks on the compounds, a continuous stream of reporting was sent to Washington from the field. All that reporting told the same story. A large-scale assault had been launched on two American-occupied compounds by a heavily armed Islamic terrorist group.

Nevertheless, in the immediate aftermath of the attacks, the Obama administration began to peddle the story in Washington that a peaceful demonstration in Benghazi had simply gotten out of hand. This was not an act of terrorism. It was regrettable but nothing more.

The backlash against this transparent lie was immediate. The Obama Administration came under scathing criticism. Enter Mike Morell.

At the time, Morell was acting Director of Central Intelligence. He stepped forward and said the erroneous claims of a peaceful demonstration gone bad were his fault. Analysts at CIA headquarters prepared an assessment that said this, and he had passed it on to the White House. President Obama and his senior officials were blameless. The CIA had given them bad intelligence.

This story is and was always absurd. Analysts at CIA headquarters do not review a mountain of reporting about ongoing attacks using heavy machine guns, mortars, and rocket-propelled grenades and then write up an assessment concluding, "We think they meant for this to be peaceful." CIA analysts also do not work in a vacuum. They look at information coming in from across the IC, from the Pentagon, and from the State Department. None of that information supported the claimed assessment.

Of note, no such written piece of analysis has ever been produced.

Morell stepped forward, in his role as Director of Central Intelligence, to take a bullet for Obama. In doing so, he covered for a blatant lie and injected himself into a domestic political dispute. He did so presumably because he believed Hillary Clinton would be the next president and that he would be named to a senior post in her administration. Interestingly, when she lost, Morell was given a post with a generous six-figure annual salary at a Washington, D.C. think tank aligned with the Democratic Party. He got his reward.

In the runup to the 2016 presidential election, Clinton's campaign officials concocted the idea of smearing Donald Trump with false accusations of colluding with Russia. Based on a dossier filled with lies, gossip, and innuendo, they fed this absurdity to federal law enforcement and intelligence officials. When they failed to stop Trump from being elected, they then used this effort to undermine the Trump presidency and hoped to remove him from office.

The involvement of the FBI in this effort, known by its codename "Crossfire Hurricane," has been documented extensively. What has been much less discussed has been the IC's role in the plot.

The investigation of what transpired during Crossfire Hurricane has shown that American intelligence reached out to and involved in the scheme several allied intelligence services, most notably the British. It has also shown that with the passage of time, the British in particular became progressively less and less enthusiastic about assisting with this "investigation." It became clear to them that this was an inappropriate and illegal activity and they wanted no part of it.

None of this interaction with some of our closest allies happened without the involvement and assistance of the CIA and other agencies like NSA. That is not the way it is supposed to work. If you are in London, for instance, meeting with the British intelligence and counterintelligence services, you are doing so not only with the knowledge of the CIA's London station chief but with his or her permission and assistance.

John Brennan, who was Director of the CIA at the time, not only had to know about Crossfire Hurricane and its purpose, but he also had to approve any of this to happen. When Brennan stepped down as director, he was replaced by Gina Haspel. She was the chief of station in London throughout Crossfire Hurricane and would have had to be directly involved in all of the interactions with the British services that were part of the plot.

Brennan made no secret of his hatred for Donald Trump and not only worked behind the scenes to destroy him but came out loudly and publicly attacking the president. In doing so, he made clear he was speaking not simply as a private citizen but as the former Director of Central Intelligence. Commenting on Trump's speech to CIA employees at Langley in 2017, Brennan said, "I couldn't take it anymore. I felt physically nauseated watching and listening to him." Immediately following the president's speech, Brennan texted a former aide with a public statement: "Former Director Brennan is deeply saddened and angered at Donald Trump's despicable display of self-aggrandizement in front of CIA's Memorial Wall of agency heroes. He should be ashamed of himself."[230]

This happened the day after Brennan stepped down as CIA Director.

Brennan went on to make a veritable crusade of attacking Trump and pushing the fictitious Russian collusion narrative. In doing so, he consistently invoked his status as the former CIA Director and implied that he "knew" things that could not be disclosed publicly that proved Trump was in bed with Moscow. When he was ultimately forced to admit that the evidence did not exist, he did so quietly and without fanfare, suggesting he had somehow been misled. Throughout this period, Brennan retained his security clearance, and his conduct became so egregious there was active consideration of removing his access to classified information as a threat to national security.[231]

We should also note that when news of Hunter Biden's "laptop from hell" threatened to derail Joe Biden's 2020 presidential campaign, 51 former intelligence officers came forward and signed a now-infamous letter branding the laptop as a fake bearing "all the classic earmarks of a Russian information operation." I have seen the contents of Hunter's laptop and retain a copy to this day. I can assure you it was immediately obvious in looking at the laptop's contents that it was real and that it suggested strongly that Joe Biden himself was compromised by a number of foreign actors, the Chinese Communist Party foremost among them.

Five former Directors or acting Directors of the CIA were among the 51 signatories to the letter, whose clear purpose was to bury the contents of the laptop and get Joe Biden elected. Both Michael Morell and John Brennan were among the five. Other signatories included James Clapper, Obama's Director of National Intelligence; Michael Vickers, former Undersecretary of Defense for Intelligence; Nicholas Rasmussen, former Director of the National Counterterrorism Center;

Russ Travers, another former director of the NCC; and Thomas Fingar, Chairman of the National Intelligence Council.[232]

This letter did not just happen to come together and magically attract the signatures of 51 well-placed individuals. Antony Blinken, now secretary of state and then a member of Joe Biden's presidential campaign, reached out to Morrell and solicited his assistance with putting together a letter that would discredit the laptop and brand it as Russian disinformation. In an effort eerily similar to that of John Brennan's collaboration with Clinton's 2016 campaign, Morrell then took the lead on getting other former intelligence officials to join forces with Biden's campaign in an effort to bury the laptop story.[233]

When asked why he signed the letter, Morrell was at least honest. He replied, "Because I wanted him (Biden) to win the election."[234]

Intelligence Community involvement in domestic politics is not confined to retired officials. Former Director of National Intelligence John Ratcliffe noted in 2021 that evidence of Chinese influence on the 2020 election had been suppressed by the IC, and analysts had been discouraged from reporting on this issue. Per Ratcliffe, evidence of Chinese influence operations inside the United States was suppressed due to domestic political considerations.[235]

CONCLUSION: A WAY AHEAD

U.S. intelligence is at a tipping point. Major intelligence failures, meddling in U.S. domestic politics, politicization of intelligence, and social engineering within agencies have alienated the American public and our elected officials. Many elected officials have lost faith and trust in the Intelligence Community. It is conceivable that a future U.S. president will ignore intelligence analysis completely. A growing number of voices from Congress and outside the Intelligence Community are calling for cuts or the outright elimination of agencies, especially the CIA and the FBI. There is a widespread belief that the $100 billion in tax dollars funding these agencies receive every year no longer promotes U.S. security interests or puts the interests of the American people first.

This is a very dangerous situation. While the effectiveness and credibility of American intelligence agencies are being undermined by mismanagement and politics, foreign threats to our nation are increasing. Presidents and other senior officials urgently need high-quality, objective, and nonpolitical intelligence to address these dangers. We also know that the intelligence capabilities of American adversaries, especially China, are surging and are not being undermined by political correctness and intelligence agency bureaucrats who think they can dictate Chinese foreign policy to Xi Jinping.

Urgent reforms to rebuild and salvage America's intelligence agencies should focus on the following areas.

Leadership

The key to reforming the Intelligence Community lies in appointing the right people to head key agencies and providing them with the necessary support for the massive reforms that are required. The individuals named to head the CIA, NSA, and other major agencies must be reform-minded, America First people, but they must also have sufficient experience in the IC to understand how the system works and what needs to change. Long, bitter experience has shown that individuals coming in from outside the community are led around by the nose and controlled by the entrenched bureaucracy. What we need are men and women who know how their agencies work and how to fix them.

These individuals, once appointed, must have the full authority of the president to do all that is required. When Franklin D. Roosevelt appointed General William "Wild Bill" Donovan to establish the Office of Strategic Services, he had the president's full support. Donovan faced much opposition in Washington, but he succeeded nonetheless because everyone knew he could call on the president when necessary and that FDR would back him to the hilt. The powerful agencies of the IC will respond vigorously and attempt to thwart efforts to reform them. Only the support of a powerful sitting president will allow for true and lasting reform.

Involvement in Domestic Politics Must End

It must be made clear from the first day of a new America First administration that the old business as usual is over. The status quo is *gone.* There will be zero tolerance for any involvement in domestic politics. Individuals who do so will be fired and prosecuted.

A significant number of senior officers should be removed immediately. Some of those officers have been complicit in actions designed to influence elections and domestic politics. Many others have stood by silently as great organizations have decayed and laws have been broken. There must be a clear sea change. Everyone in the IC must understand that real reforms are underway, and there will be a hard line against foot-dragging, slow rolling, or internal resistance.

Flatten the Structure, End Duplication of Effort

The structure of all the U.S. intelligence agencies must be flattened and simplified. The Office of the Director of Intelligence should be cut significantly to focus on coordination and effective use of resources. All ODNI components that duplicate those of other IC constituent agencies should be eliminated.

The IC must focus on the collection and production of intelligence. It is not the job of operational and analytical components to sit and wait for headquarters to finish seemingly endless rounds of meetings and reviews before moving. It is the job of headquarters to keep up. Anything and everything that prevents people at the working level from accomplishing their mission must be eliminated.

The post-9/11 bloat of the IC must be reversed. The Department of Defense's move into the collection of strategic-level human intelligence must be ended. Similar collection capabilities that have been stood up by agencies such as NSA must also be terminated. We do not need multiple junior varsity versions of CIA running around sucking up resources and crowding the operational environment. We need the key players focused on their core missions and performing those missions at significantly higher levels.

End DEI and Reform HR Practices

Hiring, promotion, awards, and assignments must be revamped completely. The IC must end quotas in personnel management, and focusing on color, gender, or sexual orientation is, at best, irrelevant. Instead, IC personnel practices must be based on merit and achievement. The American people deserve the best U.S. Intelligence Community staffed by the best and brightest officers. We must return to a strict policy of equal opportunity for the IC workforce and ban the destructive diversity, equity, and inclusion ideology.

Toughen Training

Training must be toughened. The world is a dangerous place. It is getting more dangerous by the day. We expect our operational personnel to crawl into the belly of the beast, get the intel we need, and come back alive. They need to be tough enough and well-trained enough to do that. We also need intelligence analysts who can write and brief high-quality, objective, and nonpolitical analyses. Intelligence analysts who do not know how to write quality intelligence analysis should be fired.

Demand Results

The records of every single person in a command position in the IC, at headquarters and in the field, should be reviewed. Operations officers who made rank by playing it safe and currying favor with superiors back home should be removed immediately. They should be replaced by individuals with the brains, guts, and audacity to take the necessary action. If they don't get the job done, they should be replaced. Intelligence analysts who got ahead by avoiding controversial analysis and playing the DEI game also should be removed and replaced with more capable officers.

There can be only one measure of success: results. This does not mean endless PowerPoint presentations and wiring diagrams. We need intelligence that gives our nation a decisive advantage over our adversaries.

All this needs to happen immediately upon the appointment of a new director. There can be no more blue-ribbon panels, expensive consulting firms, or interminable outside reviews. We know what the problems are. We know how to fix them. What we have lacked until now is the willingness to do what we must and confront the challenges we face.

Somewhere out there in the ether right now, a terrorist group is planning a biological attack on the United States, which could kill millions. The Afghan and Pakistani Taliban organizations are conspiring to seize functioning Pakistani nuclear weapons. The Chinese are putting the finishing touches on a plan to blockade Taiwan and crash the global economy. The Venezuelans are discussing with the Russians the idea of putting hypersonic missiles on their soil that can carry nuclear warheads and flatten dozens of U.S. cities.

Only an effective Intelligence Community has a prayer of providing the necessary insight into these and many other threats. We have no time to waste in getting our intelligence agencies back to fighting trim to best protect the American people.

12.

The Right Team, Prepared to Meet Global Challenges and an Emboldened Administrative State

By Doug Hoelscher and Michael Rigas

The earlier chapters of this book clearly communicate the global challenges the next America First administration will face and document the dangers of the administrative state within the national security apparatus. Our colleagues underscore an America First approach, putting the American people and their interests first. The success of that approach is dependent on filling critical positions quickly and choosing the right leaders: those who are loyal to the next president's agenda and have demonstrated the competence to deliver on that agenda. The members of the next president's team need to be untethered from the interests of the administrative state, the foreign policy establishment, and global special interests (the global swamp). They must also subordinate their own career ambitions to the success of the President's national security policy agenda. In short, the individuals who step forward to public service in the next America First administration need to be bold change agents ready to disrupt the status quo so the government respects and honors the will of the American people.

As President Trump said in 2017, "As president, I have no higher duty than to protect the American people." To deliver on that solemn duty a president must appoint individuals to national security posts that share his views and are willing and able to help him to faithfully implement his agenda.

The task of filling national security posts in a new presidential administration is more difficult than simply selecting the right people. Background checks for national security jobs are more intensive and invasive than for most civil service jobs. Presidential nominees or appointees for national security jobs may face a long process to obtain security clearances because of their finances, lengthy business careers, or foreign travel. Also, the pool of America First conservatives with experience in foreign affairs is not large which means there will be a learning curve for many new administration officials named to national security jobs.

In addition, as was discussed in earlier chapters, the America First approach to U.S. national security is a sea change from current U.S. policies. In the first Trump administration these policies were aggressively resisted by an entrenched national security bureaucracy, sometimes called the "deep state." Tactics included delay, ignoring administration policies and decisions, engaging in lawfare by filing baseless complaints and protests to human resources and inspectors general offices, undermining the administration by leaking information to the president's political opponents and the media, and even violating the law every federal official swears an oath to uphold by leaking intelligence, all to stop the implementation of President Trump's America First national security policies. Therefore, the men and women appointed and nominated to foreign policy jobs must be a special breed of leaders and fighters. They must be capable of working successfully with the bureaucracy but must also have thick skin and be prepared to take on those who have demonstrated they will do anything, including violating the law and their oaths, to stop an America First president.

If the past is prologue, appointees in an America First administration can expect to have to work hard for every inch of progress to overcome the inertia of the permanent national security bureaucracy as it fights to preserve their failed policies on the southern border, energy security, the Middle East, China, the environment, the United Nations, and other issues.

While some take issue with the term "deep state" and either deny its existence or alternatively attempt to conflate it with the non-partisan civil service, it is important to note that is not what we mean when we use that term. We believe that most civil servants show up to work every day and do their jobs dutifully on behalf of the president and the American people. Many career officials have tremendous institutional knowledge and expertise and are a great resource to our government, and they serve our fellow citizens well.

What we refer to when we speak of the deep state is what Senator Chuck Schumer spoke of in 2017 when he said, "Let me tell you, you take on the intelligence community, they have six ways from Sunday at getting back at you." Here we have one of the most powerful elected officials in our federal government publicly acknowledging that parts of the government are not only unaccountable to the people's elected and constitutional leadership, but he seems to accept this reality rather than calling for reform. However, we should not despair. With effective leaders who are knowledgeable and courageous, the national security establishment can return to its traditional role of safeguarding national security. This is why we believe it is important that the president appoint and nominate competent and well-prepared leaders who are aligned with his policy agenda, to take control of these agencies, and will do the job the U.S. taxpayer is paying them to do and keep politics out of their work.

Over the past few years, the America First Policy Institute (AFPI) has been working on preparing the next America First administration to be ready on Day One (Inauguration Day). This means being ready to appoint a team that is larger, dedicated to the president's policy agenda, competent, and ready to advance a robust suite of policies more quickly and effectively. This book is an example of AFPI's efforts to prepare new America First national security officials. This work, under the umbrella of the America First Transition Project and in close coordination with AFPI's Center for American Security and our other policy leaders, has been systematically documenting the policy actions, personnel actions, and management actions needed to quickly advance an America First agenda. This chapter discusses how our work will aid the next America

First administration to lead boldly and wrestle control away from the administrative state in the national security space.

A PRIMER ON ADMINISTRATION APPOINTEES

Estimates vary on the number of full-time positions subject to appointment by a president or his administration because each administration has some discretion on the number of appointees in each agency, and there is some variance in what positions are counted as appointees. Our estimate, based on an analysis of the last few administrations, puts the number of political appointees at approximately 4,800. Those 4,800 individuals are charged with aligning federal policies to the president's agenda and driving the implementation of those policies by actively managing approximately four million federal employees and military service members and perhaps over 10 million federal contractors.

Of those 4,800 appointees, approximately 1,200 are in national security-related positions. To align with the priorities of an America First administration, we broadly define national security positions. For example, we look beyond positions at the Department of Defense, the State Department, and the Intelligence Community to other positions that play key roles in advancing and protecting America's national security interests, such as critical positions in the Office of the United States Trade Representative, the Assistant Secretary for Investment Security and the Assistant Secretary for Terrorism Financing at the Department of Treasury, and the Under Secretary for International Trade at the Department of Commerce, to name just a few. Similarly, the general counsels, management officials, and chief financial officers in traditional national security agencies are also vital to national security. Such positions should be prioritized by an incoming administration to identify appointees for service and for the Senate to ensure timely confirmations for those positions that require Senate confirmation.

The individuals appointed to these critical positions that help protect our nation need to be clear on the president's priorities and how those priorities can be implemented in their specific purview. However, having clear policy objectives for each department is not sufficient—it is also vital that a new administration has mature plans on how to drive the president's priorities in the national security space. These officials must actively manage the bureaucracy, aggressively and consistently pull the levers of government, and align incentives for career employees to advance the president's policy priorities.

Knowing what you want to accomplish is the first step, but knowing how to get things done is the next critical step for sustained success. Political appointees must be willing and ready to be change agents with a relentless focus on advancing the president's agenda, fully leveraging the constitutional and statutory authorities granted to the president and other administration leaders. They must ask the right questions of the career bureaucracy and like any good leader, be willing to manage those individuals and know enough to question or reject faulty recommendations based on inaccurate or incomplete information. We know from the experience of many who served as appointees, and even from some career officials who publicly admitted as much, that career bureaucrats impeded progress and undermined the legitimate policy objectives all too often during the Trump administration.

A Look Back at Personnel in the Trump Administration

The Trump administration had many great accomplishments that benefited the American people at home and abroad. However, those accomplishments could have been even greater had there been a different and more robust approach to personnel during the transition effort. In addition, if President Obama and his administration had acted in good faith rather than trying to undermine confidence in the 2016 election and the incoming administration with the Russia collusion hoax, the Trump administration would not have been immediately consumed with this false narrative and endless investigations.[236] These actions from the intelligence community and the outgoing president and his leadership team undermined the incoming administration, particularly in its earliest days. The tumultuous transition of 2016/2017 did not serve President Trump and the nation well and slowed the advancement and implementation of his agenda.

Just one statistic helps illustrate the lack of preparation. Under the Presidential Transition Act, the nominees of the major national parties may receive pre-election resources from the federal government to prepare for transition. It is not just office space, computers, and technology provided by the General Service Administration (GSA) to each of the major candidates, but also the opportunity to begin getting security clearances for individuals who are likely to serve in a new administration, if victorious. This can help a winning candidate and their team hit the ground running after election day as they go into departments and agencies to begin their reviews, and it is vital for officials serving in national security agencies on Day One of a new administration.

In this pre-election transition window in the summer and fall of 2016, the Hillary Clinton transition team submitted approximately 1,200 names to be cleared expeditiously after the election. The Trump transition team submitted 25. This mistake cannot be repeated; we must aim higher.

In addition, the Trump administration's decision to minimize the number of appointees in some areas of government and run a "lean" government by example meant that many of these critical leadership positions were filled by career officials. This undercut the advancement of the president's priorities. Although the aspiration driving that limitation was noble – that the career bureaucracy would salute and advance the policies of the new administration – it was deeply flawed. This is true for two reasons – first, career officials can serve in acting capacities, and do so quite often and serve honorably. But their role in these instances is to maintain the smooth operation of their department. It is not the culture of our government that a career official serving in an acting capacity be a change agent. Acting career officials maintain the status quo, making sure what happened yesterday happens today while they wait for political leadership to arrive to drive a new administration's change agenda. If that political leadership never arrives, neither does the driver for change. While many career officials are capable of carrying out the policy agenda of a new administration, without political leadership to drive that change, success can be elusive. And second, there are unfortunately a not insignificant number of career officials who have their own policy preferences and do not wish to carry out the policies of a new president. James Sherk has written about this in his paper "Tales from the Swamp," citing numerous troubling examples of career officials actively thwarting the lawful policy direction of the President's appointees.[237]

Furthermore, there was little to no training for new appointees as had been the case in administrations dating back to Reagan. A training program would have tremendously aided the new team, many of whom had accomplished private sector backgrounds but lacked previous government service. While the Presidential Transition Act provides funding for training for an incoming administration's appointees, these funds were not effectively deployed in the 2016 transition. This proved to be problematic in the Trump administration as some appointees were not prepared to actively manage a bureaucracy that was not always willing to carry out the President's lawful policy. For example, some appointees at the Department of State were not well served or worse, were undermined by the knowledgeable and experienced career officials upon whom they relied to carry out the foreign policy of the president.[238] Getting the right team at the State Department and getting operational control within is critical to implementing the President's entire national security agenda. Without an aligned State Department aggressively working to implement the president's policy agenda, the administration will be mired in endless bureaucratic battles across the interagency. A training program that helps incoming officials understand how to successfully manage their departments, their budget, their personnel, and the interagency, among other things, will greatly benefit an incoming administration. These are things that even seasoned policy experts or people who have served in other capacities in Washington either on Capitol Hill or in think tanks would require training on as the rules and procedures that govern the executive branch are different than anything most people have experienced in other places in government or the private sector.

In addition, action plans and policies developed for the new team during the 2016/2017 transition – with few exceptions – were limited in depth and follow-through, further delaying policy implementation. In short, the new team was not empowered with the information it critically needed.

Early in the Trump administration, not enough care was given to changing the leadership in national security positions. For example, the

Trump National Security Council leadership kept in place almost all the career detailees chosen by the Obama administration. Many of these detailees were named late in the Obama administration – some after election day – in what appeared to be an attempt to entrench the outgoing administration's policy preferences and undermine the choice by the American people to set a new policy direction.

What followed was an unprecedented number of leaks, including leaked transcripts of the President's conversations with world leaders and other actions designed to undermine the President's national security priorities. This can be avoided by replacing current detailees on the National Security Council with detailees of the new administration's own choosing and in whom they have confidence.

This same error was repeated in many key departments and agencies. For example, at the Department of Homeland Security, upwards of 30% of the members of the Senior Executive Service were either hired or transferred into their roles just before the new administration took office. [239] These actions by the outgoing Obama administration demonstrated a level of sophistication and knowledge about how government works and an effort to cement their policy preferences within the bureaucracy by placing individuals aligned with their policy goals in key leadership positions across the government. An incoming team needs to closely examine such personnel placements made in the closing days of an administration to ensure that outgoing political officials are not working to undermine the incoming administration.

President Trump came into office with a foreign policy worldview that cut against the grain of the national security establishment. As noted in earlier chapters, this included revolutionary foreign policy initiatives such as the Abraham Accords Middle East peace agreement, moving the U.S. embassy in Israel to Jerusalem, and President Trump's personal diplomacy with North Korean leader Kim Jong Un, all of which were opposed by the permanent national security establishment. President Trump also shook up the prior foreign policy establishment approach to U.S. national security by demanding reciprocal trade and ensuring our European and other allies paid their fair share to support our shared national security interests.

Although the above initiatives were significant successes of the Trump administration, implementing them was difficult and time-consuming because of staffing problems. This, unfortunately, sometimes included actions by the administration's own appointees. To avoid such problems, a future America First administration must ensure that potential nominees and appointees to national security posts are fully on board with the president's agenda before they are offered positions. They must be mission aligned and dedicated to driving change. The new administration also must name leaders to national security agencies who are willing and able to do the hard work to manage their bureaucracies to ensure that career officials do their jobs to carry out and implement the president's policies.

Ronald Reagan's presidency was preceded by decades of conservative thought leadership that laid a policy foundation for his agenda. President Trump's new foreign policy direction was both intellectual and instinctual, moving the nation in a new direction and breaking with the entrenched and outdated foreign policy establishment. This meant he did not have a cadre of aligned think tanks, academics, or policy leaders providing support for his change agenda. While President Trump had spent decades speaking clearly and consistently, as a businessman, an author, and a candidate for office about his views on trade and foreign policy, he and the American people were breaking with the failures of the permanent establishment in Washington D.C. that largely preferred the status quo, making the change he drove harder to achieve.

Despite these personnel, cultural, and readiness challenges, those leaders who were in place and aligned with the President's policy agenda overcame tremendous obstacles to achieve what can now only be seen in retrospect as nearly miraculous results given the unrelenting opposition of the entrenched, permanent interests in Washington. Imagine how much more could have been achieved if the professional experts who control these permanent power centers and bureaucracies in Washington had worked with the president instead of against him.

No Longer the Bureaucracy of 1981

President Reagan and his team are widely credited as being one of the more organized and better-prepared administrations as they entered office in 1981. However, the bureaucracy of today is not the bureaucracy of Reagan's time. While most career civil servants continue to be honest brokers in the implementation of a president's policies, too many have abandoned their responsibility to faithfully carry out the president's lawful policies. They were often cheered on by President Trump's political opponents, the media, and so-called good-government groups. As James Sherk has documented, we have witnessed the dangers of a small but not insignificant minority of career officials who actively obstruct and even undermine the policies of the elected president.[240] Furthermore, as academic research has shown, the federal workforce has become more ideologically imbalanced. Increasing numbers of the civil and foreign service no longer reflect the views and values held by the American people.[241] While most civil servants show up every day and do a good job, this ideological imbalance between the people who administer the government and the people they serve is not healthy for our government or our country.

Conservative administrations have an inherent disadvantage in dealing with the ideological makeup of the bureaucracy they inherit – a challenge that has only grown in recent years.[242] According to academic research by Professors Brian Feinstein and Abby Wood of the Wharton School of the University of Pennsylvania and the University of Southern California Gould School of Law, the ideological makeup of the career bureaucracy has sharply shifted to the Left in recent years.[243] While many career personnel can and still do set aside this ideological difference, too many do not, and too often, personal preferences contradict the priorities of the elected president. This means that the president's team needs to be more active in the management of the bureaucracy – this is especially true for the national security agencies. The ideological makeup of the career bureaucracy also makes a strong argument for the need for a bigger political team, one that possesses the executive management skills and experience to manage large organizations and shares a strong commitment to the president's policy.

One should not underestimate the powerful corrupting influence of the foreign policy establishment on career officers and political appointees. John Ranelagh, in his authoritative 1986 book The Agency: The Rise and Fall of the CIA wrote that the CIA's Vietnam analysts during the Vietnam War slanted their work because they "especially wanted to maintain their image with academia, where they one day might seek future jobs."[244] This is what we referred to earlier when we said those who serve should have the national interest first and be untethered to the interests of the global swamp or ambitions for their next career move.

Abram Shulsky and Gary Schmitt drew a similar conclusion about CIA analysts in a 1995 article, finding that:

> ... government service, below the very top levels, is not very prestigious. Those engaged in it who have any intellectual pretensions do not wish to be seen as "Neanderthal" or "out of it" by those in the much more prestigious realms of academia or the mainstream, national-level media. This tends to reinforce a tendency toward the "conventional wisdom," it is distressing how often highly classified assessments of political issues closely resemble op-ed pieces.[245]

Another challenge for any new administration is security clearances. The security clearance process and a labyrinth of classification levels and programs controlled by career federal employees can make it difficult for an insurgent America First president to get control of national security agencies. Although the ability to grant security clearances is a presidential authority, it is delegated to agency heads and then further delegated to career employees. The experience of the Trump administration, where clearances appeared to be delayed, sometimes indefinitely, must be addressed. As part of the America First Transition Project, careful attention is being paid to this important function to ensure the president's appointees have their security clearance investigations and adjudications handled in an expeditious manner.

In addition, a new administration must ensure its national security leadership has full visibility into the classified information and activity for which they have ultimate oversight and responsibility. These programs reside in thousands of classification compartments and senior officials in a new administration often do not even know to ask to see such information because they do not know this information, or these compartments even exist. Political appointees need to know enough to ask the right questions when they walk in the door because career officials will not always volunteer important information during the transition.

Political appointees need to be willing to do the necessary, but hard work that is required in any large organization to manage the bureaucracy and drive change. Appointees to national security agencies need to quickly be told every critical thing their organizations are doing and be provided access to all classified programs and compartments over which they have ultimate responsibility. If some compartments are too sensitive to be shared with appointed agency officials, they must be immediately briefed to appointed officials cleared for such intelligence, such as the National Security Advisor.

Too often, appointees fail to actively manage career officials who are not faithfully and effectively advancing presidential policy priorities. A frequent error is not clarifying the administration's priorities quickly and incorporating those priorities into the plans and documents that the career bureaucracy oversees – such as individual performance plans, agency strategic plans, and larger governmentwide strategic plans. For national security, it is crucial that the National Security Council issue a National Security Strategy and key national security directives as soon as possible in a new administration and ensure that these strategies are incorporated as priority policies for national security agencies.

These documents must reflect the president's policy priorities and his "commander's intent" such that if the president were to read them himself, they would be documents he would agree with and endorse. For national security, the National Security Strategy should clearly explain the new president's America First approach to issues and challenges facing the United States around the world.

Another occupational hazard for any administration's political appointees is when they unwittingly become captive to the interests of their agency over the advancement of presidential policy priorities. This can result in appointees at different agencies representing the interests of their bureaucracies in intra-executive branch turf wars rather than focusing on how best to get results quickly for the president and the American people. This has often been the case in foreign policy agencies that have large and entrenched bureaucracies that are determined to maintain the status quo and maximize their influence and power. Fighting for change in any organization is difficult and time-consuming because the bureaucracy knows numerous ways to delay, appeal, and protest decisions and policies with which they disagree. This is especially true in government.

Political appointees also must have the integrity and courage not to be coopted by the prestige, glamour, and trappings of their office. While this occupational hazard exists for appointees across the board, foreign policy jobs can include travel to exotic destinations, luxurious embassies and offices, elaborate dinners and social events, and meetings with famous foreign officials and experts.

Furthermore, political appointees in foreign policy posts are under heavy pressure to side with prestigious foreign policy establishment institutions on policy issues, over the policies of their president. All too often, political appointees have given in to this pressure to increase their chances of success for their next hoped-for career move with a big corner office in academia or corporate America. America First appointees and nominees to foreign posts must resist these pressures and temptations and loyally advance the president's policy priorities and the interests of the American people.

RECOMMENDATIONS TO PUT THE RIGHT (AND PREPARED) NATIONAL SECURITY TEAM ON THE FIELD

The New Team Needs to Clarify, Relentlessly Communicate, and Keep a Laser-Like Focus on the President's Priorities

Assembling a national security team is a more difficult challenge for a new president than filling positions for other government agencies. Like presidential nominees and appointees to other government agencies, those named to serve in national security agencies must be competent, loyal to the president's policy agenda, and prepared to do the challenging work to implement it. But they also must be capable of mastering the complexities of U.S. foreign policy and an entrenched government bureaucracy resistant to change. Members of the president's national security team must know how to navigate the bureaucracy, ensure the analysis of intelligence is not being politicized, and serve the president by bringing him the best information and analysis he needs to successfully advance his foreign policy and national security agenda.

To ensure that the national security team of a new America First president fully supports his foreign policy agenda, a comprehensive framework for America First national security policies must be developed. Long before election day, work must be done to define presidential policies on a wide range of national security challenges, including border security, the Middle East, the war in Ukraine, China, energy security, the environment, and other issues. There also must be extensive plans on how to better manage and staff all national security agencies to ensure that they implement the president's policies and keep politics out of their work.

None of this work can wait until after election day. Potential presidential nominees and appointees for national security positions cannot be asked to serve in a new America First administration before a framework is established defining and explaining America First national security policies and priorities. Potential officials named to a new administration must be fully versed in this framework and declare that they will fully support it.

Given the shift in policy represented by an America First national security agenda, many officials from prior administrations may not be the best source of talent to fill national security jobs in a new administration because these former officials hold views that are inconsistent with an America First approach to national security. An America First administration should ensure that any former appointees who wish to serve are clearly aligned with the president's policy agenda. They must also ensure that those who do not have prior government service are competent with good management skills, political acumen, aligned with the president's agenda, and able to learn on the job. In addition, former military officers and some former Federal employees who are aligned with the president's policies could be good sources of personnel for these important positions.

Given the size and scope of government, a new administration needs individuals with solid executive management skills who can drive the president's agenda. Like other government agencies, presidential appointees and nominees to national security agencies should have a demonstrated track record and the capability to productively manage large bureaucracies to ensure their organizations fully implement presidential policies. This means knowing how to ask the right questions, setting clear expectations, and holding people accountable. Good leaders also know how to leverage the knowledge and abilities of those with subject matter expertise. Because secrecy, classification issues, and leaks to the media by those opposed to the president's agenda can make managing these agencies much more difficult, an America First administration will need exceptionally qualified and well-prepared candidates to manage these agencies.

Once governing, some actions are simple, such as immediately updating performance plans to align with the new administration's priorities rather than waiting until month nine at the end of the first fiscal year of the administration, or worse, simply approving a performance plan drafted by the career incumbent that is not sufficiently updated to reflect the new administration's policy priorities.

Agency leaders should also move swiftly to update strategy documents that guide agency officials, such as the National Security Strategy, the National Defense Strategy, and key national security directives. Agency budgets and funding should be shifted, to the maximum extent allowable by law, to reflect and support the new administration's policy priorities. Agency heads should review delegations of authority to ensure they are comfortable with who is exercising authority on their behalf or should rescind such delegations as they see fit to retain such authority for themselves. All authorities within each department and agency flow from the constitutional powers of the president or via statute through the president's appointees.

Appointees must boldly protect those authorities and ensure they are fully leveraged to advance the priorities of the duly elected president.

The transition team overall, including the national security personnel, needs to be hyper-disciplined to align their work to the policy priorities of the nominee/president-elect. Having mature policy documents prepared in advance allows the newly elected president's team to have a head start on developing, coordinating, and implementing the president's preferred policies faster to better serve the American people and respect their will as expressed in the election.

The Senate Should Do Its Job (But a President Must Act in Its Absence)

In the last few decades, the number of Senate-confirmed positions has continued to grow despite periodic efforts to reduce that number.[246] The Senate confirmation process has slowed to a point where a new president waits months and even years for his full team to be in place. This key failure was recognized in the 9/11 Commission report as a national security vulnerability. The Senate attempted to address this in the Intelligence Reform and Terrorism Prevention Act of 2004 by committing to confirmation votes on national security positions at the undersecretary level or above within 30 days of the nominations.[247] This problem appeared to worsen during the Trump administration which saw lengthy delays in confirmations for national security posts or ambassadorships. Delays of over a year were common.

Because of the importance of national security posts, it is incumbent that an incoming administration identify, vet, and nominate their key national security personnel quickly. In addition, the administration must hold the Senate publicly accountable to its commitment to hold a confirmation vote on those positions within 30 days.

While we can hope the Senate acts quickly to confirm the president's nominees, hope is not a strategy. Indeed, the experience of administrations of both parties is that their nominees will routinely wait months, if not years, to be confirmed. As such, it is incumbent upon the president to act with energy, beginning on January 20th by filling critical senior non-Senate-confirmed positions in the executive branch with appointees to advance presidential policy priorities. This will also serve to deter our adversaries by showing them the new president has a competent and aligned team in place in national security positions. Therefore, we recommend the formal transition team have robust plans for both Senate nominations and non-confirmed appointments on Day One. Conservatives can no longer focus only on Senate-confirmed positions during transition planning. The Biden administration did not. We must play by the new rules and reality.

Robust Plans for Needed Management Actions

Getting the right team in place is the key foundational action, but by itself is insufficient to advance the president's policy agenda. Appointees also need to have clear action plans that outline the priority management, budget, and policy actions required to wrestle control away from the administrative state and advance an America First agenda. This is what is groundbreaking about AFPI's America First Transition Project. We are leveraging the experience of our nearly 700 volunteers, who have worked in nearly every department and agency in the federal government, to develop a level of depth and sophistication into the planning of how departments and agencies work, so that the leadership of a new administration can successfully implement its agenda. AFPI has paid special attention to management, budget, and policy actions in the national security space.

To the credit of many conservative administrations, the ethos of a government led by ordinary citizens who hail from outside the capital still prevails. While some appointees have had prior experience serving in the federal government, as explained earlier, many appointees are needed for national security posts who lack government experience but who are successful and accomplished in other walks of life. However, inexperienced officials who may not be aware of the unique rules and culture that prevail in Washington or know when they are being given inaccurate or incomplete information can quickly get themselves into trouble.

Such missteps, however innocent, can derail their appointments and the president's policy agenda. This is why the America First Transition Project is developing in-depth training and orientations for future executive branch appointees about their statutory authorities, obligations, rules and regulations, and other fundamentals of how the executive branch works. Like the action plans we are developing for every department and agency, this training program is being developed by subject matter experts with substantial experience as political appointees and will be handed off to a formal transition team for it to deploy. By preparing an incoming team in this way, a new administration can take successful citizens and leaders from across the country and position them for success as change agents in the executive branch and for the American people.

Increase the Focus on Implementation

The next America First administration also has an opportunity to increase the focus on the implementation of the president's policy priorities. Doing so is even more important in the national security space as implementation is solely the responsibility of the federal government, whereas implementation of domestic priorities is often a shared responsibility with state, local, tribal, and even private sector entities. The need to enhance the focus on aggressive implementation of policy priorities should be a key factor when selecting appointees – each team should ensure that there are strong implementors driving change on behalf of the president. This is a key component of AFPI's America First Transition Project. As part of our personnel management effort, we have worked with prior leadership at every department and agency to identify the key personnel positions that must be filled (or created) on Day One to ensure that the new administration's team controls each department's personnel, budget, spending, policymaking, and policy implementing apparatus.

Having the right people in key personnel positions is the first step to successful implementation. Knowing that America First policies are ascendant also informs the action plans we are developing. These plans are informed by individuals with deep knowledge of these departments and agencies who know from experience how things get done and understand the obstacles to doing so. This will empower a new America First administration to implement the new president's policy agenda quickly.

CONCLUSION: A FULL TEAM OF NATIONAL SECURITY CHANGE AGENTS READY TO DRIVE THE PRESIDENT'S POLICY PRIORITIES

Tremendous work has been done by AFPI and other organizations to better prepare the next America First administration to advance the duly elected president's policy priorities. That work boils down to having a larger team of appointees that is better prepared, aligned to the president's policy agenda, in place quickly, ready to be relentless change agents for the president's policy agenda, and having a more robust suite of policies and action plans ready to execute on behalf of the new president. Implementing such change will be difficult but even more important in national security agencies charged with protecting the American people and our homeland. Transition preparedness is about being ready to govern effectively on Day One by learning from the past and planning for the future. The American people deserve nothing less, as the status quo has not served them well.

America First Press

222

About the Authors

FRED FLEITZ, Editor, is Vice Chair of AFPI's Center for American Security. He served in 2018 as a Deputy Assistant to President Donald Trump and Chief of Staff of the National Security Council. Fleitz served in U.S. national security positions for 25 years with the CIA, DIA, the Department of State, and the House Intelligence Committee staff. He is the author or editor of eight books on national security issues.

SAMUEL BUCHAN is an energy and foreign policy strategist. He served as Senior Advisor to Secretaries of Energy Rick Perry and Dan Brouillette and Director of International Economic Policy at the National Security Council and National Economic Council. He is a Senior Fellow at the America First Policy Institute's Center for Energy & Environment.

ELLIE COHANIM is a Senior Fellow with the Independent Women's Forum focusing on Iran, Israel, and global antisemitism; and is a national security contributor for the Christian Broadcasting Network. During the Trump Administration, she served as U.S. Deputy Special Envoy to Monitor and Combat Antisemitism. In 2021, Ellie launched and hosted for Jewish News Syndicate 30+ episodes of the show "Global Perspectives with Ellie Cohanim." Ellie spent 15 years in media and NGO management before serving in the public sector

SAM FADDIS is a former U.S. Army combat arms officer and retired CIA operations officer who spent 20 years undercover in South Asia and the Middle East working against rogue states, terrorist groups, and WMD smuggling networks. After his retirement from the CIA, he spent 10 years running training courses for operatives employed by the NSA, DIA, DOE, military counterintelligence units, and other components of the Intelligence Community. He is the author of seven books and the senior editor for *AND Magazine*, an online publication focused on national security issues.

DOUG HOELSCHER is Chair of AFPI's America First Transition Project and previously served as Assistant to the President and Director of White House Intergovernmental Affairs in the Trump Administration. He previously served as the Director of the Iowa Office of State-Federal Relations.

Hoelscher also worked at PricewaterhouseCoopers and held several positions within the George W. Bush Administration at the White House and at the U.S. Department of Homeland Security.

LT. GEN. (RET.) KEITH KELLOGG is co-Chair of the Center for American Security at AFPI. Kellogg is a highly decorated, retired three-star Army General and has extensive experience in the military and international business. Most recently, he served as National Security Advisor and National Security Council Chief of Staff in the Trump Administration. General Kellogg has wide-ranging experience in Europe, the Pacific, the Middle East, and Africa. He is an author and a Fox News contributor.

ROBERT LAW is Director of the AFPI Center for Homeland Security & Immigration and a senior editor. From 2017 to 2021, he served in the Trump Administration as a senior policy advisor and chief of policy at U.S. Citizenship and Immigration Services within the Department of Homeland Security. Law has over a decade of immigration law, regulation, and policy expertise and has held leadership positions at other immigration-focused think tanks.

ROBERT LIGHTHIZER is Chair of the America First Policy Institute Center for American Trade. Prior to joining AFPI, Lighthizer served as the 18th United States Trade Representative (USTR) under President Donald Trump. Prior to joining the Trump Administration, Lighthizer was a partner at Skadden, Arps, Slate, Meagher & Flom, LLP (Skadden), where he practiced international trade law for over 30 years. Before joining Skadden, Lighthizer served as Deputy USTR for President Ronald Reagan. Prior to that, he was the chief of staff for the Senate Foreign Relations Committee under Chairman Bob Dole.

MORGAN ORTAGUS is the founder of Polaris National Security, host of "The Morgan Ortagus Show" on SiriusXM, and a national security expert on Fox News. She is an active U.S. Navy Reserve Officer and a business executive. During the Trump Administration, she served at the U.S. Department of State Press Spokesperson. During the Obama Administration, she was an intelligence analyst at the U.S. Treasury in the Office of Intelligence and Analysis and from 2010-2011, was the deputy U.S. Treasury attaché in Riyadh, Saudi Arabia.

RICK PERRY served as the 14th U.S. Secretary of Energy from 2017 to 2019, the 47th and longest-serving Governor of the State of Texas, and a member of the Texas state House of Representatives. Governor Rick Perry is a veteran of the United States Air Force, having flown C-130 tactical airlift aircraft in Europe and the Middle East. He is the Chair of the Center for Energy & the Environment at the America First Policy Institute.

MICHAEL RIGAS is Vice Chair and Director of AFPI's America First Transition Project and was Acting Director of the Office of Personnel Management and Acting Deputy Director for Management at the Office of Management and Budget in the Trump Administration. Rigas also served as the chair of the federal government's Agency Transition Directors Council. Rigas spent more than a decade in the private sector in banking before serving in the public sector.

ADAM SAVIT is the Director of the China Policy Initiative at the America First Policy Institute. He previously served as China Program Coordinator at the Center for Security Policy and is a John Quincy Adams Fellow at the Common Sense Society.

MICHAEL WALTZ has represented the 6th District of Florida in the U.S. House of Representatives since 2019. He is the first Green Beret to be elected to Congress and a member of the House Armed Services, Foreign Affairs, and Intelligence Committees. Congressman Waltz is a retired National Guard colonel and combat-decorated Green Beret, former White House and Pentagon policy advisor, a small business owner, and an author.

ROBERT WILKIE is a Distinguished Fellow with AFPI's Center for American Security. He served as the tenth Secretary of Veterans Affairs (VA) during the Trump Administration after previously serving as the acting Secretary of VA. Before confirmation as VA Secretary, Wilkie was the Under Secretary of Defense for Personnel and Readiness. Wilkie is a Colonel in the United States Air Force Reserve. He holds an Honors degree from Wake Forest University, a Juris Doctor from Loyola University College of Law in New Orleans, a Master of Laws in international and comparative law from Georgetown University, and a master's in strategic studies from the United States Army War College.

CHAD WOLF is Executive Director and Chief Strategy Officer of the America First Policy Institute and Chair of the AFPI Center for Homeland Security & Immigration. Wolf served as Acting Secretary of the U.S. Department of Homeland Security during the Trump Administration. Wolf is a Member of the Texas Public Policy Foundation Border Security Coalition, serves as President and Founder of Wolf Global Advisors, and is a recognized leader in national security, border security, immigration, China, and counterterrorism issues.

STEVE YATES is Chair of AFPI's China Policy Initiative. His appointments in government include Radio Free Asia president and deputy national security advisor to Vice President Cheney. Since 2006, Yates has been a senior advisor to presidential campaigns, a frequent media commentator, and CEO of D.C. International Advisory. He previously served as a Professor in the Practice of International Business and Politics at Boise State University, chairman of the Idaho Republican Party, co-chair of the 2016 Republican Platform Subcommittee on National Security, and an analyst at the National Security Agency.

Endnotes

[1] "National Security Strategy of the United States of America," December 2017, Trump Administration archives, https://trumpwhitehouse.archives.gov/wp-content/uploads/2017/12/NSS-Final-12-18-2017-0905.pdf

[7] Jonathan Masters and Will Morrow, "How Much Aid Has the U.S. Sent Ukraine? Here Are Six Charts." Council on Foreign Relations, February 23, 2023. https://www.cfr.org/article/how-much-aid-has-us-sent-ukraine-here-are-six-charts.

[3] "National Security Strategy of the United States of America," December 2017," op. cit.

[4] "Remarks by President Trump to the 74th Session of the United Nations General Assembly," White House press release, September 26, 2019. https://trumpwhitehouse.archives.gov/briefings-statements/remarks-president-trump-74th-session-united-nations-general-assembly/

[5] "Executive Order on Combating Race and Sex Stereotyping," September 22, 2020, Trump Administration archives, https://trumpwhitehouse.archives.gov/presidential-actions/executive-order-combating-race-sex-stereotyping/

[6] "Remarks by President Trump in State of the Union Address," February 4, 2020, Trump Administration archives, https://trumpwhitehouse.archives.gov/briefings-statements/remarks-president-trump-state-union-address-3/

[7] Robert Wilkie, The Steep Cost of Mishandling Our Withdrawal From Afghanistan, The Heritage Foundation, Washington D.C., August 22, 2021

[8] The Human Cost of Failed Deterrence, The Wall Street Journal editorial, January 30, 2024

[9] James Mattis, Secretary of Defense, Summary of the 2018 National Defense Strategy of the United States of America: Sharpening the American Military's Competitive Edge, U.S. Department of Defense, https://dod.defense.gov/Portals/1/Documents/pubs/2018-National-Defense-StrategySummary.pdf

[10] Patrick Savage, "What If It Doesn't End Quickly? Reconsidering US Preparedness For a Protracted Conventional War," Modern War Institute, United States Military Academy, July 23, 2020.

[11] Lara Seligman, "Biden prepares largest Pentagon budget in history as spending cuts loom," Politico, February 10, 2023.

[12] "About that "Record" Defense budget, Biden's 3.2% increase is a cut in real terms despite rising threats," Wall Street Journal editorial March 9, 2023.

13 "8 Things to Know About Biden's Fiscal 2024 Budget, From Bad to Worse," The Daily Signal, March 14, 2023

14 Robert Wilkie, "Failing to Take China At Its Word Will Mean More Global Catastrophes The United States Can't Afford," The Federalist, August 14, 2021.

15 Ibid.

16 Mackenzie Eaglen, Wars of Mass and Attrition Demand a Military Sized for Three Theaters, The American Enterprise Institute, October 16, 2023.

17 "2024 Index of U.S. Military Strength," The Heritage Foundation, Washington D.C., p 627.

18 Ibid.

19 Ibid. p.13. The Heritage Index estimates that we are short of 60% of the active force required to deter and, if need be, contest peer actors. The force would look something like this: Army: 50 brigade combat teams (BCTs); l Navy: 400 battle force ships and 624 strike aircraft; l Air Force: 1,200 fighter/ground-attack aircraft; l Marine Corps: 30 battalions.

20 T.S. Allen and Jackson Perry, "Task Force Smith and the Problem with "Redlines," Modern War Institute, United States Military Academy, July 17, 2020 https://mwi.westpoint.edu/task-force-smith-and-the-problem-with-readiness/

21 Colin L. Powell, MTV Global Discussion, 14 February 2002.

22 Ronald Reagan, A Time for Choosing, October 27, 1964, NBC Television Network

23 Robert Wilkie, "Americans Must Resist Rising Anti-Semitism," The National Interest, June 2021 https://nationalinterest.org/blog/politics/americans-must-resist-rising-anti-semitism-187164

24 Letter to House Speaker Kevin McCarthy from Flag Officers for America, May 20, 2023.

25 In FY 2023 the military fell 41,00 recruits short of its overall goals. The data below represents the Services' annual goals and accessions/gains for FY23. Army Accessions: Goal: 65,500; Attained 50,181 (76.61 percent/-15,319). Navy Accessions: Goal 37,700; Attained 30,236 (80.20 percent/-7,464). Marine Corps Accession: Goal 28,900; Attained 28,921 (100.07 percent/+21). Air Force Accessions: Goal 26,977; Attained 24,100 (89.34 percent/-2,877). Space Force Accessions: Goal 492; Attained 537 (109.15 percent/+45). DOD Press Release EOM SEP 23 Recruiting and Retention Report

26 Beacon Research, "US National Survey of Defense Attitudes on Behalf of the Ronald Reagan Foundation—Final Topline Results," November 9–17, 2022, https://www.reaganfoundation.org/media/359964/rndf-survey-2022-topline.pdf

27 U.S. Army Recruiting Command, Army Public Affairs Office, "Facts and Figures," https://recruiting.army.mil/pao/facts_figures (February 2023).

[28] "Biden's Army Secretary Doesn't Want 2nd Gen Military Recruits For Fear Of A Warrior Caste", Main Street Digest, July 10, 2023. https://mainstreetdigest.com/2023/07/bidens-army-secretary-doesnt-want-2nd-gen-military-recruits-for-fear-of-a-warrior-caste/

[29] Christine E. Wormuth, Secretary of the Army, "Message from the Secretary of the Army to the Force," February 8, 2022, https://www.army.mil/article/253814/message_from_the_secretary_of_the_army_to_the_force

[30] Pentagon Leaders Testily Defend Efforts on Racism and Extremism, Robert Burns and Lolita C. Baldor, The Associated Press, June 23, 2021. https://apnews.com/article/ny-state-wire-race-and-ethnicity-racial-injustice-government-and-politics-45214130da3db8418ad8a9e19254544a

[31] Dakota Wood, "Caught Red-Handed: Critical Race Theory Taught at West Point," The Daily Signal, June 24, 2022, https://www.dailysignal.com/2022/06/24/caught-red-handed-critical-race-theory-is-being-taught-at-west-point/

[32] "Has the Military Gone Woke", Wall Street Journal editorial, June 25, 2021

[33] Dominic Pino, *"Ideas Matter, and So Do the Books We Read,"* National Review, June 27, 2021https://www.nationalreview.com/2021/06/ideas-matter-and-so-do-the-books-we-read/

[34] Senator Tom Cotton, "Critical Race Theory Inside the U.S. Military", Letter to the Editor, Wall Street Journal, July 5, 2021

[35] Mike Pompeo quoted in *Service members sound alarm against 'extremely woke' military,* by Mike Lee Fox News, Oct. 11, 2022, https://www.foxnews.com/politics/service-members-speak-out-against-woke-military

[36] Secretary of the Air Force Memorandum, *Officer Source of Commission Applicant Pool Goals,* Department of the Air Force, Washington, DC August 9. 2022.

[37] "Heritage 2024 Index of Military Strength, pp. 617-628.

[38] John Venable, "The Air Force Is About to Lower Its Already Low Standards," Heritage Foundation Reports, April 28, 2021. https://www.heritage.org/defense/commentary/the-air-force-about-lower-its-already-low-standards

[39] Students for Fair Admissions, Inc., v. President and Fellows of Harvard College, https://www.supremecourt.gov/DocketPDF/20/20-1199/232539/20220801205901633_20-1199%20Harvard%20FINAL%20Revised.pd

[40] Scott Sturman, "How DEI Infiltrated the Military," Washington Examiner June 19, 2023.

[41] Remarks by President Biden on the Continued Battle for the Soul of the Nation, Philadelphia, Pennsylvania, September 1, 2022.

https://www.whitehouse.gov/briefing-room/speeches-remarks/2022/09/01/remarks-by-president-bidenon-the-continued-battle-for-the-soul-of-the-nation/

[42] Mike Lee, *Air Force Base warns service members to avoid "patriot" rally with speaker from pro-Trump group,* Fox News.com, November 21, 2023. https://www.foxnews.com/us/air-force-base-warns-service-members-avoid-rally-speaker-pro-trump-group

[43] Eleanor Watson, "Pentagon updates extremism policy and says nearly one hundred members engaged in extremist activity in 2021," CBSNews.com, December 21, 2021, *https://www.cbsnews.com/news/pentagon-extremism-military-policy-updates/*

[44] "The Military's Phantom "Extremists," Wall Street Journal editorial, January 1, 2024.

[45] "Prohibited Extremist Activities in the U.S. Department of Defense," Institute for Defense Analysis, Report P-33076, December 2023, p. iv.

[46] General George C. Marshall, quoted. In The Military Leader https://themilitaryleader.com/quote-marshall-combat-leader/

[47] Ibid.

[48] Lieutenant General Thomas Spoehr, "America's Army: "Equitable" but Not Combat-Ready," The Heritage Foundation, May 20, 2022, https://www.heritage.org/defense/commentary/americas-army-equitable-not-combat-ready

[49] Jeff Crawley, "Cannoneers participate in TRADOC MOS Study," U.S. Army Website, June 19, 2013, https://www.army.mil/article/105863/Cannoneers_participate_in_TRADOC_MOS_study

[50] Ibid Spoehr

[51] Ibid.

[52] Major General Amos Yadlin, The Day After—in Israel, Foreign Affairs, March 8, 2024

[53] Ibid.

[54] Ibid.

[55] Captain Kristen M. Griest, "With Equal Opportunity, Comes Equal Responsibility: Lowering Fitness Standards, To Accommodate Women Will Hurt The Army— And Women," Modern War Institute, United States Military Academy, February 25, 2021. https://mwi.westpoint.edu/with-equal-opportunity-comes-equal-responsibility-lowering-fitness-standards-to-accommodate-women-will-hurt-the-army-and-women/

[56] "Thomas Spoehr, "The Administration and Congress Must Act Now to Counter the Worsening Military Recruiting Crisis," Heritage Foundation, July 28, 2022. https://www.heritage.org/sites/default/files/2022-07/IB5283.pdf

[57] National Commission on Terrorist Attacks, The 9/11 Commission Report (2004), available at https://govinfo.library.unt.edu/911/report/911Report.pdf.

[58] Pub. L. 107-296 (Nov. 25, 2002), https://www.dhs.gov/sites/default/files/publications/hr_5005_enr.pdf.

[59] U.S. Department of Homeland Security. Core Values. https://www.dhs.gov/core-values.

[60] U.S. Customs and Border Protection. CBP Enforcement Statistics. https://www.cbp.gov/newsroom/stats/cbp-enforcement-statistics.

[61] Donald J. Trump. Executive Order 13767. Border Security and Immigration Enforcement Improvements, Jan. 25, 2017. 82 FR 8793. https://www.federalregister.gov/documents/2017/01/30/2017-02095/border-security-and-immigration-enforcement-improvements.

[62] See Muzaffar Chishti & Jessica Bolter, "Border Challenges Dominate, But Biden's First 100 Days Mark Notable Under-the-Radar Immigration Accomplishments," Migration Policy Institute, April 26, 2021. https://www.migrationpolicy.org/article/biden-100-days-immigration.

[63] U.S. Customs and Border Protection. Southwest Land Border Encounters. https://www.cbp.gov/newsroom/stats/southwest-land-border-encounters.

[64] Ibid.

[65] U.S. Customs and Border Protection. CBP Enforcement Statistics. https://www.cbp.gov/newsroom/stats/cbp-enforcement-statistics.

[66] See, e.g., Josh Hawley, "Hawley Blasts Mayorkas for Record Number of Illegal 'Gotaways' Crossing the Border Without CBP Apprehension," Jan. 24, 2024 ("All told, nearly 2 million illegal immigrants have successfully evaded border officials during the Biden Administration."). https://www.hawley.senate.gov/hawley-blasts-mayorkas-record-number-illegal-gotaways-crossing-border-without-cbp-apprehension.

[67] See Current Authorities the Biden Administration is NOT Using to Secure the Border. (15 Feb. 2024). America First Policy Institute available at https://americafirstpolicy.com/issues/current-authorities-the-biden-administration-is-not-using-to-secure-the-border.

[68] Inspectors General of the Intelligence Community, Central Intelligence Agency, Department of Justice, and Department of Homeland Security. Unclassified Summary of Information Handling and Sharing Prior to the April 15, 2013 Boston Marathon Bombings. https://oig.justice.gov/reports/2014/s1404.pdf.

[69] Office of Public Affairs, U.S. Department of Justice. Man Sentenced to Life in Prison for ISIS-inspired Bombing in New York City Subway Station in 2017. April 22, 2021. https://www.justice.gov/opa/pr/man-sentenced-life-prison-isis-inspired-bombing-new york city subway station 2017.

70 "National Security Presidential Memorandum – 7," The White House, October 5, 2017 https://trumpwhitehouse.archives.gov/presidential-actions/national-security-presidential-memorandum-7/.

71 "National Security Presidential Memorandum – 9," The White House, February 6, 2018. https://irp.fas.org/offdocs/nspm/nspm-9.pdf.

72 See Ellen Nakashima and Joseph Menn, "China's cyber army is invading critical U.S. services," Washington Post, December 11, 2023. https://www.washingtonpost.com/technology/2023/12/11/china-hacking-hawaii-pacific-taiwan-conflict/.

73 See National Security Agency/Central Security Service. Russian Cyber Actors are Exploiting a Known Vulnerability with Worldwide Impact. December 13, 2023. https://www.nsa.gov/Press-Room/Press-Releases-Statements/Press-Release-View/Article/3616384/russian-cyber-actors-are-exploiting-a-known-vulnerability-with-worldwide-impact/.

74 See Center for Strategic & International Studies. Survey of Chinese Espionage in the United States Since 2000. https://www.csis.org/programs/strategic-technologies-program/survey-chinese-espionage-united-states-2000.

75 See, e.g., Rachel Hatzipanagos, "Laws banning Chinese from buying property dredge up old history," Washington Post, August 21, 2023. https://www.washingtonpost.com/nation/2023/08/18/florida-chinese-land-laws/.

76 See "Chinese Medical Student Accused of Trying To Smuggle Cancer Research From Boston Hospital," Associated Press, December 31, 2019. https://www.wbur.org/news/2019/12/31/chinese-medical-student-accused-of-trying-to-smuggle-cancer-research-from-boston-hospital.

77 See, e.g., Alexandra Yoon-Hendricks, "Visa Restrictions for Chinese Students Alarm Academia," New York Times, July 25, 2018. https://www.nytimes.com/2018/07/25/us/politics/visa-restrictions-chinese-students.html.

78 Jay Greene, PhD, Adam Kissel and Lindsey Burk, "Protecting American Universities from Undue Foreign Influence," Heritage Foundation, February 13, 2004. https://www.heritage.org/education/report/protecting-american-universities-undue-foreign-influence

79 Phillip Shishkin, "Ukraine to Get More U.S. Aid, but Not Weapons," Wall Street Journal, September 18, 2014.

80 Charles Cogan, "You Have to Understand, George. Ukraine Is Not Even a Country," Huffington Post, March 16, 2014. https://www.huffpost.com/entry/you-have-to-understand-ge_b_4976198

81 Timothy Snyder, "Putin's rationale for Ukraine invasion gets the history wrong," Washington Post, February 25, 2022.

82 "Contextualizing Putin's 'On the Historical Unity of Russians and Ukrainians,'" Harvard University Ukrainian Research Institute, August 2, 2021. https://huri.harvard.edu/news/putin-historical-unity

83 Tucker Carlson interview with Vladimir Putin, X (formerly Twitter), February 8, 2024. https://x.com/TuckerCarlson/status/1755734526678925682?s=20

84 "Kremlin says NATO expansion in Ukraine is a 'red line' for Putin," Reuters, September 27, 2024, https://www.reuters.com/world/kremlin-says-nato-expansion-ukraine-crosses-red-line-putin-2021-09-27/

85 James Marson and Daniel Michaels, "Ukraine War Slips Toward Violent Stalemate," Wall Street Journal, November 12, 2023.

86 Natasha Bertrand, Oren Liebermann and Jennifer Hansler, "US and NATO grapple with critical ammo shortage for Ukraine," CNN.com, July 18, 2023.

87 Kaitlin Lewis, "NATO Ally Gives Ukraine's F-16 Program Additional Boost," Newsweek, January 5, 2024. https://www.newsweek.com/nato-ally-gives-ukraines-f-16-program-additional-boost-1857982; Lara Jakes, "Ukraine Could Deploy F-16s as Soon as July, but Only a Few," New York Times, March 11, 2024.

88 "Remarks by President Biden on the United Efforts of the Free World to Support the People of Ukraine." White House Briefing Room, March 26, 2022. https://www.whitehouse.gov/briefing-room/speeches-remarks/2022/03/26/remarks-by-president-biden-on-the-united-efforts-of-the-free-world-to-support-the-people-of-ukraine/

89 Jennifer Agiesta, "Majority of Americans oppose more aid for Ukraine in war with Russia," August 4, 2023. https://www.cnn.com/2023/08/04/politics/cnn-poll-ukraine/index.html

90 "U.S. Security Cooperation with Ukraine." U.S. Department of State Bureau of Political-Military Affairs, December 27, 27, 2023. https://www.state.gov/u-s-security-cooperation-with-ukraine/

91 Eric Lipton, "From Rockets to Ball Bearings, Pentagon Struggles to Feed War Machine." The New York Times, March 24, 2023. https://www.nytimes.com/2023/03/24/us/politics/military-weapons-ukraine-war.html

92 Karen DeYoung, Dan Lamothe and Isabelle Khurshudyan, "Inside the monumental, stop-start effort to arm Ukraine," Washington Post, December 23, 2022. https://www.washingtonpost.com/national-security/2022/12/23/ukraine-weapons-biden/

93 Ibid.

94 Greg Wehner, "Pentagon prepares to make 'tough choices' between U.S. readiness and Ukraine support as funding package lingers." FoxNews.com, December 14, 2023. https://www.foxnews.com/politics/pentagon-prepares-make-tough-choices-between-us-readiness-ukraine-support-funding-package-lingers

[95] Rohac Dalibor, "Biden's Lack of Leadership Is Galvanizing US Critics of Ukraine Aid," New York Post, October 5, 2023.

[96] James Landale, "Ukraine War: Western allies say they are running out of ammunition." BBC News, October 3, 2023. https://www.bbc.com/news/world-europe-66984944?at_campaign=KARANGA

[97] Pieter D. Wezeman, Justine Gadon and Siemon T. Wezeman, "Trends in International Arms Transfers, 2022." Stockholm International Peace Research Institute, March 2023. https://www.sipri.org/publications/2023/sipri-fact-sheets/trends-international-arms-transfers-2022

[98] Antoinette Radford & Adam Easton, "Poland no longer supplying weapons to Ukraine amid grain row." BBC News, September 21, 2023. https://www.bbc.com/news/world-europe-66873495

[99] Elisabeth Gosselin-Malo and Jaroslaw Adamowski, "Slovakia shift, elections in Poland dampen support for Ukraine," Defense News, October 3, 2023. https://www.defensenews.com/global/europe/2023/10/03/slovakia-shift-elections-in-poland-dampen-support-for-ukraine/

[100] Yaroslav Trofimov, "Did Ukraine Miss an Early Chance to Negotiate Peace With Russia?," Wall Street Journal, January 5, 2024.

[101] Peter Baker, "Top U.S. General Urges Diplomacy in Ukraine While Biden Advisers Resist," New York Times, November 10, 2022.

[102] Susie Blann and Matthew Lee, "Blinken warns Ukraine cease-fire now would result in 'Potemkin peace,' legitimizing Russian invasion," Associated Press, June 2, 2023. https://apnews.com/article/russia-ukraine-war-kyiv-attack-16ee160a9ac7fc27b9974c2887b15a8d

[103] "Remarks by President Biden on the United Efforts of the Free World to Support the People of Ukraine." White House Briefing Room, March 26, 2022. https://www.whitehouse.gov/briefing-room/speeches-remarks/2022/03/26/remarks-by-president-biden-on-the-united-efforts-of-the-free-world-to-support-the-people-of-ukraine/

[104] Jon Jackson, "Biden Compares Putin to Hamas as US Navy Takes Rare Action to Defend Israel," Newsweek, October 19, 2023. https://www.newsweek.com/biden-compares-putin-hamas-us-navy-takes-rare-action-defend-israel-1836309

[105] Bojan Pancevski and Laurence Norman, "NATO's Biggest European Members Float Defense Pact with Ukraine," Wall Street Journal, February 24, 2023.

[106] Richard Haass and Charles Kupchan, "The West Needs a New Strategy in Ukraine," Foreign Affairs, April 13, 2023.

[107] Video of this interview is available at https://twitter.com/i/status/1727015665780060233.

[108] "Henry Kissinger explains how to avoid world war three," The Economist, May 17, 2023.

[109] Anton Troianovski, Adam Entous and Julian E. Barnes, "Putin Quietly Signals He Is Open to a Cease-Fire in Ukraine," New York Times, December 23, 2023; Guy Faulconbridge and Darya Korsunskaya, "Exclusive: Putin's suggestion of Ukraine ceasefire rejected by United States, sources say," Reuters, February 13, 2024. https://www.reuters.com/world/europe/putins-suggestion-ukraine-ceasefire-rejected-by-united-states-sources-say-2024-02-13/

[110] Kurt Schlichter tweet, February 17, 2024. https://x.com/KurtSchlichter/status/1758881662975594611?s=20

[111] Daris Shekina, "Ukrainian Intelligence discloses number of Russian soldiers in Ukraine." RBC-Ukraine, October 23, 2023. https://newsukraine.rbc.ua/news/ukrainian-intelligence-discloses-number-of-1698087629.html

[112] Klain, D. (2022, September 15). "Russia is Seeding Ukraine's Soil with Land Mines." Foreign Policy. https://foreignpolicy.com/2022/09/15/russia-ukraine-land-mines/

[113] Jason Jay Smart, "Analysis: Ukraine's Impending Demographic Crisis," Kyiv Post, December 24, 2023. https://www.kyivpost.com/analysis/25730

[114] Maria Kostenko, Daria Tarasova-Markina, et al, "As the war grinds on, Ukraine needs more troops. Not everyone is ready to enlist," CNN.com, November 19, 2023. https://www.cnn.com/2023/11/19/europe/ukraine-difficulties-in-military-recruitment-intl/index.html

[115] Hanna Arhirova and Samya Kullab, "Ukraine lowers its conscription age to 25 to replenish its beleaguered troops," Associated Press, April 3, 2024. https://apnews.com/article/russia-ukraine-war-conscription-mobilization-251058a942a253f3eaec2c53373adf03

[116] Richard Haass and Charles Kupchan, "The West Needs a New Strategy in Ukraine," Foreign Affairs, April 13, 2023.

[117] James A. Dorn, "China's Post-1978 Economic Development and Entry into the Global Trading System." CATO Institute, October 10, 2023. https://www.cato.org/publications/chinas-post-1978-economic-development-entry-global-trading-system#plan-market-overview

[118] "China Exports to the United States." Trading Economics. https://tradingeconomics.com/china/exports/united-states

[119] CPA Data Shows Federal Retirement Funds Flowing to CCP Companies." Coalition for a Prosperous America, August 3, 2022. https://prosperousamerica.org/cpa-data-shows-federal-retirement-funds-flowing-to-ccp-companies/

[120] "CPA Data Shows Federal Retirement Funds Flowing to CCP Companies." Coalition for a Prosperous America, August 3, 2022. https://prosperousamerica.org/cpa-data-shows-federal-retirement-funds-flowing-to-ccp-companies/

121 "Committee Report: American VC Firms Investing Billions into PRC Companies Fueling the CCP's Military, Surveillance State, and Uyghur Genocide." The Select Committee on the Chinese Communist Party. February 8, 2024. https://selectcommitteeontheccp.house.gov/media/press-releases/committee-report-american-vc-firms-investing-billions-prc-companies-fueling

122 Emily Benson and Gregory C. Allen, "A New National Security: The Executive Order on Outbound Investment." Center for Strategic and International Studies, August 10, 2023. https://www.csis.org/analysis/new-national-security-instrument-executive-order-outbound-investment

123 Catharine Adams, "China's Shipbuilding Capacity is 232 Times Greater Than That of the United States." Alliance for American Manufacturing, September 18, 2023. https://www.americanmanufacturing.org/blog/chinas-shipbuilding-capacity-is-232-times-greater-than-that-of-the-united-states/

124 Mallory Shelbourne, "Davidson: China Could Try to Take Control of Taiwan In 'Next Six Years'," USNI News, March 9, 2021. https://news.usni.org/2021/03/...; Joseph Huitson, "CIA Director William Burns says President Xi Jinping 'unsettled and sobered' by Russia's performance in Ukraine," Sky News Australia, February 27, 2023. https://www.skynews.com.au/world-news/china/cia-director-william-burns-says-president-xi-jinping-unsettled-and-sobered-by-russias-performance-in-ukraine/news-story

125 Iain Marlow, "What is the 'Quad' Alliance and Why Doesn't China Like It?" Bloomberg News, May 16, 2023. https://www.bloomberg.com/news/articles/2023-05-16/what-is-the-quad-alliance-and-why-doesn-t-china-like-it

126 Jesse Jiang, "Laos Faces Debt Crisis After Borrowing Billions From China," VOA.com, July 1, 2022. https://www.voanews.com/a/laos-faces-debt-crisis-after-borrowing-billions-from-china-/6641633.html

127 Elias Biryabarema, "China rejects allegations it may grab Ugandan airport if country defaults on loan," Reuters, November 29, 2021. https://www.reuters.com/markets/rates-bonds/china-rejects-allegations-it-may-grab-ugandan-airport-if-country-defaults-loan-2021-11-29/

128 Lauren Frayer, "Why a Chinese ship's arrival in Sri Lanka has caused alarm in India and the West," NRP.com, August 19, 2022. https://www.npr.org/2022/08/19/1118113095/sri-lanka-china-ship-hambantota-port

129 "How China's Belt and Road Initiative Is Changing." The Economist, October 17, 2023. https://www.economist.com/the-economist-explains/2023/10/17/how-chinas-belt-and-road-initiative-is-changing

130 Chengyi Lin, "3 Drivers of China's Booming Electric Vehicle Market." Harvard Business Review, January 3, 2024. https://hbr.org/2024/01/3-drivers-of-chinas-booming-electric-vehicle-market

131 Sylvia Pfeifer, "We Can De-risk but Not Decouple' from China, Says Raytheon Chief," Financial Times, June 19, 2023. https://www.ft.com/content/d0b94966-d6fa-4042-a918-37e71eb7282e

132 John G. Ferrari and Mark Rosenblatt. "How to End China's Chokehold on the Pentagon's Supply Chains." Defense News, February 15 2024. https://www.defensenews.com/opinion/2024/02/15/how-to-end-chinas-chokehold-on-the-pentagons-supply-chains/

133 Jeffrey Nadaner and Tara Dougherty, "Numbers Matter: Defense Acquisition, U.S. Production Capacity, and Deterring China," Govini, January 2024. https://govini.com/wp-content/uploads/2024/01/Govini_2024_Numbers-Matter.pdf.

134 Ryan McCrimmon, "China is buying up American farms. Washington wants to crack down," Politico, July 19, 2021. https://www.politico.com/news/2021/07/19/china-buying-us-farms-foreign-purchase-499893; "Foreign Holdings of U.S. Agricultural Land Through December 31, 2020," U.S. Department of Agriculture report, https://www.fsa.usda.gov/Assets/USDA-FSA-Public/usdafiles/EPAS/PDF/2020_afida_annual_report.pdf.

135 "States' Role in Addressing Foreign Threats in U.S. Critical Energy Infrastructure Sectors," National Governors Association, January 26, 2022. https://www.nga.org/publications/states-role-in-addressing-foreign-threats-in-u-s-critical-energy-infrastructure-sectors/

136 "Insider Threat Mitigation for U.S. Critical Infrastructure Entities," National Counterintelligence and Security Center, March 2021. https://www.dni.gov/files/NCSC/documents/news/20210319-Insider-Threat-Mitigation-for-US-Critical-Infrastru-March-2021.pdf

137 H.R. 4577, "Protecting U.S. Farmland and Sensitive Sites from Foreign Adversaries Act." U.S. House of Representatives, July 12, 2023. https://www.congress.gov/bill/118th-congress/house-bill/4577?s=1&r=14

138 H.B. 2766, "Kansas Land and Military Installation Protection Act." Kansas House of Representatives, February 8, 2024. https://www.kslegislature.org/li/b2023_24/measures/hb2766/

139 Nathan Owens, "Missouri bans Chinese-owned farmland near military bases." Agriculture Dive, January 5, 2024. https://www.agriculturedive.com/news/missouri-bans-chinese-owned-farmland-near-military-bases/703785/

140 Lawrence Richard, "US forces attacked at least 160 times in the Middle East since mid-October after Sunday's drone strike," Fox News, January 29, 2024. https://www.foxnews.com/politics/us-forces-attacked-least-160-times-middle-east-since-mid-october-sundays-drone-strike

141 "Press Release Announcing U.S. Recognition of Israel (1948)," U.S. National Archives. https://www.archives.gov/milestone-documents/press-release-announcing-us-recognition-of-israel

142 "Kerry warns Trump: Moving US embassy would cause regional 'explosion,'", Times of Israel, January 7, 2017. https://www.timesofisrael.com/kerry-moving-us-embassy-would-cause-a-regional-explosion/

143 See "Peace to Prosperity: A Vision to Improve the Lives of the Palestinian and Israeli People," The White House, January 2020. Available at: https://trumpwhitehouse.archives.gov/wp-content/uploads/2020/01/Peace-to-Prosperity-0120.pdf

144 Edward Lawrence, Andrew Miller, and Lauren Shank, "Palestinian group accused of harboring terrorists received $1B from Biden admin: report," FoxBusiness.com, October 18, 2023. https://www.foxbusiness.com/politics/palestinian-group-accused-harboring-terrorists-received-1b-biden-admin

145 Alexander Ward and Nahal Toosi, "Biden made final decision to keep Iran's IRGC on terrorist list," Politico, May 24, 2022. https://www.politico.com/news/2022/05/24/biden-final-decision-iran-revolutionary-guard-terrorist-00034789

146 Laurence Norman, "Differences Splinter U.S. Team Negotiating with Iran on Nuclear Deal," Wall Street Journal, January 24, 2022.

147 David Albright, "How quickly could Iran make nuclear weapons today?" Institute for Science and International Security, January 8, 2024. https://isis-online.org/isis-reports/detail/how-quickly-could-iran-make-nuclear-weapons-today

148 Tyler O'Neil, "$6B Prisoner Swap Was 'Just a Drop in the Bucket' for Iran. Here's How Much Tehran Has Raked in Under Biden," Daily Signal, October 18, 2023. https://www.dailysignal.com/2023/10/18/not-just-6b-heres-how-much-money-biden-admin-freed-iran-hamas-terror-attack-israel/

149 Barak Ravid, "Scoop: Bibi says U.S. and Iran held indirect talks on 'mini agreement,'" Axios, June 13, 2023; Yonah Jeremy Bob, "Are Iran, the West still moving toward unofficial nuclear understanding? – analysis," Jerusalem Post, July 20, 2023; Amos Harel, "Iran Gets an Unwritten Deal From the U.S. as Israel Gets a Bear Hug," Haaretz, July 14, 2023.

150 "China-led SCO pushes multipolar world as Xi warns of 'color' revolts," Nikkei Asia. September 17, 2022. https://asia.nikkei.com/Politics/International-relations/China-led-SCO-pushes-multipolar-world-as-Xi-warns-of-color-revolts

151 Summer Said, Sha Hua, and Dion Nissenbaum, "Saudi Arabia Eyes Chinese Bid for Nuclear Plant," August 25, 2023. https://www.wsj.com/world/middle-east/saudi-arabia-eyes-chinese-bid-for-nuclear-plant-e4a56f

152 Michael Scollon, "Iranian Economy Buoyed By 'Dark Fleet' Oil Shipments to China," Radio Free Europe/Radio Liberty, January 7, 2024. https://www.rferl.org/a/iran-economy-oil-shipments-dark-fleet-china-sanctions/32764518.html

153 "Iran & Russia: New Land & Sea Networks," The Iran Primer, May 18, 2023. https://iranprimer.usip.org/index.php/blog/2023/may/18/iran-russia-new-network-land-sea-routes

154 Mark Armstrong, "Putin welcomes Assad to Moscow for talks to reaffirm mutual support," Euronews, March 15, 2023. https://www.euronews.com/2023/03/15/syrias-president-bashar-al-assad-in-moscow-for-talks-with-ally-vladimir-putin

155 Jeff Mason and Steve Holland, "Russia received hundreds of Iranian drones to attack Ukraine, US says," Reuters, June 9, 2023. https://www.reuters.com/world/europe/russia-has-received-hundreds-iranian-drones-attack-ukraine-white-house-2023-06-09/

156 "Exclusive: Iran sends Russia hundreds of ballistic missiles," Reuters, February 21, 2024. https://www.reuters.com/world/iran-sends-russia-hundreds-ballistic-missiles-sources-say-2024-02-21/

157 Barak Ravid, "Scoop: State Department reviewing options for possible recognition of Palestinian state," Axios, January 31, 2024. https://www.axios.com/2024/01/31/palestine-statehood-biden-israel-gaza-war

158 "The Iranians Pay a Price in Syria," Wall Street Journal editorial, April 1, 2024.

159 Barak Ravid, "Scoop: Biden told Bibi U.S. won't support an Israeli counterattack on Iran," Axios, April 14, 2024. https://www.axios.com/2024/04/14/biden-netanyahu-iran-israel-us-wont-support

160 Arie Egozi, "Israel asks the United States to expedite supply of aircraft," Zona Militar, 28 January, 2024. https://www.zona-militar.com/en/2024/01/28/israel-asks-the-united-states-to-expedite-supply-of-aircraft/

161 Brad Lendon, Radina Gigova, Fred Pleitgen and Kostyantin Gak, "Western ammo stocks at 'bottom of the barrel' as Ukraine war drags on, NATO official warns," CNN, October 4, 2023. https://www.cnn.com/2023/10/04/europe/uk-nato-ukraine-war-ammunition-intl-hnk-ml/index.html

162 Jacob Nagel, "The 2016 MOU on U.S. Defense Aid to Israel," Foundation for Defense of Democracies, August 19, 2020. https://www.fdd.org/analysis/2020/08/19/the-2016-mou-on-us-defense-aid-to-israel/

163 Nadeen Ebrahim, "Saudi crown prince says normalization deal with Israel gets 'closer' every day," CNN, September 21, 2023. https://www.cnn.com/2023/09/21/middleeast/saudi-arabia-mbs-interview-

fox-intl/index.html; "Netanyahu, Mossad chief fly to Saudi, hold first known meet with crown prince," Times of Israel, November 23, 2020. https://www.timesofisrael.com/netanyahu-mossad-chief-said-to-travel-to-saudi-arabia-meet-with-crown-prince/

164 "President Donald J. Trump at the United Nations General Assembly: Outlining an American First Foreign Policy," Trump Administration Fact Sheet, September 20, 2017.

165 Baron Weinberger, Foreign Policy, "The Return of the Pentagon's Yoda," Foreign Policy, September 12, 2018.

166 Fabrice Pothier and Alexander Vershbow, "NATO and Trump," Atlantic Council, May 23, 2017. https://www.atlanticcouncil.org/in-depth-research-reports/issue-brief/nato-and-trump-2/

167 James Frater and Joshua Berlinger, "Record 18 NATO states expected to meet 2% defense spending threshold this year," CNN.com, February 13, 2024. https://www.cnn.com/2024/02/14/europe/nato-defense-spending-target-intl/index.html

168 "2024 Index of U.S. Military Strength," The Heritage Foundation, January 24, 2024. https://www.heritage.org/military-strength/assessing-the-global-operating-environment/europe

169 Ibid

170 Ryan Browne, "Trump Administration to cut its financial contribution to NATO," CNN.com, November 28, 2019. https://www.cnn.com/2019/11/27/politics/trump-nato-contribution-nato/index.html

171 "NATO Secretary General meets President Trump ahead of Leaders 'meeting," NATO website, December 3, 2019. https://www.nato.int/cps/en/natohq/news_171617.htm.

172 Nahal Toosi, "Trump demands other NATO members pay their fair share," Politico, February 28, 2017. https://www.politico.com/story/2017/02/donald-trump-congress-speech-nato-235543

173 Marshall Billingslea Twitter post, February 17, 2024. https://twitter.com/m_s_billingslea/status/1758876715315564845?s=46&t=ml h8UXn8BG2EfWLttml95w

174 Wayne Schroder, "NATO at seventy: Filling NATO's critical defense-capability gaps," Atlantic Council, April 4, 2019. https://www.atlanticcouncil.org/in-depth-research-reports/report/nato-at-seventy-filling-nato-s-critical-defense-capability-gaps/

175 "Trump Administration Accomplishments," Trump Administration Fact Sheet, January 2021. https://trumpwhitehouse.archives.gov/trump-administration-accomplishments/

[176] Pothier and Vershbow, op. cit.

[177] "Shoring Up the US-Japan Alliance under the Trump Administration," Japan Center for International Exchange, December 12, 2016. https://www.jcie.org/analysis/east-asia-insights/eai201612/

[178] "Remarks by President Trump at APEC CEO Summit | Da Nang, Vietnam," November 10, 2017. Trump White House Archives. https://trumpwhitehouse.archives.gov/briefings-statements/remarks-president-trump-apec-ceo-summit-da-nang-vietnam/

[179] Alastair Gale and Chieko Tsuneoka, "Japan Heeds Trump's Call with American-Made Defense Spending Spree," *The Wall Street Journal*, December 18, 2018.

[180] Lindsay Maizland and Nathanael Cheng, "The U.S. Japan Security Alliance," Council on Foreign Relations, November 4, 2021. https://www.cfr.org/backgrounder/us-japan-security-alliance

[181] U.S. Strategic Framework for the Indo-Pacific," declassified Trump Administration strategy paper, available at https://trumpwhitehouse.archives.gov/wp-content/uploads/2021/01/IPS-Final-Declass.pdf.

[182] "Trump Administration Accomplishments," op. cit.

[183] "Trade Agreements," Japan – Country Commercial Guide, International Trade Administration, January 1, 2024. https://www.trade.gov/country-commercial-guides/japan-trade-agreements

[184] "U.S. Agricultural Reaps Benefits of Free Trade Agreement with Korea," U.S. Department of Agriculture, December 18, 2017. https://fas.usda.gov/data/us-agriculture-reaps-benefits-free-trade-agreement-korea

[185] "Trump Administration Accomplishments," op. cit.

[186] "Resolved: Abe's Investment in His Relationship with President Trump Has Advanced Japanese Interests," Center for Strategic & International Studies, January 30, 2020.

[187] Lindsey Ford, "The Trump Administration and the 'Free and Open Indo-Pacific,'" Brookings Foundation, May 2020. https://www.brookings.edu/wp-content/uploads/2020/05/fp_20200505_free_open_indo_pacific.pdf

[188] Garima Mohan, Bonnie Glaser, and Kristi Govella, "Expanding Engagement among South Korea and the Quad Countries in the Indo-Pacific," German Marshall Fund, June 6, 2022. https://www.gmfus.org/news/expanding-engagement-among-south-korea-and-quad-countries-indo-pacific; Premesha Saha and Angad Singh, "Securing Two Oceans: Bolstering India-Australia Defence Cooperation in the Indo-Pacific," Observer Research Foundation, January 21, 2023. https://www.orfonline.org/research/securing-two-oceans-bolstering-india-australia-defence-cooperation-in-the-indo-pacific

[189] Quad Joint Leaders' Statement," White House press release, May 24, 2022. https://www.whitehouse.gov/briefing-room/statements-releases/2022/05/24/quad-joint-leaders-statement/

[190] Jonathan E. Hillman, "Corruption Flows Along China's Belt and Road," Center for Strategic & International Studies, January 18, 2019. https://www.csis.org/analysis/corruption-flows-along-chinas-belt-and-road

[191] Noah Barkin, "Five Eyes intelligence alliance builds coalition to counter China," Reuters, October 12, 2018. https://www.reuters.com/article/idUSKCN1MM0N2/

[192] Marc Polymeropoulos, "Trump's Impact on the Five Eyes and Beyond," Cipher Brief, October 4, 2019. https://www.thecipherbrief.com/column_article/trumps-impact-on-the-five-eyes-and-beyond

[193] Barkin, op. cit.

[194] Tyler O'Neill, "$6B Prisoner Swap Was 'Just a Drop in the Bucket' for Iran. Here's How Much Tehran Has Raked in Under Biden," Daily Signal, October 18, 2023. https://www.dailysignal.com/2023/10/18/not-just-6b-heres-how-much-money-biden-admin-freed-iran-hamas-terror-attack-israel/

[195] By Edward Lawrence, Andrew Miller, and Lauren Shank, "Palestinian group accused of harboring terrorists received $1B from Biden admin: report," FoxBusiness.com, October 18, 2023. https://www.foxbusiness.com/politics/palestinian-group-accused-harboring-terrorists-received-1b-biden-admin

[196] "President Donald J. Trump Keeps His Promise To Open U.S. Embassy In Jerusalem, Israel," White House press release, May 14, 2019.

[197] The Abraham Accords," U.S. State Department 2017-2021 archive. https://2017-2021.state.gov/the-abraham-accords/

[198] Trump Administration Accomplishments," op. cit.

[199] Statement from the President on the Liberation of ISIS-Controlled Territory," White House Press release, March 23, 2019. https://trumpwhitehouse.archives.gov/briefings-statements/statement-president-liberation-isis-controlled-territory/#

[200] "Trump Administration Accomplishments," op. cit.

[201] "Trump Administration Accomplishments," op. cit.

[202] "2022 UNGA Resolutions on Israel vs. Rest of the World," UN Watch, November 22, 2022. https://unwatch.org/2022-2023-unga-resolutions-on-israel-vs-rest-of-the-world/.

[203] For a discussion of these policies, see "The United States Needs to Strategically Decouple from China," Testimony of Robert Lighthizer Before the House Select Committee on Strategic Competition between the United Statas and the Chinese

Communist Party," May 17, 2023; Barry Naughton, The Chinese Economy: Adaptation and Growth (Cambridge, MA: MIT Press, 2018).

204 Ibid.

205 "Trade in Goods with China," U.S. Census Bureau, https://www.census.gov/foreign-trade/balance/c5700.html. Accessed March 1, 2024.

206 Ibid.

207 Charles Benoit, "Falsehoods & Facts: The Truth About De Minimis," Coalition for a Prosperous America, August 14, 2023; Conversation with Mike Orlando, Intelligence Matters Podcast, May 12, 2021. https://www.cbsnews.com/news/foreign-espionage-threats-u-s-intelligence-matters-podcast/.

208 For a discussion of these sectors alongside discussion of how Made in China 2025 industrial policies impact their growth, please see: Marco Rubio, "Made in China 2025 and the Future of American Industry," U.S. Senate Committee on Small Business and Entrepreneurship, February 2019.

209 Paul McLeary, "China is Ahead in Ship, Missile & Air Defense Tech: DOD Report," Breaking Defense, September 1, 2020.

210 Sylvia Pfeifer, "We Can De-risk but Not Decouple' from China, Says Raytheon Chief," Financial Times, June 19, 2023.

211 Jeffrey Nadaner and Tara Dougherty, "Numbers Matter: Defense Acquisition, U.S. Production Capacity, and Deterring China," Govini, January 2024. https://govini.com/wp-content/uploads/2024/01/Govini_2024_Numbers-Matter.pdf.

212 For my testimony, see "The United States Needs to Strategically Decouple from China," Testimony of Robert Lighthizer Before the House Select Committee on Strategic Competition between the United States and the Chinese Communist Party," May 17, 2023. https://docs.house.gov/meetings/ZS/ZS00/20230517/115974/HHRG-118-ZS00-Wstate-LighthizerR-20230517.pdf

213 Trade in Goods with China, U.S. Census Bureau, available at https://www.census.gov/foreign-trade/balance/c5700.html, accessed on February 25, 2024.

214 Alexander Hamilton, "Report on Manufacturers," December 5, 1791.

215 Franklin D. Roosevelt, "Annual Budget Message," January 5, 1942.

216 James Manyika, Katy George, Eric Chewning, Jonathan Woetzel, and Hans-Werner Kaas, "Building a More Competitive U.S. Manufacturing Sector," McKinsey Global Institute, April 15, 2021, pp. 8-9.

217 Ibid.

218 Trade in Goods with World, Seasonally Adjusted, U.S. Census Bureau, available at https://www.census.gov/foreign-trade/balance/c0004.html.

219 Ibid.

220 In the late 1970s, the United States had twenty-two large shipyards that built a variety of oceangoing vessels including cargo ships, tankers, regional containerships, drill rigs, and barges. For a discussion of the shipbuilding sector in the late 1900s, see: Tim Colton and LaVar Huntzinger, "A Brief History of Shipbuilding in Recent Times," Center for Naval Analyses, September 2002, p. 18, www.cna.org/CNA_files/PDF/D0006988.A1.pdf.; for a discussion of U.S. Navy shipbuilding woes, see: Mallory Shelbourne, "OSD Comptroller Says U.S. Shipyards Can't Build 3 Destroyers a Year," U.S. Naval Institute News, March 21, 2023.

221 John Hill, "China's Navy Launches New Destroyers at Dalian Shipyard," Naval Technology, March 14, 2023.

222 Eric Lipton, "From Rockets to Ball Bearings, Pentagon Struggles to Feed War Machine," New York Times, March 24, 2023.

223 Seth Jones, "Empty Bins in a Wartime Environment: The Challenge to the U.S. Defense Industrial Base," CSIS International Security Program, January 2023.

224 Strategic Homeland Investment in Economic and Logistical Defense (SHIELD) Act, H.R. 5703, 118th Congress (introduced September 26, 2023).

225 The Mountain Valley pipeline is a natural gas pipeline being constructed from northwestern West Virginia to southern Virginia. After over a decade of legal and regulatory delays, Senator Joe Manchin (D-West Virginia) negotiated a deal in 2022 under which the Biden Administration and Congress cleared the hurdles blocking the completion of this pipeline in exchange for his vote for the Inflation Reduction Act. On June 3, 2023, President Biden signed legislation ratifying and approving all permits and authorizations necessary for the construction and initial operation of the Mountain Valley Pipeline and directed federal officials and agencies to maintain such authorizations. In addition, not later than June 24, 2023, the legislation requires the Secretary of the Army to issue all permits or verifications necessary to complete project construction and allow for MVP's operation and maintenance. Source: "Mountain Valley Pipeline to Proceed," Equitrans press release, June 3, 2023. https://ir.equitransmidstream.com/news/news-details/2023/Mountain-Valley-Pipeline-To-Proceed/default.aspx

226 "Statement of CIA Objectives and Principles," internal CIA memo, February 16, 1984. CIA website. Available at: https://www.cia.gov/readingroom/docs/CIA-RDP86B00885R000901030005-9.pdf

227 "Director of National Intelligence (DNI), Congressional Research Service, report March 16, 2023. https://crsreports.congress.gov/product/pdf/IF/IF10470/12

228 "The Pentagon's Spies," National Security Archive, July 6, 2015. https://nsarchive2.gwu.edu/NSAEBB/NSAEBB520-the-Pentagons-Spies/

[229] Varej Filhanessian, "HT-JCOE's Training Administration and Assessment Program," Military Intelligence Professional Journal, (October-December 2010). https://www.ikn.army.mil/apps/MIPBW/MIPB_Issues/MIPB%20OCT-DEC%2010.pdf

[230] Greg Myre, "After Chasing Threats Abroad, Former CIA Chief Brennan Says The Risk Is At Home," NPR.com, October 5, 2020. https://www.npr.org/2020/10/05/ 918667854 /after-chasing-threats-abroad-former-cia-chief-john-brennan-says-the-risk-is-at-h

[231] Mark Moore, Mark, Brennan Blasts Trump's No "Collusion" claims as "hogwash," New York Post, August 16, 2028. https://nypost.com/2018/08/16/brennan-blasts-trumps-no-collusion-claims-as-hogwash/

[232] "Public Statement on the Hunter Biden Emails," (Letter signed by 51 former intelligence officers published by Politico), October 19, 2020. https://www.politico.com/f/?id=00000175-4393-d7aa-af77-579f9b330000

[233] Brooke Singman, Biden campaign, Blinken orchestrated intel letter to discredit Hunter Biden laptop story, ex-CIA official says, Senate Judiciary Committee press release, April 21, 2023. https://judiciary.house.gov/media/in-the-news/biden-campaign-blinken-orchestrated-intel-letter-discredit-hunter-biden-laptop#:~:text=Morell%20testified%3A%20%22There%20were%20two,the%20election%2C%22%20Morell%20testified

[234] Ibid

[235] Bill Gertz, "Ratcliffe: Intel on China Politicized," Washington Times, January 19, 2021. https://www.washingtontimes.com/news/2021/jan/20/john-ratcliffe-intel-on-china-politicized/

[236] House Permanent Select Committee on Intelligence, "Report on Russian Active Measures," https://intelligence.house.gov/uploadedfiles/final_russia_investigation_report.pdf; John H. Durham, "Report on Matters Related to Intelligence Activities and Investigations Arising Out of the 2016 Presidential Campaigns," May 12, 2023 https://www.justice.gov/storage/durhamreport.pdf; Gregg Jarrett, "The Russia Hoax: The Illicit Scheme to Clear Hillary Clinton and Frame Donald Trump," (Broadside Books, 2018).

[237] James Sherk, "Tales From the Swamp: How Federal Bureaucrats Resisted President Trump," America First Policy Institute, February 1, 2024. https://americafirstpolicy.com/issues/20222702-federal-bureaucrats-resisted-president-trump.

[238] AFPI interviews with former senior State Department officials.

[239] AFPI interviews with former senior Trump administration officials.

[240] Ibid.

[241] Jorg Spenkuch et al., "Ideology and Performance in Public Organizations," Working Paper 28673, National Bureau of Economic Research, April 2021.

242 *See* AFPI letter to U.S. Office of Personnel Management, "Comment of the America First Policy Institute in Opposition to the Proposed Rule Upholding Civil Service Protections and Merit System Principles, 88 Fed. Reg. 63862 (Sept. 18, 2023)," America First Policy Institute, November 15, 2023. https://americafirstpolicy.com/assets/uploads/files/AFPI_Comment_on_OPM_R IN_3206%E2%80%93AO56-Anti-Schedule_F_NPRM-FINAL.pdf.

243 Brian Feinstein and Abby Wood, "Divided Agencies," Southern California Law Review, Vol. 95, NO.4. December 2022. https://southerncalifornialawreview.com/2022/12/21/divided-agencies/.

244 John Ranelagh, "The Agency: The Rise and Decline of the CIA." New York: Simon and Schuster, 1986, p. 463.

245 Abram Shulsky and Gary Schmitt, "Intelligence Reform: Beyond the Ames Case," in US Intelligence at the Crossroads: Agendas for Reform, Roy Godson, Ernest May and Gary Schmitt, Editors, (Washington, DC: Brassey's, 1995), p.54.

246 Senate Committee on Homeland Security and Governmental Affairs, Presidential Appointment Efficiency and Streamlining Act of 2011, report to accompany S. 679, to reduce the number of executive positions subject to Senate confirmation, 112th Congress, 1st session, June 21, 2011, Senate Report 112-24 (Washington: GPO, 2011)

247 Section 7601 (2) for all such national security nominees received by the date of inauguration, the Senate committees to which these nominations are referred should, to the fullest extent possible, complete their consideration of these nominations, and, if such nominations are reported by the committees, the full Senate should vote to confirm or reject these nominations, within 30 days of their submission.

Index

A

Abraham Accords · 8, 23, 33, 39, 124, 126, 136, 154, 173, 210
Abrams Tanks · 86
Afghanistan · 15, 24, 29, 30, 31, 32, 33, 34, 37, 42, 44, 50, 51, 57, 77, 79, 103, 121, 129, 146, 188
Al-Qaeda · 25, 31, 63, 156, 188, 189, 193
America First Transition Project · 205, 213, 219, 220
Arghandab river valley · 31
Arkansas · 119
Army Tactical Missiles (ATACMS) · 85, 88
Asia-Pacific Economic Co-operation (APEC) · 148
AUKUS · 106, 118, 147
Austin, Lloyd · 53
Australia · 32, 105, 106, 147, 150, 151, 241
Axis,China, Russia, Iran · 28, 81, 139, 146

B

Bahrain · 72, 124, 154, 155
Bauer, Robert · 88
Belt and Road Initiative · See China
Biden Administration · 53
    and AUKUS agreement · 146–47
    and Iran · 42, 79, 103, 125, 126–28, 138, 152
    and Israel · 126, 127, 130, 131, 135, 152
    and JCPOA · See Joint Comprehensive Plan of Action
    and North Korea · 24
    and Saudi Arabia · 79, 126, 152
    and the U.S. military · 58
    and the United Nations · 158
    and Ukraine · 79–92
Biden, Hunter · 196
Big Inch pipeline · 169
Billingslea, Marshall · 144
Bin Laden, Osama · 188
Blinken, Antony · 90, 197
Boston Marathon bombing · 68
Bradley, Omar · 55
Brazil · 108, 109
Brennan, John · 195, 196, 197
BRICS group · 108
Brouillette, Dan · 9
Burke, Edmund · 51
Burns, William · 104
Bush Administration, George W. · 15, 24, 64, 76
Bush, George W. · 81
ByteDance · 114, 120

C

Camp David · 146, 147
CapCut · 72
Carlson, Tucker · 81
Carter, Administration · 47
Carter, Jimmy · 42
Center for Strategic and International Studies · 165
Central Intelligence Agency · 10, 190, 192, 193, 195, 197
Chiang Kai-shek · 98
China · 29, 34, 42, 81, 94, 129, 141, 154, 178

abuse of U.S visas · 71
and abusive trade practices · 160–66
and de-dollarization · 108
and energy security · 180–84
and international organizations · 157
and rare earth elements · 110, 180
and U.S. military readiness · 45
and war in Ukraine · 94
Belt and Road Initiative · 70, 107, 110, 151, 176
Chinese spy balloon · 112
Cyber warfare by · 69
threats from · 97–120
Chinese Communist Party (CCP) · 8, 32, 69–72, 97–120, 141, 143, 161, 177, 196
Chinese Student and Scholar Associations · 113, 118
Chornobyl · 171
Churchill, Winston · 156, 167
Clapper, James · 196
Clausewitz, Claude von · 32
Climate change · 19, 42, 45, 50, 51, 79, 129, 178, 182
Clinton Administration · 30, 45, 54
Clinton, Hillary · 194, 208
CNN · 92
Cold War · 31, 37, 44, 79, 105, 106, 142, 156, 159
Colombia · 29
Committee on Foreign Investment in the United States (CFIUS) · 111, 119
Confucius Institutes · 72, 113, 118
Consolidated Appropriations Act of 2016 · 173
Cotton, Tom · 57
COVID-19 · 13, 65, 69, 79, 189
Creighton, Abrams · 43
Critical Infrastructure · 69
Crossfire Hurricane · 195

Cultural Marxism · 49
Currency manipulation · 160
Custer, George · 54
Cyber threats · 32, 55, 69, 70, 117, 147, 152, 160, 232

D

Dabbar, Paul · 174
Davidson, Phillip · 104
Defense Clandestine Service · 192
Defense Production Board · 59
Department of Health and Human Services · 45
Department of Justice
China Initiative · 113
Diversity, Equity and Inclusion (DEI) · 43, 49–53, 55, 58, 60, 79, 187, 200
Doha Agreement · 25
Donovan, William · 198

E

Egypt · 109, 123, 126, 137, 152
Eisenhower, Dwight · 55
Environmental Protection Agency · 45

F

F-16 · 86
FARC · 29
FBI · 64, 65, 195, 197
Federal Energy Regulatory Commission · 179
Feinstein, Brian · 212
Fentanyl · 27, 94, 116, 120, 161
Financial Intelligence Unit · 72

Fingar, Thomas · 197
First Island Chain · 102
Five Eyes alliance · 152
Florida · 119
Fort Bragg · 47, 50
Fort Huachuca · 192
Fox, Jeremy · 111
France · 18, 91, 142, 143, 147
FuFeng Group · 112, 120

G

Gallagher, Mike · 112
Gallium · 110
Gates, Robert · 80
Gavin, James · 55
Gaza · 23, 57, 104, 115, 123, 130, 131, 135, 137
Georgia · 35
Geranium · 110
Germany · 18, 48, 77, 78, 80, 91, 109, 142, 143, 144, 180
Gibson, Andrew · 56
Gilday, Michael · 50
Golan Heights · 23, 123, 127
Granholm, Jennifer · 180
Griest, Kristen · 58
Group of 7 (G7) · 178

H

Haass, Richard · 91, 95
Hagerty, Bill · 149
Hamas · 28, 39, 57, 72, 91, 115, 121, 124, 125, 126, 130, 131, 135, 153
Hamilton, Alexander · 164
Harvard University · 53
Haspel, Gina · 195
Hawaii · 69
Heritage Foundation · 128, 142, 153

Hezbollah · 72, 121, 130, 135, 153
High Mobility Artillery Rocket System (HIMARS) · 85, 94
Homeland Security Act · 63
House Select Committee on Strategic Competition between the United States and the Chinese Communist Party · 100
Houthi rebels · 39, 121, 130, 153
Huawei · 152, 163
Hypersonic missiles · 102, 147, 201

I

Immigration and Customs Enforcement (ICE) · 64
Immigration and Nationality Act · 64, 68
Immigration and Naturalization Service · 63, 64
India · 32, 104, 106, 108, 145, 150, 176, 241
   Arunachal Pradesh region · 104
Indo-Pacific · 145
Indo-Pacific Economic Vision · 150
industrial spying · 160
Institute for Defense Analysis · 53
Intermediate-Range Nuclear Forces (INF) treaty · 78
International Energy Agency · 170, 177
Iran · 43, 69, 72, 122, 125–29, 138, 152–55, 160, 173, 177
Iran Experts Initiative · 72
Iraq · 27, 29, 30, 31, 32, 33, 34, 38, 44, 51, 57, 121, 122, 128, 130, 139, 152, 153, 156, 157
ISIS · 15, 27, 31, 38, 42, 77, 156, 231
Israel · 8, 18, 22, 28, 33, 39, 57, 79, 115, 121–36, 152–56, 170, 173
Italy · 143

J

Japan · 32, 33, 46, 48, 102, 105, 109,
    118, 145, 146, 147, 148, 149, 150,
    167, 180, 241
Jerusalem Act of 1995 · 23
Jerusalem embassy · *See* U.S. Embassy
    to Israel
Johnson, Boris · 90
Joint Comprehensive Plan of Action
    (JCPOA) · 135, 138
    Biden policies on · 127, 146, 153
    Obama policies on · 125, 152
    Trump policies on · 125, 126, 153,
    155
Jordan · 121, 123, 152

K

Kendall, Frank · 52
Kennedy, Paul · 16
Kerry, John · 123, 125
Khashoggi, Jamal · 126
Kim Jong Un · 77, 146, 210
King, Martin Luther Jr. · 50
Kissinger, Henry · 92, 98, 234
Korean War · 45
Kuwait · 72, 157
Kyrgyzstan · 35

L

Laughlin Air Force Base · 112
Le Drian, Jean-Yves · 147
Lebanon · 104, 175
Lexington Green · 47
Libya · 15, 175, 193
Lincoln, Abraham · 41, 47, 61
Liquified natural gas · 173, 178, 179
Lithium · 109, 161, 181

Little Big Inch pipeline · 169
Liu Yunshan · 113

M

MacArthur, Douglas · 54
Maduro, Nicolas · 107
Maliki, Nuri · 38
Mao Zedong · 98
Marshall, Andrew · 141
Marshall, George · 54, 55
McCarthy, Kevin · 49
McClellan, George · 54
Mercantilism · 98, 159, 160, 165
Mexico · 64, 162
    Mexican drug cartels · 27, 64, 161
Michigan · 131
MiG-29 · 85, 88
Miller, Keith · 170
Milley, Mark · 90
Mohammed bin Salman · 126, 136
Montana · 70, 119
Moon Jae-in · 149
Morell, Michael · 194, 196
Morocco · 124, 154
MSNBC · 91

N

National Defense Strategy · 217
National Security Agency · 192, 195,
    198, 199
National Security Presidential
    Memorandum 7 · 68
National Security Presidential
    Memorandum 9 · 68
National Security Strategy · 20, 21,
    214, 217
National Vetting Center · 68

NATO · 14, 20, 33, 75, 76, 77, 78, 79, 80, 81, 82, 83, 84, 85, 86, 88, 91, 92, 95, 142
2008 Bucharest Summit · 80, 82
Nazi Germany · 164
Neoconservatives · 15
Netherlands · 142
New Development Bank · 108
New START treaty · 78
New York City · 157
New Zealand · 151
Nigeria · 175
Nixon, Richard · 43, 98
Nord Stream II Pipeline · 38, 77, 80
North Dakota · 70, 119
North Korea · 21, 22, 23, 24, 28, 43, 69, 77, 81, 94, 106, 107, 115, 145, 146, 147, 148, 149, 157, 158, 160
Norway · 142

O

Obama Administration · 42, 51, 64, 76, 78, 79, 151, 173, 176, 194
Obama, Barack · 193, 194, 210
Office of Naval Intelligence · 46
Office of the Director of National Intelligence (ODNI) · 192
Okinawa · 45
Oman · 72
Open Skies Treaty · 78
Organization of the Petroleum Exporting Countries (OPEC) · 170, 173, 174, 183
Oslo Accords · 132

P

Palestine Liberation Organization · 29

Panama · 44
Paris Climate Accords · 22, 141
Patton, George · 55, 164
Pearl Harbor · 167
Philippines · 102, 104
Pielke, Robert Jr. · 177
Pivot to Asia · 146
Poland · 85, 89, 180
Pompeo, Mike · 51
Pope Air Force Base · 47
Powell, Colin · 48
Putin, Vladimir · 42, 103
Putin,Vladimir · 76

Q

Quadrilateral Security Dialogue · 32, 106, 118, 145

R

Ranelagh, John · 213
Rare earth elements · 110, 119, 180, 181
Rasmussen, Nicholas · 196
Ratcliffe, John · 197
Raytheon Technologies · 109, 162
Reagan, Ronald · 30, 32, 43, 44, 48, 59, 211, 224
Reserve currency · 81, 108
Ridgway, Matthew · 47, 55
Robinson, Roger · 100
Roosevelt, Franklin · 54, 156, 164, 198
ROTC · 60
Russia · 8, 20, 29, 34, 38, 42, 44, 69, 102, 106, 108, 115, 129, 134, 135, 139, 142, 145, 146, 152, 157, 160, 174, 176, 178, 183, 195, 196, 201
and war in Ukraine · 43, 75–96

Cyber warfare by · 69

S

Saddam Hussein · 29, 30, 167
Saudi Arabia · 23, 79, 109, 121, 124, 125, 126, 127, 129, 136, 152, 153, 155
Scarborough, Joe · 91
Schlichter, Kurt · 92
Schlieffen Plan · 164
Schmitt, Gary · 213
Schumer, Chuck · 131
Shale Revolution · 169, 173, 174, 182
SHEIN · 72
Sherk, James · 208, 212
Shulsky, Adam · 213
Singapore Summit · 149
Soleimani, Qasem · 26, 39, 122
South China Sea · 104, 105, 106, 118, 145, 146, 147, 148
South Korea · 46, 89, 105, 107, 145, 149, 180
South Sudan · 175
Sri Lanka · 108
Sternberg, Joseph · 178
Stinger anti-aircraft missiles · 87
Strategic decoupling · 162, 163
Strategic Petroleum Reserve · 170
Sudan · 154, 175
Sun Guangxin · 112
Supply chains · 17, 32, 77, 98, 109, 116, 119, 129, 162, 163, 166, 182, 184
Syria · 27, 77, 121, 122, 128, 129, 130, 139, 153, 156

T

Taiwan · 28, 45, 75, 94, 97, 98, 102, 103, 104, 105, 106, 115, 117, 118, 129, 145, 146, 193, 201
Taiwan Relations Act · 117
Taliban · 25, 193, 201
Tariffs · 99, 116, 120, 149, 162, 163
Task Force Smith · 46
Tedros Adhanom Ghebreyesus · 157
Temurm · 72
Tennessee · 119
Terrorism
  9/11 Commission · 63
  9/11 terrorist attacks · 24, 63, 68, 188, 192
  Hamas terrorist attack of Oct. 7, 2023 · 39, 57, 91, 121, 124, 130, 135, 153
Three Mile Island · 171
Thrift Savings Plan · 100
Tiananmen Square · 29
TikTok · 71, 72, 114, 120
Travers, Russ · 197
Truman, Harry · 47, 122
Trump Administration
  and Asian allies · 152
  and NATO · 144
  and Saudi Arabia · 121, 122, 124, 154, 155
  and the United Nations · 158
  and Ukraine · 76–79
  Iran policies · 126
  Israel policies · 122–25, 154
  Maximum Pressure policy on Iran · 9, 125, 128, 138, 155
  national security priorities · 17
  National Security Strategy · 20, 21
Trump, Donald
  friendship with Shinzo Abe · 150
  on ending the killing in Ukraine · 96

on Iraq War · 33
on JCPOA · 125
on securing the U.S. southern
    border · 64
personal diplomacy with Kim Jong
    Un · 23, 149
speech to 2017 APEC summit ·
    148

U

U.S. Air Force · 46, 52
    1st Fighter Wing · 55
    Air Force Academy · 52
U.S. Army · 46
    1st Fighter Wing · 55, 56
    21st Infantry Regiment · 46
    Secretary of the Army · 57
U.S. Border Patrol · 64, 66
U.S. Citizenship and Immigration
    Services · 64
U.S. Congress · 59
U.S. Customs and Border Protection ·
    64
U.S. Department of Agriculture · 111
U.S. Department of Commerce · 206
U.S. Department of Defense · 44, 50,
    56, 57, 87, 101, 110, 192, 194,
    199, 206
U.S. Department of Energy · 168, 170,
    171, 179
U.S. Department of Homeland
    Security · 63, 64, 66, 68, 69, 73
U.S. Department of Justice · 64, 113,
    119, 163
U.S. Department of State · 8, 103,
    123, 138, 194, 206, 209
U.S. Department of the Treasury ·
    101, 144, 206, 224
U.S. Embassy to Israel

Move of embassy to Jerusalem by
    the Trump Administration · 23,
    39, 77, 123, 127, 154, 173
U.S. Intelligence Community · 63, 68,
    114, 120, 161, 187, 188, 191, 193,
    187–93, 197, 198, 201
U.S. Marine Corps · 45, 49, 53
    Second Marine Division · 55
U.S. Navy · 45, 101
U.S. Senate · 218
U.S. Supreme Court · 53
U.S. Trade Representative · 206
U.S.-Japan Digital Trade Agreement ·
    150
U.S.-Japan Trade Agreement · 149
U.S.-South Korea Free Trade
    Agreement · 150
Uganda · 108
Ukraine · 142, 174
    NATO membership · 82, 83, 95
    Obama policies toward · 78, 79
    Trump policies toward · 76–79
Ukraine War · 75, 79–96
    Biden policies on · 79–92
    Possible ways to end · 92–96
United Arab Emirates · 72, 109, 124,
    137, 154, 155
United Kingdom · 91, 106, 147, 151
United Nations · 78, 156, 158
    UN Security Council · 38, 107, 157,
    158
United Nations Educational,
    Scientific and Cultural
    Organization (UNESCO) · 22, 158
United Nations Relief and Works
    Agency (UNRWA) · 124, 137, 153
University of Pennsylvania · 212
University of Southern California ·
    212
USS Cole · 188
Utah · 119

V

Venezuela · 72, 173, 175, 177
Vickers, Michael · 196
Vietnam · 162
   Vietnam War · 42, 213
Virginia · 70, 119
Vladivostok · 146

W

Wagner Group · 77
WeChat · 72
Weinberger Doctrine · 30
Weinberger, Casper · 30
White House Council of Economic
   Advisers · 173
Wisconsin · 131
Wood, Abby · 212
World Bank · 108, 183
World Health Organization · 157
World Trade Center · 188
World Trade Organization · 99, 148
World War I · 35

World War II · 18, 44, 46, 48, 54, 59,
   95, 145, 156, 164, 169, 172, 178,
   179
Wuhan Institute of Virology · 189

X

Xi Jinping · 99, 102, 104, 105, 106,
   107, 109, 191, 198, 238

Y

Yadlin, Amos · 57
Yemen · 39, 104, 121, 130, 153, 188
Yoon Suk Yeol · 146, 147

Z

Zelenskyy, Volodymr · 82, 83, 85, 89,
   90
Zheng, Zaosong · 71
ZTE · 152

Made in the USA
Coppell, TX
14 October 2024

38606579R00144